Roseville Public Library
Roseville CA 95678

☝ **W9-BNS-854**

APR —2003—

595.789 BRO
Brock, James P.
Butterflies of North America

z#   3509650

KAUFMAN FOCUS GUIDES

BUTTERFLIES

OF

NORTH

AMERICA

JIM P. BROCK
and
KENN KAUFMAN

With the collaboration of
RICK and NORA BOWERS
and
LYNN HASSLER KAUFMAN

Illustrated with
more than 2,200 images
digitally edited
by the authors
and based on photos
by more than
70 top photographers

HOUGHTON MIFFLIN COMPANY

Roseville Public Library
Roseville CA 95678

PICTORIAL TABLE OF CONTENTS

WHEN YOU SEE AN UNFAMILIAR BUTTERFLY:

1. Try to place it in one of the groups shown on the next four pages. Its **shape, size,** and **behavior** may be better clues than color.
2. Refer to the page numbers or color tabs and go to that section of the book. Look for the pictures that match your butterfly most closely.
3. Make sure the size is right. Always check the "actual size" figure in the upper right-hand corner of each plate.
4. Check the range maps to see which species are likely in your area. This will help to narrow down the choices.
5. Read the text for additional pointers on habitat, behavior, flight season, and comparisons to similar species.

SWALLOWTAILS AND PARNASSIANS, pages 20–45

Swallowtails are mostly large, with sailing or fluttering flight. Many have "tails" on hindwings. They rest with wings open or closed. Parnassians are only in parts of west and far northwest.

WHITES AND SULPHURS, pages 46–77

Very small to very large, but mostly medium-sized. Rapid fluttering flight. Most kinds are white, yellow, or orange. Whites may sit with wings open, but sulphurs sit with wings folded above their back.

COPPERS AND HARVESTER, pages 80–91
Coppers are fairly small, visiting flowers, often sitting with wings open. Harvester is scarce, found around alders in the east.

HAIRSTREAKS, pages 92–123
Small butterflies with fast, erratic flight. Most sit with their wings folded above their back; only a few bask with wings spread.

BLUES, pages 124–141
Small to very small, with fluttering, erratic flight. They may sit with wings folded or partly open. Often seen on flowers or at puddles.

METALMARKS, pages 142–151
Mostly tropical; ours are mostly small. Some have metallic marks on wings. They visit flowers and sit with their wings spread.

LONGWINGS AND FRITILLARIES, pages 154–175

Longwings are fairly large and mostly tropical. Fritillaries are mostly medium-sized, mostly orange and black, and most diverse in the north and west. They visit flowers and usually sit with their wings spread.

CRESCENTS AND CHECKERSPOTS, pages 176–195

Mostly rather small butterflies. They fly fast and low, usually sit with their wings spread, often at flowers or puddles.

TYPICAL BRUSHFOOTS, pages 196–229

A highly varied group, from small to large, but mostly medium-sized. Some are common at flowers, while others avoid them. Some have irregular wing shapes. Many fly with alternating flaps and glides.

SATYRS, pages 230–253
Mostly medium-sized brown butterflies with floppy flight, in woods, field, tundra. They tend to sit with wings folded above their back. Only a few are regular visitors to flowers.

SPREAD-WING SKIPPERS, pages 256–299
Fairly small, with stout bodies, fast flight, and usually dull colors. Most kinds sit with the wings spread, but some keep wings folded.

GRASS SKIPPERS, pages 300–357
Mostly very small, with stout bodies, short wings, and fast flight. Often seen at flowers, they usually sit with the wings folded, or with the hindwings spread farther than the forewings.

GIANT-SKIPPERS, pages 358–363
Medium-sized butterflies with very heavy bodies. Usually rare, seen near yucca or agave plants or at puddles, but not at flowers.

TO MY WIFE, JOAN, AND MY DAUGHTER, JOY
— J.P.B.

TO LYNN, MY OWN ELUSIVE BUTTERFLY
—K.K.

Copyright © 2003 by Hillstar Editions L.C.

All rights reserved

For information about permission to reproduce selections from
this book, write to Permissions, Houghton Mifflin Company,
215 Park Avenue South, New York, New York 10003.

Visit our Web site: www.houghtonmifflinbooks.com.

Library of Congress Cataloging-in-Publication Data

Brock, James P.
Butterflies of North America / Jim P. Brock and Kenn Kaufman.
p. cm. — (Kaufman focus guides)
ISBN 0-618-25400-5 (cloth)
ISBN 0-618-15312-8 (flexi)
1. Butterflies — North America — Identification.   2. Butterflies —
North America — Pictorial works.   I. Kaufman, Kenn.   II. Title.
QL548 .B76   2003
595.78'9'097—dc21   2002027622

Book design by Anne Chalmers
Typefaces: Minion, Univers Condensed

Illustrations and maps for this guide were produced in
Tucson, Arizona, by Hillstar Editions L.C. and Bowers Photo.

Printed in Singapore

TWP 10 9 8 7 6 5 4 3 2 1

ENJOYING BUTTERFLIES
A Note from Kenn Kaufman

Most people seem to be aware of butterflies more as symbols than as real living creatures. Although there are hundreds of species of butterflies in North America, they somehow escape public notice most of the time. Out in plain sight, they lead secret lives.

I still recall how surprised I was when I began to notice them myself. At the age of fourteen, having learned a lot of my local birds, I decided to see if there were any butterflies in the neighborhood. Amazingly, as soon as I began looking for them, they appeared: Little Wood-Satyrs flopping through the woods, tiny Reakirt's Blues on weed flowers in vacant lots, and dozens more. Although I had been outside looking for birds, up to that time I had utterly missed these other winged creatures.

Butterflies are not birds, of course. They are very different in their habits, yearly cycles, and population dynamics. And they're a lot smaller. The biggest ones, like Monarchs and Giant Swallowtails, may grab our attention, but most of the diversity is among the smaller butterflies. We have far more species of little hairstreaks, blues, skippers, and the like than we do of the big guys. Small can be beautiful: even the tiniest butterflies have intricate patterns that are well worth appreciating. But until recently, it has been extremely difficult to identify many of these butterflies in the field. Even separating some larger species has been problematic, because their identification often depends on small details. Until the recent development of good close-focusing binoculars and cameras, many butterflies could be recognized only by expert lepidopterists with vast experience.

I have been lucky enough to have one such lepidopterist as a good friend for years, and luckier still that he is the kind of expert who is always ready to share his knowledge. Jim Brock has studied butterflies from Alaska to Brazil, and in the field he dazzles everyone with his ability to find and identify even the rare and little-known species; but he will also patiently point out the most common butterflies to anyone who wants to know them. Jim agreed to coauthor this book as a way of helping newcomers to the field. In doing so, he graciously accepted the challenge of our Focus Guide format: boiling his vast knowledge down to just the essentials that would be most useful in a pocket-sized book. If any serious lepidopterists are displeased by the treatments here, they should blame me, not Jim Brock.

But of course serious lepidopterists (who already have their technical reference works) are not the primary audience for this book. The Focus Guides are shortcuts, intended to be the best and fastest way to get started in a subject, to send you outside quickly, putting names on what you find. Slip this book into your pocket the next time you go exploring, and start discovering the secret world of butterflies for yourself.

IDENTIFYING BUTTERFLIES

In naming a butterfly, the first step is to make sure that it really is one. The order Lepidoptera includes the moths as well as the butterflies, and some moths are active by day and are quite colorful. Usually they sit or behave in an obviously different way from butterflies. If in doubt, look at the antennae. On butterflies, the tip of each antenna has a thickened area, or "club." North American moths lack this feature; their antennae are either thread-like to the tip, feathery, or fringed along the edges.

Butterflies have four wings: two on each side, the forewing and the hindwing. The upperside and underside of each wing usually has a different pattern. To describe a color pattern on a butterfly, therefore, we have to say where it is—for example, on the upperside of the forewing. Lepidopterists can describe butterfly patterns in great detail using a system of numbering the wing veins and the spaces between them. It's hard to apply that system to an active butterfly in the wild, so we don't use it in this guide, except to point out the cell, an area outlined by veins near the base of each wing. However, a few terms are necessary for communicating about the intricate patterns of some species; see the diagrams below for the simplified terminology used in this guide.

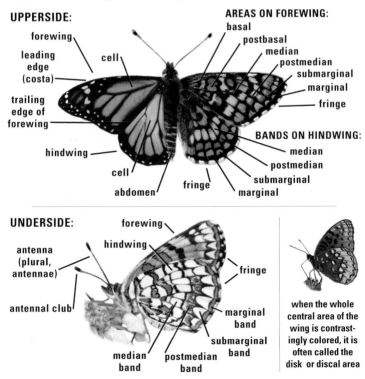

UPPERSIDE:

- forewing
- leading edge (costa)
- cell
- trailing edge of forewing
- hindwing
- cell
- abdomen
- fringe

AREAS ON FOREWING:
- basal
- postbasal
- median
- postmedian
- submarginal
- marginal
- fringe

BANDS ON HINDWING:
- median
- postmedian
- submarginal
- marginal

UNDERSIDE:

- forewing
- hindwing
- antenna (plural, antennae)
- antennal club
- fringe
- marginal band
- submarginal band
- median band
- postmedian band

when the whole central area of the wing is contrastingly colored, it is often called the disk or discal area

What to look for: Wing patterns are obviously important in identifying butterflies, but they are not the only clues. Here are some other points to consider.

Size: Some swallowtails are six inches or more from one wingtip to the other, while some blues are much less than an inch across. Since these wingspan measurements are hard for most people to visualize, we have treated sizes in this guide by showing one individual on each color plate at actual life size in gray outline. The illustrations are in correct scale relative to the others on that page, but not necessarily to those on other pages; be sure to check the "actual size" figure each time you turn the page, to get an idea whether the butterflies shown are actually big, medium-sized, or small.

Little butterflies do not grow up to be big ones: once they complete the transformation to winged adult, their size does not change. However, there are variations within a species. Early spring individuals are often smaller than those of summer; females are often larger than males. And occasionally we see a "runt" individual that is oddly small. But with experience, you will find that size is usually a good quick clue to identification.

Shape: At a glance, most butterflies may seem to be roughly the same shape. With closer study, you will begin to see differences in wing shapes that help to create the distinctive look of each species. Some have extended "tails" on the hindwings, or jagged or scalloped outer wing margins. Other differences are much more subtle, such as the wingtips being slightly more rounded or pointed. But with practice you will find that a butterfly's shape is an important identifying mark.

Posture: The way a butterfly sits is always worth noticing. Sulphurs almost always perch with their wings folded tightly above their backs; metalmarks usually have their wings spread out flat; cloudywings usually hold their wings half open in a shallow V; and grass skippers often hold their hindwings spread farther than their forewings. Any butterfly may sit in an odd position at times, but the typical posture can be a good clue to identification. We have tried to illustrate and describe this for all species.

Flight style: Experts often can recognize a butterfly as it flits past—not because they can actually see detailed field marks on its fast-moving wings, but because the way it flies is a field mark in itself. Some species fly erratically, others more directly; some flutter along with regular steady flaps, while others flap a few times quickly and then glide. These flight styles are hard to describe in words, but with practice you will learn to recognize many of them.

Fine details: Some field marks involve very small details, such as the colors of the eyes, the color or pattern on the antennae, or the color of the "face" (the palps, on the front of the head). These things really can be seen in the field, but for wary species you may need to use binoculars. Good binoculars are now available that can focus as close as just a few feet away, allowing incredible views of butterflies and other small creatures. One good source of information on binoculars for butterfly-watching can be found online at www.eagleoptics.com.

Variation in butterflies: As with humans and other living things, no two individual butterflies look exactly alike. Most of the variation within a species is so minor that you won't notice it in the field, but sometimes it's enough to cause confusion. Occasionally you'll see an individual that looks totally unlike the normal color pattern for its species; these aberrant butterflies may be identifiable only by shape or other clues.

Many species vary from place to place, and if these variations are well marked, a local or regional population may be designated as a subspecies; see p. 14 for more information. There are also seasonal variations. For example, Zebra Swallowtails flying in spring are smaller and paler than those flying in summer, even though they all belong to the same species; Goatweed Leafwings flying in fall have more sharply pointed forewings than those flying in early summer. Males and females often differ in pattern or even in shape — sometimes subtly, sometimes so strikingly that they appear to be unrelated. And finally, every individual butterfly gradually changes in appearance as its condition becomes more worn and faded. The two Painted Ladies shown here, for example, were sitting on flowers in the same meadow. The ragged one on the right can still be identified, because Painted Ladies have lots of field marks, but some butterflies in this condition would be unrecognizeable.

It's a tough life: two Painted Ladies, one in fairly fresh condition, the other very worn

Habitat and season: Many butterflies are restricted to particular habitats, and this is a key not only to finding them but to identifying them. We give habitat descriptions for most species in this guide, and these should always be considered. Seasons are important as well. Even in warm climates, only a few species are on the wing year-round; in most species, adults are present only in certain seasons. We usually describe these flight seasons in general terms, such as "early summer," and these designations relate to local conditions, not arbitrary calendar dates. The Sara Orangetip, for example, is an early spring butterfly. It may appear by late January in Arizona and not until the end of May in the Yukon Territory, but those dates qualify as "early spring" in both locations.

About the illustrations: Naturalists have debated for years whether field guides should be illustrated with paintings or photographs. This book uses a third method, introduced in 2000 with the first Kaufman Focus Guide, *Birds of North America:* we begin with photos and edit them digitally to make them all directly comparable, as paintings would be.

Some butterflies, such as sulphurs, never bask with their wings open; but it is still useful to know the colors of their uppersides, because even at a glimpse in flight, a pale yellow one will look different from an orange one with black borders. For most species like this, we provide illustrations at reduced size showing their uppersides as an aid to identification.

Understanding the range maps: One of the most important clues to identification involves knowing where you are. Most butterflies have very specific ranges and are unlikely to be seen anywhere else. This is a good thing, because some groups include similar species that are much easier to tell apart by range than by field marks. For example, Eastern and Western Tailed-Blues look very much alike, but in most places you will find only one or the other, not both. In identifying any butterfly, always check the range maps to see which ones are likely in your region.

Most of the range maps in this guide have the distributions of the butterflies indicated in green. This color means that the species is flying in summer (the peak butterfly season in most areas) *or* in more than one season (for example, spring and summer, or even most of the year). We use a darker shade of green for areas where the species is most common, and a paler shade for areas where it is less likely to be seen. These designations are quite arbitrary, but we hope they will be helpful in giving a general idea of which species are most expected.

A few species fly mainly in spring or mainly in fall; these are mapped in blue for spring, orange for fall, again with a darker shade for the areas where they are more common.

Some butterflies, especially from southern regions, sometimes stray far from their normal haunts. If there is a regular pattern of such straying, we indicate it on the map with a dashed line beyond the typical range.

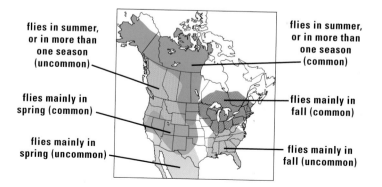

flies in summer, or in more than one season (uncommon)

flies in summer, or in more than one season (common)

flies mainly in spring (common)

flies mainly in fall (common)

flies mainly in spring (uncommon)

flies mainly in fall (uncommon)

FINDING BUTTERFLIES

Some butterflies are adaptable and may show up almost anywhere, but most prefer a particular habitat. You will not see Salt Marsh Skippers in a forest or Desert Elfins in a marsh. To see a wide variety of butterflies, therefore, it's necessary to visit many habitats. You should go at various seasons, because many species have rather short flight periods: Falcate Orangetips fly only in spring, Apache Skippers only in fall. This adds to the enjoyment of butterfly watching, because you can hope to see different species on repeat visits to the same place during the year.

Flowers: Not all butterflies fit the classic image of visiting flowers to sip nectar—some species are rarely or never seen at flowers. Still, to get started, the easiest way to find butterflies is to find a good patch of blooms in a garden or meadow, or by a roadside. Some flowers seem to be more attractive than others, and some butterflies prefer certain types of flowers, so it pays to look in a variety of places.

Mud: Males of some butterflies, including blues, swallowtails, and sulphurs, are strongly attracted to damp soil. They are apparently taking in salts and other chemicals from the mud. Sometimes these "puddle parties" involve several species and hundreds of individuals, while at other times only a few individuals will be present, but you should always check puddles and pond edges for the presence of butterflies.

Other baits: Many butterflies are attracted to odd things such as flowing sap, rotting fruit, or animal dung. (This is especially true of some species that tend to ignore flowers, such as the Goatweed Leafwing and the Question Mark.)

Aside from these feeding behaviors, adult butterflies put most of their energy into activities related to reproduction. Males spend a lot of time looking for females; females spend much time looking for the right places to lay their eggs. Knowing their behaviors can help you find them.

Hilltopping: Male butterflies of some species look for mates by flying to the top of a hill and patrolling or waiting there for the females to show up. If we check the tops of low hills, especially from late morning to afternoon, we may see butterflies that are hard to find in the surrounding country.

Patrolling: Males of other species fly back and forth along linear pathways, such as trails or gullies, looking for females. They may come back time after time to the same perches, allowing for repeated views.

Foodplants: Many butterflies are closely tied to the plants on which their larvae feed. Hessel's Hairstreaks are seldom seen away from Atlantic white cedars; Square-spotted Blues are usually seen sitting on buckwheats. A skilled lepidopterist is often able to find particular butterflies by learning to recognize their larval foodplants.

THE BUTTERFLY'S LIFE CYCLE

The amazing process of metamorphosis—the butterfly's transition from egg to caterpillar to pupa to winged adult—is well known and fairly well understood, but it is still rightly regarded as a miracle.

The process begins with the egg laid by the adult female on or near the plants that will serve as food for the caterpillars. Most butterfly caterpillars cannot survive on the wrong plants, so the adult's choice of where to lay her eggs is critically important. But given the right plant, the caterpillar or larva (plural: larvae) is a little eating machine, and as it grows it passes through about five stages, or instars, each one larger than the last. Because the larva's skin can stretch only so far, it sheds its skin each time it passes to the next instar. The last time it sheds its skin, it reveals not a larger larva but the next phase in its life, the pupa (plural: pupae).

Monarch larva

Monarch pupa

The pupa, also called the chrysalis, is the stage in which the larva is transformed into the adult butterfly. Unlike many moths, most butterflies do not spin a protective cocoon; their pupa is smooth but often colored for camouflage. When the development inside is complete, the pupa splits open and the adult crawls out; after an hour or two for the wings to expand and dry, the butterfly is ready for flight.

In cooler climates, butterflies have the challenge of surviving through winter. Some pass the winter as eggs, others as partly grown larvae or as pupae. A few overwinter as adults, emerging to fly about on unusually warm winter days. But aside from such hibernators, and a few large species such as Monarchs and longwings, most butterflies do not live very long in the adult stage—a couple of weeks is a long life for a small butterfly.

In some cases, a butterfly passes through all four stages in a matter of weeks, and the whole cycle is repeated several times during the year. In this guide we note how many generations, or broods, a species may have per year. Many species have only one brood per year, and these usually have short flight seasons. Some have fewer than one brood per year: in the far north, where summers are short, some species take two years to develop, hibernating through one winter as a small larva and the next winter as a nearly full-grown larva; adults may appear only every other year.

Monarch adult

Some butterflies found in northern climates cannot survive the winter there in any stage. Instead, they invade northward every summer, with some of their offspring surviving to move south in fall. These migrations generally seem far more haphazard than those of birds, but so far they are not well known.

HOW BUTTERFLIES ARE CLASSIFIED AND NAMED

The sheer variety of nature is wonderful, but it can also be very confusing. To make sense of this diversity, scientists classify living things in categories such as order, family, subfamily, genus, and species. All butterflies (and all moths) are classified in the order Lepidoptera. The color-coded sections in this guide are built around families or subfamilies of butterflies. For most of us, the most interesting category is the species—the basic "kind" of butterfly that we write on our list of sightings.

Species of butterflies: Whole books have been written to define exactly what a species is. No definition will fit perfectly, because there are many borderline cases, populations that appear to be in the process of becoming species but are not yet quite distinct enough. In general, members of a species are isolated from members of other species in terms of reproduction. Different species often *can* interbreed (and may even produce fertile offspring), but they generally *don't*. For example, Crossline and Tawny-edged Skippers (p. 324) look very similar to us, but they occur together over a wide area without interbreeding, so they are clearly separate species. On the other hand, the Red-spotted Purple and the White Admiral (p. 210) look quite different, but they seem to interbreed randomly where their ranges meet, forming a broad blend zone in the northeast; they are regarded as forming just one species. Lorquin's and Weidemeyer's Admirals (p. 212) also may interbreed in the narrow zone where they meet, but much less frequently; they are still considered to be separate species.

Subspecies: Members of a species do not all look the same. Aside from the kinds of individual variation mentioned on p. 9, they may vary consistently from one place to another. These regional variations, if they are well marked, may be formally described by scientists as subspecies. Subspecies within a species will interbreed wherever their ranges come in contact, so the divisions between them are not precise. In some cases a species will vary gradually over a wide area (becoming gradually paler from east to west, for example), and dividing this kind of clinal variation into subspecies is arbitrary and not very useful. But if a subspecies has an isolated range and is not in contact with other populations of its species, it may be very distinctive, and may eventually become a full species.

In most cases we ignore subspecies in this guide, since the differences are usually not obvious in the field. But if you develop a serious interest in butterflies, you will discover a whole additional level of diversity by delving into their subspecific variation.

Scientific names are applied to every known species. Mainly Latin or Latinized Greek, these names are recognized by scientists working in any language. The names are written in italics: *Limenitis archippus* is the Viceroy. The first word is the genus: *Limenitis*. The Lorquin's Admiral, *Limenitis lorquini,* belongs to this same genus, so it is a close relative of the Viceroy in spite of its different colors. If the scientific name consists of three words, the third one is the subspecies. *Limenitis archippus floridensis* is the dark subspecies of Viceroy living in Florida.

Standardized names: For some other groups of organisms, such as birds and dragonflies, there are official publications (produced by committees of expert scientists) that list all valid species and give standardized scientific and English names for each. For butterflies, however, this has not been done, and many different classifications and names have been used — you might find the same butterfly called by three different names in three books. To address this confusing situation, a committee of enthusiasts from the North American Butterfly Association (NABA) has compiled *The NABA Checklist & English Names of North American Butterflies* (second edition, 2001). Although this is not really an "official" list and is not followed by all lepidopterists, it has proven to be tremendously useful for amateur butterfly watchers. In this book, for the sake of convenience, we have followed the NABA list in almost all cases.

Most people who use English names for butterflies today use names that identify them only to species, not to subspecies, except in a few cases involving populations that are very notable for some reason (such as the San Bruno Elfin, an endangered subspecies of Moss's Elfin). Unless you plan to become deeply involved in taxonomic issues, it is usually easier to stick with species names. However, some lepidopterists with a strong interest in subspecies have suggested that each one should have its own English name. We don't follow this practice, but we should point out that a list of suggested English names for all North American subspecies of butterflies can be found online at http://tils-ttr.org/lepnames.html.

The unknown: In this guide we have presented all North American butterflies in a way that reflects our current understanding of how they should be classified. However, no one should assume that this is the final word. Scientific understanding of some groups is still developing. For example, the little Spring Azure was long regarded as one variable species found all over North America. There is now good evidence that it is actually a complex of species, perhaps seven or more. Similar complexes may exist within what we now call the Square-spotted Blue, Dotted Blue, Juniper Hairstreak, Common Ringlet, Mormon Metalmark, Mustard White, and others. We still have much to learn about them.

As an example of how much remains unknown, as this book was going to press, we received word of a new species described to science. It was not a drab, small butterfly from a remote wilderness, but a large, spectacular one in the eastern United States! This creature, the Appalachian Tiger Swallowtail *(P. appalachiensis),* had been overlooked because of its similarity to the Eastern Tiger Swallowtail; but it flies only in spring, has no black form of the female, is larger than the spring brood of Eastern Tiger, and has a narrower black and blue outer edge on the hindwing. Opinions are still divided as to whether this is really a valid species, but it looks promising, and it hints at exciting discoveries remaining to be made.

OTHER ACTIVITIES INVOLVING BUTTERFLIES

Butterfly gardening: This is becoming tremendously popular in many parts of North America, as people discover that they can add the beauty of butterflies to their gardens. Whole books have been written on how to do it. The details vary from one region to another, but the basics are the same everywhere: plant some flowers for nectar to attract the adults, and plant some foodplants for the larvae (caterpillars). The latter aspect is sometimes neglected, but it is very important. By planting to feed the larvae, you can actually increase local populations of butterflies, not just attract a few adults that happen to be passing through.

And whatever you do, don't spray pesticides in your garden. Butterflies are insects; pesticides kill insects (along with lots of other things). A living garden with butterflies and bugs and other creatures may have holes chewed in the leaves, but it will still be far more beautiful than a "perfect" garden that has been sprayed and poisoned into sterility.

Butterfly photography: While bird photography usually requires bulky, expensive telephoto lenses, butterflies can be approached closely and photographed without much special equipment. A good macro lens is needed for the smaller species, and flash is helpful. Our colleagues Rick and Nora Bowers, who contributed more images to this book than any other photographers, almost always use artificial light—a ring flash or a bracket with two flash units—to get the best detail, color, and depth of field. But in some situations it is possible to get very pleasing shots with natural light.

Digital cameras have added a new dimension to butterfly photography. They are improving rapidly, and the latest models do an amazingly good job of capturing sharp closeups. We (Bowers, Brock, and Kaufman) are all still using film and then making digital scans from the slides, but we suspect that our conversion to straight digital photography is not far off.

The field is wide open for aspiring butterfly photographers. While Monarchs and a few others have been photographed many times, there are very few images available for many of the skippers, hairstreaks, and others (as Nora Bowers discovered in trying to track down all the images for this guide). If you seek out some of the less common butterflies, you may wind up taking the world's best photos of those species.

Visiting butterfly houses: In recent years, live butterfly exhibits have opened in many parts of North America. While we generally prefer to search for butterflies in the wild, these exhibits can be fascinating places to visit. They usually feature large, showy species from tropical regions. Often the "livestock" is supplied by firms in the developing countries of the tropics, and these companies provide local people with a good income and an incentive to preserve some pieces of natural habitat for butterfly populations. Therefore, in addition to their educational value for visitors, these butterfly houses are often supporting good social and conservation causes as well.

Conservation: The most important thing you can do with butterflies is to help preserve their wonderful diversity. One of our main objectives in writing this guide was to inspire more people to notice and appreciate butterflies so that there would be more support for their conservation.

The main threat facing butterfly populations is loss of habitat. Some of our most beautiful butterflies, such as the Regal Fritillary and the Hermes Copper, have disappeared from much of their former range because their specific habitats have been destroyed. Preserves for butterflies do not have to be very large, but without them we will certainly lose some species.

Pollution of their surroundings, especially with insecticides, poses another problem. Widespread, indiscriminate spraying for gypsy moths has undoubtedly killed billions of butterflies, along with countless numbers of our beautiful silk moths and others. Several butterflies in southern Florida have become quite rare in recent years, and we have to wonder whether heavy, continuous spraying for mosquitoes may have been a factor.

Uninformed persons sometimes imagine that butterfly collectors pose a threat also, but there is scant evidence for this. During an average *week* in summer there are probably more butterflies killed by cars on American roads than the total taken by all the collectors in history. For any would-be protectors of butterflies, harassment of net-wielding lepidopterists is a waste of time; habitat protection is a more worthwhile effort.

Two conservation groups especially deserve support.

THE XERCES SOCIETY, 4828 Southeast Hawthorne Blvd., Portland, Oregon 97215. Named for the Xerces Blue, a butterfly that was driven to extinction by habitat loss in the 1940s, this organization works for the conservation of butterflies and other invertebrates.

THE NATURE CONSERVANCY, 1815 Lynn Street, Arlington, Virginia 22209. This pragmatic organization protects habitat in a very direct way, by buying it. The Nature Conservancy has many good biologists on staff, including some expert lepidopterists, and in working to save particular habitats they take into account the needs of rare butterfly species.

Relations between watchers and collectors: We assume that most users of this guide want to watch butterflies, not collect them. Collecting requires a lot of equipment and a lot of work, and most people find it easier just to enjoy live butterflies in the wild. However, these new watchers or "butterfliers" should recall that essentially all of our knowledge of butterfly classification and distribution is based on the work of collectors. They are the pioneers and discoverers, and their work is not finished.

Not all butterflies can be identified in the field, and collected specimens are essential for study. Species of butterflies new to science are still being discovered, and they must be scientifically documented before their habitat can be protected, so collecting is an essential part of both science and conservation. We have no evidence that collectors have ever caused the extinction of a butterfly species—but a strident anticollecting attitude might result in some species going extinct without having been discovered.

ACKNOWLEDGMENTS

Our first debt is to the generations of lepidopterists who have gathered the information distilled in this guide. Over the years JPB has learned from many of these individuals; it would take a larger book than this to list them all. Some who gave specific help on this book include George T. Austin, Ken Hansen, Sterling Mattoon, Bruce O'Hara, and Andy Warren. In working on this guide, KK gained valuable information (either by direct communication or via Internet discussions) from Barb Beck, John Calhoun, Ken Davenport, Chris Durden, Ron Gatrelle, Michael Gochfeld, Alex Grkovich, Norbert Kondla, Harry LeGrand, Paul Opler, Harry Pavulaan, Ken Philip, Mike Quinn, John Shuey, Felix Sperling, and Dale A. Zimmerman. We benefited from the pioneering work on butterfly distribution done by Paul Opler and others, including the information presented on the U.S. Geological Survey Web site (see p. 19). In recent years, Jeffrey Glassberg has done much to advance the field identification of butterflies, and we are grateful for his influence as well. Thanks also to Michael Godfrey for early pointers on map-making and on presenting information.

Like its predecessor (the *Kaufman Focus Guide to Birds*), this guide was assembled in Tucson, Arizona, by the team at Hillstar Editions L.C. Rick and Nora Bowers again contributed the largest percentage of the photographs used and performed the research to find the others, contacting scores of photographers, juggling thousands of slides, and helping to choose the ones we used in the book. In addition, Nora did much of the digital editing of images and designed many of the color plates, while Rick drew the initial drafts of many of the maps. Stacy M. Fobar came on board partway through the project, and her talents and hard work made a tremendous contribution to all aspects of the final book. Lynn Hassler Kaufman's botanical skills sharpened our treatment of plants; she compiled the larval foodplant index and advised on many other aspects of the book. Others who helped in various ways included Eric Eaton, Leslie Holmes, Linda Leonard, Sam Macomber, and Juliet Niehaus.

As always, it was a pleasure to work with the professionals at Houghton Mifflin. The overall layout of the guide is that of designer Anne Chalmers, the best in the business, who again helped with details as well as with the big picture. Lisa White's editorial skills greatly improved the clarity of our treatment throughout the book, while Harry Foster gave superb advice on the general approach; Peg Anderson and Liz Duvall both helped to improve parts of the text. The talented Megan Butler developed the ideal plan for presenting this guide to the public, with excellent input from Nancy Grant, Lori Glazer, and Larry Mallach. Thanks also to Michaela Sullivan, Beth Kluckhohn, Becky Saikia-Wilson, Julie Burns, and Martha Kennedy. Thanks most of all to Wendy Strothman, who played the key role in establishing the plan for this book and provided good counsel throughout the project (as well as allowing KK to photograph Harris's Checkerspots in her yard). We hope that Wendy, and everyone else at Houghton Mifflin, will approve of the final result.

SOURCES OF FURTHER INFORMATION

This guide was designed for quick identifications in the field, but only so much information can be crammed into a pocket-sized book. If you develop a serious interest in butterflies, you will want to check other sources.

Books: In the Peterson Field Guide series (Houghton Mifflin), *Eastern Butterflies* (1992) and *Western Butterflies* (1999) are excellent. Both are by Paul A. Opler, a scientist who has done much to popularize butterfly study. The Butterflies Through Binoculars series (Oxford University Press) includes volumes for the East (1999), West (2001), and Florida (2000), with fine photos and many field marks (south Texas and the far north are excluded). All are by Jeffrey Glassberg, founder of the North American Butterfly Association. *The Audubon Society Guide to North American Butterflies* (Knopf, 1981) has wonderful text by Robert Michael Pyle.

More detailed or technical references include *The Butterflies of Canada* (University of Toronto Press, 1998), an excellent resource by Ross A. Layberry, Peter W. Hall, and J. Donald Lafontaine, and *The Butterflies of North America* (Stanford University Press, 1986) by James A. Scott. Out of print but worth seeking for its illustrations of subspecies is *The Butterflies of North America* by W. H. Howe (Doubleday, 1975).

A number of books have been published on butterflies of a single state or province, such as the excellent volumes on Alberta, British Columbia, New Jersey, Georgia, and Ohio. Such books may not stay in print for long, but they are worth seeking out for their wealth of specific local data. Of special note among regional books, useful throughout the northwest and beyond, is *The Butterflies of Cascadia* (Seattle Audubon Society, 2002) by Robert Michael Pyle, the father of butterfly-watching.

Web sites: One of the best is provided by the U.S. Geological Survey at http://www.npwrc.usgs.gov/resource/distr/lepid/bflyusa/bflyusa.htm, coordinated and edited by lepidopterists Paul Opler, Ray Stanford, and Harry Pavulaan, with details on all species in the lower 48 states. Sometimes offbeat but worth checking for news, alternate names, and alternate views of butterfly classification is http://tils-ttr.org. For help in getting started watching butterflies, check Kenn Kaufman's www.kknature.com.

Organizations: The Lepidopterists' Society is the world's leading association for people interested in butterflies and moths. Membership is open to all, at any level of interest. Write to The Lepidopterists' Society, 9417 Carvalho Court, Bakersfield, California 93311.

The North American Butterfly Association (NABA) is a private enterprise to promote a particular view of butterfly-watching, but anyone can send in dues and receive their publications. Local chapters operate somewhat independently, offering field trips and other worthwhile activities. Write to NABA, 4 Delaware Road, Morristown, New Jersey 07960.

SWALLOWTAILS

(family Papilionidae) are our largest butterflies, most with "tails" on the hindwings. Tropical relatives (the Birdwings) are the largest butterflies in the world. Swallowtails are popular for their beauty and for the ease with which they can be attracted to gardens. A few of our species are tailless or nearly so, including the Parnassians of the west and north (see p. 44). Young caterpillars of many swallowtails resemble bird droppings.

EASTERN TIGER SWALLOWTAIL *Papilio glaucus*

One of the most familiar eastern butterflies. Common in forests and along streams, it is equally at home in gardens. Avidly visits flowers; also gathers at mud, sometimes in large congregations. Often seen sailing high across roads or clearings. Flies from spring to fall; most of year in deep south (2 or 3 broods). Males are always yellow, but females can be yellow or all black. The black forms are more common southward, especially in areas shared with Pipevine Swallowtail, which they apparently mimic. ▶ Yellow adults have *black tiger stripes.* In the west, see species on next page. Underneath the forewing, the yellow marginal band is *broken up into spots.* Females generally have more extensive blue on the hindwing than males. Black females mimic Pipevine Swallowtail (p. 26); compare to other Pipevine mimics like Spicebush Swallowtail and females of Black and Ozark Swallowtails (p. 28). Black female Eastern Tigers usually show a shadow of the tiger stripes, and have a different pattern on the underside of the hindwing. Note: one large, spring-flying population was very recently described as a new species, Appalachian Tiger Swallowtail *(P. appalachiensis);* see p. 15 for more information. 🐛 **Larval foodplant:** Leaves of trees and shrubs, including cottonwood, tuliptree, sweet bay, cherry, and others.

CANADIAN TIGER SWALLOWTAIL *Papilio canadensis*

This smaller species replaces the Eastern Tiger Swallowtail along the northern tier of states and up into Canada and Alaska. It is common over most of its range, especially around woodland edges, flying in spring and early summer (1 brood). ▶ Similar to Eastern Tiger; usually noticeably smaller, but identification can be difficult along the lengthy, narrow strip where their ranges meet, and some individuals appear intermediate. Underneath the forewing, the yellow marginal band is *continuous,* not broken as on Eastern Tiger. On the hindwing below, the black stripe nearest the body is wider. Black form females are rare. 🐛 **Larval foodplant:** Birch, aspen, black cherry and others.

male

actual size

larva

Eastern Tiger Swallowtail

yellow female

intermediate female

dark female

Canadian Tiger Swallowtail

TIGERS OF THE WEST

Like the tiger swallowtails on the previous page, these two are wide-spread and common, often seen flying high along woodland edges, streamsides, canyons, and even suburban streets.

WESTERN TIGER SWALLOWTAIL *Papilio rutulus*

From the east slope of the Rocky Mountains westward, this is one of our most familiar butterflies. It is found along streamsides, in urban gardens, and in mountain woodlands. More limited in habitat at southern end of range; rarely ventures below 7,000 feet in Arizona, even though it frequents residential areas on the floor of the San Joaquin Valley in California. Can sometimes be found with the Two-tailed Swallowtail. May congregate at mud in large numbers. Replaced by the Canadian Tiger to the north and the Eastern Tiger east of the Rockies. Flies early to midsummer (1 brood) in most areas, but most of year (2–4 broods) along Pacific Coast. ▶ Similar to Eastern Tiger (previous page), but on underside of forewing, yellow marginal band is continuous, not broken into spots. Sexes similar; has no black form of female. Black tiger stripes wider than those of the Two-tailed Swallowtail. Single tails on each hindwing (but note that worn or damaged Two-taileds may be missing these tails). See also Pale Swallowtail (next page). 🌿 **Larval foodplant:** Cottonwood, ash, willow, alder, aspen, and other trees.

TWO-TAILED SWALLOWTAIL *Papilio multicaudata*

The largest of all western butterflies. Often common, ranging widely through open woods with high, lazy, soaring flight. Males sail up and down streamside canyons searching for females. Flies mostly late spring and early summer (1 brood) in northern areas, spring to fall or most of the year farther south (several broods). ▶ The twin tails on each hindwing are unique among western swallowtails. Sexes similar, although females have more blue and orange on the hindwing. This species has narrower black stripes than the Western Tiger Swallowtail and, except in the hot southwest, usually has a more restricted habitat, being found mainly in mountain streamside areas. 🌿 **Larval foodplant:** Chokecherry, ash, and hoptree.

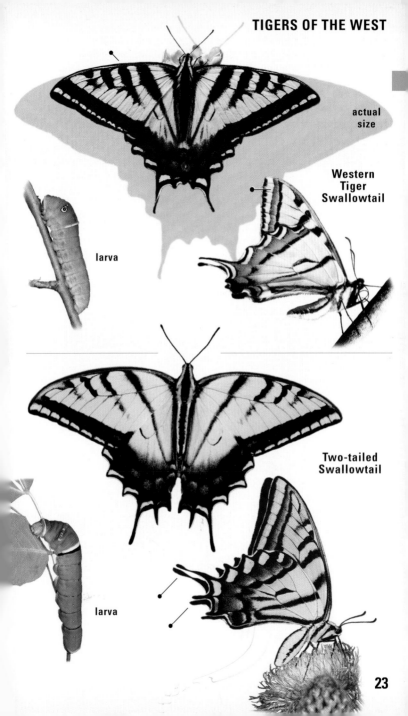

actual
size

Western
Tiger
Swallowtail

larva

Two-tailed
Swallowtail

larva

23

Easily known by their whitish ground color, Zebra and Pale Swallowtails are not found together and are not close relatives. The Zebra Swallowtail belongs to a tropical group often referred to as kite-swallowtails. Pale Swallowtail is related to the species on the previous page.

ZEBRA SWALLOWTAIL   *Eurytides marcellus*

A beautiful long-tailed butterfly of moist woods and brushy fields of the east. The flight is swift and direct, with a side-to-side waver, and usually only a few feet above the ground. Absent in most of New England and from the central Great Plains westward. Flies in spring and summer in the north, most of the year in deep south (2–3 broods). In most areas, seems to be most common in spring. ▶ No other white swallowtails share its range. Easily identified by the greenish white ground color, zebra stripes, and long narrow tails. Underside of hindwing shows a bright red median stripe. Summer individuals tend to be larger and darker, with longer tails (can be up to an inch long). Sexes similar. 🌿 **Larval foodplant:** Pawpaws and squirrel-bananas.

DARK KITE-SWALLOWTAIL   *Eurytides philolaus*

A tropical relative of the Zebra Swallowtail. Normally found in Mexico and Central America, it has strayed into extreme southern Texas several times; midsummer seems to be the most likely season to look for it. ▶ Suggests Zebra Swallowtail (black and white with long tails, red spots on hindwings) but *mostly black,* with white stripes very narrow. 🌿 **Larval foodplant:** Shrubs in the family Annonaceae.

PALE SWALLOWTAIL   *Papilio eurymedon*

The only whitish and black swallowtail in the west. Flies with both Western Tiger and Two-tailed Swallowtails, but is less inclined to remain in riparian areas than the other two. Males patrol hillsides, canyons, and even mountain summits to seek females. Found from sea level to timberline. Flight is fast and erratic. Flies mostly in late spring and early summer in most areas (1 brood), but early spring to fall in some areas along Pacific Coast (2 or more broods). ▶ Pale creamy or whitish with heavy black stripes. Some may have a light yellow flush. Looks similar to Western Tiger Swallowtail (previous page) when perched with wings closed, but is whiter and has orange in the crescent spot leading into the tail. Sexes similar. 🌿 **Larval foodplant:** Buckthorn, coffeeberry, alder, wild plum, and others.

WHITISH SWALLOWTAILS

actual size

spring form

summer form

Zebra Swallowtail

summer form

Dark Kite-Swallowtail (rare)

Pale Swallowtail

DARK SWALLOWTAILS

The first of several. Check range maps in identifying dark swallowtails.

PIPEVINE SWALLOWTAIL   *Battus philenor*

In the southern U.S., the most familiar dark swallowtail next to the Black Swallowtail (next page). Because the caterpillars feed on noxious pipevines, adults are poisonous (or at least distasteful) and predators learn to avoid them. Some other butterflies gain protection by mimicking the pattern of this species; mimics include Spicebush Swallowtail, female Black and Ozark Swallowtails, female Eastern Tiger Swallowtail (black form), Red-spotted Purple (p. 210), and female Diana (p. 158). Common in a variety of open habitats, including gardens. Males patrol hilltops in search of females in the southwest. Flight is rapid and generally low, with fluttery wingbeats, and even when perched they usually continue to flutter wings. It is worth seeking out individuals at mud, who after some time will sit still and reveal an incredibly patterned underside. Flies from spring to fall, most of year in deep south (2–4 broods). Rarely strays north of mapped range. ▶ Black above with a single row of pale spots near wing margins. Hindwing above on male with lovely blue-green iridescence, more subdued on female. Hindwing below with a single row of bright orange spots on iridescent blue background. Individuals from northern California are smaller and hairier. Compare to other dark swallowtails (following pages), also to other mimics mentioned above. 🐛 **Larval foodplant:** Pipevines.

SPICEBUSH SWALLOWTAIL   *Papilio troilus*

An attractive eastern swallowtail, most common in the south. Tends to stick close to wooded areas; flight is slow and close to the ground. Mimics Pipevine Swallowtail but more closely related to Palamedes Swallowtail (p. 36). Flies from spring to fall, most of year in deep south (2–3 broods). Rarely strays north of mapped range. ▶ Differs from most dark swallowtails by overall greenish appearance. Hindwings on males are especially flushed with green while on females this area is more bluish. Note the *large, light green submarginal spots.* Hindwing below has two orange spot bands (only one on Pipevine and dark female Eastern Tiger Swallowtails), and the median spot band lacks one orange spot (band is complete on Black and Ozark Swallowtails). Other dark swallowtails do not overlap in range. 🐛 **Larval foodplant:** Spicebush, sassafras, and other laurels.

DARK SWALLOWTAILS

actual size

male

Pipevine Swallowtail

pupa

larva

female

Spicebush Swallowtail

male

female

BLACK SWALLOWTAIL   *Papilio polyxenes*

A "garden" butterfly, widespread in east and in desert southwest. Occurs from sea level to mountains in a variety of habitats. Absent from Pacific Coast and most of mountain west. Desert populations mostly yellow (see below). Flies spring to fall, most of year in deep south (2–3 broods). ▶ Above males are mostly black with yellow spots along wing edge and a submarginal yellow band of varying width. On females this band is reduced to small spots on forewing and replaced by blue scaling on hindwing (mimicking Pipevine Swallowtail, previous page). Note yellow spot near tip of forewing. Hindwing eyespot with black pupil usually centered and not touching margin. Hindwing below has submarginal and median orange spotbands, plus a yellow/orange cell spot (sometimes faint). Abdomen with rows of yellow spots. 🦋 **Larval foodplant:** Many plants in parsley family, including cultivated, weedy, and native species.

"DESERT" BLACK SWALLOWTAIL   *Papilio polyxenes coloro*

Replaces widespread race in Mojave and Colorado deserts. This and Indra (p. 34) are usually the only swallowtails in desert mountains of southeast California and southern Nevada. From about Phoenix west and northwest, percentage of mostly yellow form increases; northwest edge of range nearly devoid of black forms. Males patrol hilltops. Flies mainly in spring. Later broods (late spring and fall) are rainfall dependent, may not occur some years. Can remain in pupal stage for years until rains bring about good breeding conditions. ▶ Smaller than typical Black Swallowtail. Usually with broad yellow wing band, yellow stripe on abdomen. Similar Anise Swallowtail (next page) barely overlaps; forewing marginal spots rounded on "Desert" Black, flattened distally on Anise. Darkest forms in desert resemble the typical Black, and intermediate black/yellow forms are rare. 🦋 **Larval foodplant:** Primarily turpentine broom, rarely plants in parsley family.

OZARK SWALLOWTAIL   *Papilio joanae*

Ozark Mountain region only, apparently rare or uncommon. Essentially identical to Black Swallowtail and probably not reliably separable in the field. More associated with closed woods. Flies from spring to early fall. ▶ Pupil in hindwing eyespot often touches the margin. Below very little or no yellow in the hindwing orange spots. 🦋 **Larval foodplant:** Meadow parsnip, yellow pimpernel, and golden alexander.

BLACKISH SWALLOWTAILS

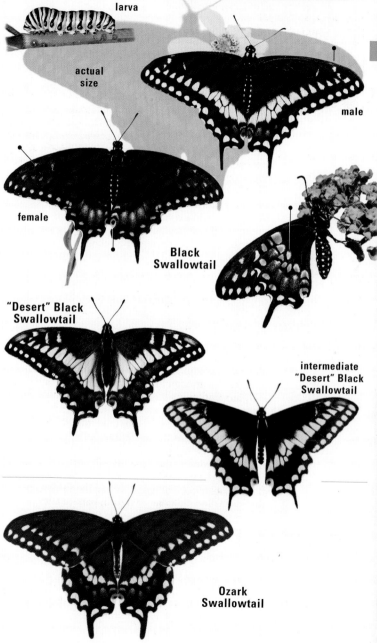

larva

actual
size

male

female

Black
Swallowtail

"Desert" Black
Swallowtail

intermediate
"Desert" Black
Swallowtail

Ozark
Swallowtail

29

One western, one limited to eastern Canada.

ANISE SWALLOWTAIL   *Papilio zelicaon*

A widespread swallowtail of the west, occupying most habitats except arid desert regions. A common garden visitor along the Pacific Coast. Males patrol hilltops, both on lower foothills and on high mountain summits. Along the east edge of the Rocky Mountains, from Alberta through Colorado, part of the population belongs to a scarce black form ("nitra"), which may result from past interbreeding with Black Swallowtails. Over most of range, flies for a brief period between spring and late summer (1 brood). Has 2–4 broods along Pacific Coast, flying from spring to fall, or all year in southern California. ▶ Broad yellow submarginal band. Forewing yellow spots flattened on outer edge. Eyespot on hindwing has centered pupil. Black form ("nitra") similar to Black Swallowtail (previous page) but usually with a basal scattering of black scales into the yellow submarginal band. In arid country, compare to Indra Swallowtail (p. 34). Sexes similar. 🐛 **Larval foodplant:** Plants in the parsley family, including parsley and dill. Along Pacific Coast feeds especially on the introduced sweet fennel (anise), also cultivated citrus.

SHORT-TAILED SWALLOWTAIL   *Papilio brevicauda*

Localized in Maritime Provinces of Canada only, where it barely overlaps the range of Black Swallowtail. Usually flies close to the ground. Found on open grassy hills and in wooded areas, also visits gardens. Flies in early summer (1 brood); may sometimes have a partial second brood in late summer. ▶ Resembles Black Swallowtail (previous page), but tails are *short,* and the lower outer edge of the forewing is more rounded. The band of yellow spots across the upperside of the wings is often *invaded by orange,* especially in Newfoundland and especially on the hindwing, but not always; orange is often lacking on individuals from the western part of the range. Sexes similar. 🐛 **Larval foodplant:** Cow parsnip, scotch lovage, and other plants in the parsley family.

actual
size

Anise Swallowtail

black form
Anise Swallowtail
("nitra")

Short-tailed
Swallowtail

OLD WORLD SWALLOWTAIL

Despite the name, this butterfly is native to large areas of North America as well as to Europe and Asia.

OLD WORLD SWALLOWTAIL *Papilio machaon*

This variable black and yellow species of the west and north can be difficult to identify with certainty in the field, managing to confuse even experienced butterfly watchers. May look similar to Anise, Black, or even Indra Swallowtail in regions where they overlap. Position of the pupil on the hindwing eyespot is a key mark, but often difficult to see in the field. Northern individuals are mostly yellow, southern populations are mostly black. Some regional variations and intermediate forms have been named. Included here are "Oregon" and "Baird's" Swallowtails, both at one time considered separate species. "Oregon" Swallowtail (the official state insect of Oregon) occurs from southern British Columbia to southern Oregon and Idaho; "Baird's" occupies most other parts of the range south of Canada. All forms are usually uncommon and less likely than some other swallowtails to be found in gardens in most areas. Absent from coastal regions and most of California except San Bernardino Mountains. Males are avid hilltoppers. Flies from late spring to early fall in most of range (2 broods), early to midsummer in north (1 brood). ▶ Northern populations: Both sexes have broad yellow bands. Hindwing eyespot with oblong black patch along lower margin, no centered pupil. Broadly overlaps range of Anise Swallowtail, but both yellow and black forms of Anise show a hindwing eyespot with a rounded, centered black pupil. Southern populations: Hindwing eyespot rounded or oblong but extending to and touching the inner angle. Both sexes are usually mostly black. Male usually with narrow yellow median band. Female with little or no yellow median band and more extensive blue on the hindwing. Some individuals (form *brucei*) show a broad yellow median band. Black forms are very similar to Black Swallowtail and to some populations of Indra Swallowtail, but in those two species, the hindwing eyespot usually has the pupil rounded and centered. Forewing marginal spots rounded outwardly on Black, more flattened outwardly on Old World Swallowtail. 🌿 **Larval foodplant**: Wild tarragon, wormwood, and rarely plants in the parsley family.

actual
size

northern
population

"Oregon"
Swallowtail

"Oregon"
Swallowtail

"Baird's"
Swallowtail

"Baird's"
(southern male)

"Baird's"
(southern female)

33

This variable species is a prize find for butterfly watchers in rugged western country.

INDRA SWALLOWTAIL   *Papilio indra*

Fortunate is the observer who gets a good glimpse of this widespread but local and elusive western swallowtail. Most populations occur in rugged, arid, mountainous country accessible only to bighorn sheep and to those humans with good hiking ability. However, like other swallowtails, the Indra is fond of flowers and will seek mud and damp soil, where one may even obtain a photograph or two of this wary species. Males avidly patrol hilltops, where they may be found in company with Anise, Old World, and Pale Swallowtails in the mountain west, and with the "Desert" Black Swallowtail in the desert southwest. Indra Swallowtails usually occupy territory just below the summit, leaving the top for "the others." The flight is rapid and adults are difficult to approach when at rest. Only 1 brood in most areas, spring in southern and lowland regions, early summer farther north and at higher elevations. During wet years in southerly desert areas, may have a partial second brood in mid- to late summer. ▶ Variable in appearance. At least a dozen subspecies have been described on the basis of differing widths of the yellow postmedian wing bands, differing tail lengths, or both; we illustrate five of the most distinctive here. In most areas, mostly black wings with pale yellow bands; *tails usually short or very short* in northern populations, longer in southwestern populations. Abdomen is all black in some regions, or has yellow on the side near the tip. On the eyespot on the upperside of the hindwing, the black pupil is centered (like the pattern of Anise Swallowtail, but unlike that of Old World Swallowtail). Individuals from the north rim of the Grand Canyon (subspecies *kaibabensis*) are nearly all black with extensive blue scaling. Delightful! 🌿 **Larval foodplant:** Wild members of the parsley family.

INDRA SWALLOWTAIL

actual size

fordi

indra

minori

pergamus

kaibabensis

Five regional variations on Indra Swallowtail (labeled by name of subspecies)

SOUTHERN SWALLOWTAILS

Two striking and distinctive species of the southeastern states.

PALAMEDES SWALLOWTAIL   *Papilio palamedes*

This large, brightly marked swallowtail is at home in the swamplands of the southeast. Common in Florida, it also ranges northward in woodlands along the east coast to southern New Jersey and westward to eastern Texas. Like other swallowtails, the Palamedes avidly visits flowers and mud. Rivals the Eastern Tiger in terms of size and splashy pattern. Adults coursing slowly through swampy woodlands are a sight to behold! Flies from spring to fall in most areas, with a longer season in more southerly areas, throughout the year in southern Florida (2–3 broods). ▶ Dark brown to blackish above with a yellow postmedian band crossing both wings, especially broad and unbroken on the hindwing. From below, shows a very bright pattern on the hindwing, with a thin yellow stripe paralleling the base of the hindwing. Sexes similar. 🌿 **Larval foodplant:** Redbay and other laurels.

POLYDAMAS SWALLOWTAIL   *Battus polydamas*

A dark, tailless species of tropical affinity, found throughout the Caribbean region and tropical America. A garden butterfly in much of peninsular Florida and to a lesser degree in southern Texas. Strays northward rarely. Flight consists of constant, rapid wingbeats, and it continues to flutter wings rapidly even while attending flowers (like the Pipevine Swallowtail, p. 26, which is related but not very similar). Flies from mid-spring to late fall (2 or 3 broods). ▶ Identified by the absence of tails and by the greenish yellow spot band rimming the wing edges on the upperside (this butterfly is also known as the "Gold Rim"). Hindwing below brownish black with curved red lines along the margin. Sexes similar. Note that other swallowtails in worn or damaged condition can be missing the tails on the hindwing, so be sure to see color pattern as well as wing shape. 🌿 **Larval foodplant:** Pipevines.

actual
size

Palamedes
Swallowtail

Polydamas
Swallowtail

Giant Swallowtail is very common in many areas and is mostly easy to recognize. However, several tropical species, rare in our area, resemble it closely. Near the Mexican border or in southern Florida, experienced butterfly-watchers may want to look out for the rare species mentioned below and on the next two pages.

GIANT SWALLOWTAIL   *Papilio cresphontes*

This large, dark brown and yellow swallowtail is nearly always found in association with plants in the citrus family. It is equally at home in gardens and in natural wooded areas, and although it is common, the first sighting of one never fails to dazzle the observer. Ranges throughout most of the east; more limited distribution in the southwest, but has expanded into the Los Angeles basin within the past 20 years. Considered a pest of ornamental citrus by growers, as its larvae feed on the foliage. Flight is a graceful series of strong flaps and short glides, usually flying at eye level or above. Adults are on the wing all year in southern Florida, most of year in deep south, spring to fall farther north. Sometimes strays north of mapped range. ► Mostly dark above and pale below (including body). On upperside, the yellow bands cross, forming an **X** near the tip of the forewing. Tails on hindwing have *yellow centers*. On hindwing below, the small rusty brown patch does not invade the median band. Sexes similar. 🌿 **Larval foodplant:** Ornamental citrus, torchwood, wild lime, hoptree, and other citrus relatives.

THOAS SWALLOWTAIL   *Papilio thoas*   (not illustrated)

Very similar to Giant Swallowtail and difficult to distinguish from it reliably in the field. Rare in extreme southern Texas, straying northward into the plains. Associated with piper plants in the tropics. ► Essentially identical to Giant Swallowtail. Yellow bands can be paler than those on Giant Swallowtail but worn Giants make this field mark unreliable. 🌿 **Larval foodplant:** Piper; possibly also some plants in the citrus family.

ORNYTHION SWALLOWTAIL   *Papilio ornythion*

Local and scarce in extreme southern Texas, rarely straying northward onto plains and through Big Bend to southeastern New Mexico. Habits and flight similar to Giant Swallowtail. ► Males have paler yellow bands on the forewing than Giant Swallowtail, and these bands do not cross near the wingtip. Females with pale yellow bands reduced or obscured by black. Compare to Broad-banded Swallowtail (p. 42). 🌿 **Larval foodplant:** Ornamental and native citrus.

SWALLOWTAILS

actual size

Giant Swallowtail

larva

males

Ornythion Swallowtail

Any possible sightings of these should first rule out the Giant Swallowtail (previous page), which is very common in Florida.

SCHAUS'S SWALLOWTAIL   *Papilio aristodemus*

Extreme south Florida only, an endangered species. This attractive and much sought after butterfly lives only in hardwood hammocks of native vegetation, now mainly in a few areas of the Florida Keys (Biscayne National Park, Key Largo). Destruction of habitat was probably responsible for its disappearance from much of its former range, but now a captive breeding and reintroduction program has brightened its future. Usually flies close to the ground. Adults are on the wing only in late spring (late April to early June). Other races exist in the Greater Antilles. ▶ Similar to the Giant Swallowtail (previous page), but tails on hindwing lack yellow in the center, and yellow bands on the forewing above do not form an X near the wingtip. Below, the hindwing shows a large rusty brown median patch. Males have yellow antennal clubs. 🌱 **Larval foodplant:** Torchwood and rarely wild lime.

BAHAMIAN SWALLOWTAIL   *Papilio andraemon*

Extreme south Florida only. Not considered a regular resident, but may be found in the same places and habitats as Schaus's Swallowtail when present. Also known from the Bahamas and Cuba. ▶ Upperside pattern similar to both Giant and Schaus's Swallowtails, but yellow median bands are arranged differently, especially on hindwing, where the band does not angle in so sharply toward the base of the wing; also note the short yellow bar near the end of the forewing cell. Tails have yellow centers. Hindwing below with single rusty brown triangle invading the median band. Males have yellow antennal clubs. 🌱 **Larval foodplant:** Torchwood and other members of the citrus family.

ANDROGEUS SWALLOWTAIL   *Papilio androgeus*

Formerly southern Florida, not seen in many years. Became established in Broward and Dade Counties, where it colonized overgrown citrus groves during its brief tenure (1976 to 1983). Flight is darting, fast, and close to the ground. Known from the Greater Antilles, also Mexico to South America. ▶ Sexes strikingly different: Males with broad yellow band and without marginal spots. Females mostly black, with blue iridescence on the upperside of the hindwing, and with a series of short, pointed tails on the hindwing. 🌱 **Larval foodplant:** Members of the citrus family.

actual size

Schaus's
Swallowtail

Bahamian
Swallowtail

females

male

Androgeus
Swallowtail

These should be watched for, but not expected, in areas near the border. They may even stray farther north — these strong-flying butterflies occasionally wander long distances — but colorful butterflies found far out of range may have been brought there by humans.

RUBY-SPOTTED SWALLOWTAIL *Papilio anchisiades*

Widespread in the tropics, from Mexico to Brazil, seen along woodland edges and in semiopen country. In our area found mainly in extreme southern Texas, where it is apparently scarce or irregular, flying at various times from spring to late fall. Strays have reached southern Arizona and have wandered as far north as Kansas. ▶ Large and long-winged, with an irregular margin on the hindwing but no well-developed tails. Mostly blackish, with a ruby red spot or patch (of variable size) on the hindwing. Females have variable amounts of white on the forewing. ❧ **Larval foodplant:** Ornamental and native citrus.

WHITE-DOTTED CATTLEHEART *Parides alopius*

Native to western Mexico, where it flies mostly in mountain forests. Found once in July in southeastern Arizona. The one found here was in fresh condition, suggesting it had not strayed far, and the species might be expected to occur again. ▶ A relatively small swallowtail. Mostly black, with a single row of small white dots (fewer on male) and a larger row of pinkish-red spots on the hindwing, more obvious on underside than on upperside. ❧ **Larval foodplant:** Watson's pipevine.

BROAD-BANDED SWALLOWTAIL *Papilio astyalus*

Widespread in the tropics, from Mexico to Argentina. A regular stray into extreme southern Texas, occurring there at most times of the year; also wanders very rarely into southern Arizona (in late summer) and to northern Texas. ▶ Males with broad yellow bands and with a large yellow spot within the cell on the forewing. Females mostly black with multiple spot-bands on the hindwing: blue, gray-green, and orange. Both sexes with large submarginal yellow crescents on hindwing. Tails are often short on females. Compare to Ornythion Swallowtail (p. 38). ❧ **Larval foodplant:** Ornamental and native citrus.

THREE-TAILED SWALLOWTAIL *Papilio pilumnus*

Widespread in Mexico, but reaches our area only as a rare stray in southern Texas and a very rare stray in southern Arizona. Inhabits tropical woodlands in native range. ▶ Smaller than Two-tailed Swallowtail and has three tails on each hindwing. In flight appears to be a much duskier yellow swallowtail than the other "tigers" (pp. 20–23), because of the broad black forewing stripes. ❧ **Larval foodplant:** Laurels.

TROPICAL RARITIES

males

Ruby-spotted Swallowtail

actual size

White-dotted Cattleheart

males

Broad-banded Swallowtail

female

Three-tailed Swallowtail

PARNASSIANS

These enchanting members of the swallowtail family, denizens of the west and north, are certain to become favorites of most who lay eyes on them. Parnassians are tailless, yellow or white, and, to varying degrees, translucent with variable black and red markings. The flight is usually slow and close to the ground, making for easy observation. Mated females have a visible waxy plug, known as a sphragis, placed there by the male to prevent further fooling around. Parnassian caterpillars, unlike those of most butterflies, pupate in ground litter in a cocoonlike case.

CLODIUS PARNASSIAN — *Parnassius clodius*

A large white butterfly of western woodlands. Flies slowly, constantly flapping its wings, occasionally gliding with wings held in a shallow V. Occurs rather locally from sea level to higher mountain forests. Avidly visits flowers. Usually found at lower elevations than Phoebus Parnassian. Flies from late spring to early fall, mostly in summer. ▶ Antennae black. The bar within the forewing cell is gray, rectangular, and *crosses the entire cell*. Size of the red hindwing spots varies. Outer forewing margins broadly transparent gray. 🐛 **Larval foodplant:** Bleeding heart.

PHOEBUS PARNASSIAN — *Parnassius phoebus*

This lovely species of midsummer brightens up any high-altitude rocky landscape. Generally flies slowly and close to the ground, often stopping at various alpine flowers. Occurs locally from open high-mountain woodlands to rocky alpine areas and tundra. A variable butterfly with many named populations from northern New Mexico, the Black Hills, and California north to Alaska. Those at high elevations in the Sierra Nevada (with hindwing spots centered in orange) may be a separate species, and other populations may merit species status as well. ▶ Antennae banded black and white. The bar within the forewing cell is black, rounded on the bottom, and *rarely crosses the entire cell*. Outer forewing margins mostly white in males, transparent gray in females except gray in both sexes in colder regions. 🐛 **Larval foodplant:** Various stonecrops.

EVERSMANN'S PARNASSIAN — *Parnassius eversmanni*

Our only yellow Parnassian. A "must see" butterfly found only in Alaska and northwestern Canada (and in northern Asia). Flies close to the ground over open tundra. ▶ Male yellow with two red spots on the hindwing. Female yellow or white with three red hindwing spots. Forewing margin transparent in both sexes. 🐛 **Larval foodplant:** Bleeding heart and corydalis (in Asia).

PARNASSIANS

female

actual size

Clodius Parnassian

male

frequent posture

Rocky Mountains

high-elevation Rockies

Phoebus Parnassian

Sierras

Alaska female

male

female

Eversmann's Parnassian

45

and sulphurs **(family Pieridae)** are among our most abundant and conspicuous butterflies, drawing attention as they flutter about gardens, fields, and other open areas. Whites are found from coastal beaches to mountain summits. They are avid flower visitors. Most are rather plain, but some orangetips and marbles are among our most beautiful butterflies. Caterpillars of most whites feed on mustards or capers, but two species eat pine needles.

CABBAGE WHITE   *Pieris rapae*

One of our most common butterflies. Introduced from Europe in the 19th century and has spread across the continent. Very much at home in cities, frequently found in gardens where it is considered a pest of cabbage, nasturtium, and cultivated mustards. Less likely to be found in natural habitats or in arid regions. Flight is high or low, swerving side to side and up and down. Flies spring to fall (many broods). ▶ Above shows a *horizontal black patch* at wingtip. Male with one spot, female with two in the *middle of the forewing*. Hindwing below *unmarked pale yellow, grayish white, or white*. 🐛 **Larval foodplant:** Cabbage, nasturtium, watercress, various capers and mustards.

MUSTARD WHITE   *Pieris napi*

This butterfly brightens up many a shady woodland with sunlit white wings. Mainly inhabits moist forest, also on alpine tundra in Alaska. Strongly attracted to flowers. Flight is erratic, not very fast, close to the ground. Quite variable, and thought by some to consist of two or three different species. Flies early spring to summer (1 or 2 broods). ▶ Variable. Below hindwing veins usually *outlined in dark green in spring,* but can be *nearly unmarked* in summer. Above generally plain although forewing may have one or two spots at center and black scaling from tip down outer margin and inward along veins. 🐛 **Larval foodplant:** Wide variety of mustards, including toothwort, rock cress, and others.

WEST VIRGINIA WHITE   *Pieris virginiensis*

A springtime butterfly of woodland in the Appalachian and Great Lakes regions, usually uncommon. Seldom strays from moist shaded woodlands where its foodplant grows. Flight is slow, close to the ground. Flies in spring (1 brood). ▶ Above white, mainly unmarked. Female slightly duskier than male. Below, veins are *softly lined in brownish gray.* Spring-flying Mustard Whites usually show much darker hindwing veins. 🐛 **Larval foodplant:** Toothwort, also rock cress and other mustards.

WHITES

variations

actual size

Cabbage White

male

female

Mustard White
(quite variable)

West Virginia White

CHECKERED WHITE *Pontia protodice*

Widespread, most common in south and west. Occurs in wider variety of habitats than other whites, colonizing exotic mustards in disturbed areas. Males gather on hilltops but are as easily found in fields and roadsides. Both sexes visit flowers. Flight is rapid, low, erratic but direct. Flies most of year in south, spring to fall northward (1–3 broods). ► Above white marked with gray, more so on female. Hindwing below with *extensive yellow-brown veining.* Smaller in early spring, with darker veining below. Some summer males are all white below. 🌿 **Larval foodplant:** Many native and exotic mustards.

WESTERN WHITE *Pontia occidentalis*

Mostly upper elevations. Flies spring to fall (2 broods) at mid elevations, summer (1 brood) at high elevations and in north. Males hilltop. ► Very similar to Checkered White, especially in spring. Above forewing marginal spots tend to be *gray,* contrasting with black submarginal band (but some have black marginal spots). Male Western White has 5–6 marginal spots; male Checkered White has 2–3, rarely 5. Female Western usually has submarginal band more black above than Checkered. Hindwing below usually with strong gray-green veining. 🌿 **Larval foodplant:** Many native mustards.

BECKER'S WHITE *Pontia beckerii*

A nicely marked butterfly of arid habitats, including some where few other butterflies live. Adults seem continually on the move, stopping only for an occasional sip of nectar. Often along roadsides. Flies from spring to fall (2–4 broods). ► Above both sexes white. Female with more black markings. Often forewing cell with *bold black spot centered with white.* Hindwing below with green scaling along *yellow veins.* 🌿 **Larval foodplant:** Bladderpod, prince's plume, and other mustards.

SPRING WHITE *Pontia sisymbrii*

Widespread in the west, flying early in the season. Tends to avoid arid lowlands and open, high desert. Males avidly hilltop and will come to mud. Flies in spring in lowlands, early summer at high elevations (1 brood). ► Above white with black markings, some females tinged yellow. The forewing cell bar is *narrow* (can be thicker in southwest), *notched on the outside edge.* Hindwing below has brown scaling along yellow veins, the postmedian area *interrupted by white.* 🌿 **Larval foodplant:** Rock cress, lace pod, many other mustards.

WHITES

lightly marked
males

actual size

female

**Checkered
White**

heavily marked spring
Checkered or Western
(very similar)

male

**Western
White**

female

**Becker's
White**

male

female

Spring White

heavily marked
Las Vegas
population

male

female

49

These distinctive and unusual butterflies are rarely found away from evergreen forests.

PINE WHITE *Neophasia menapia*

White butterflies flying high around western pine trees from mid- to late summer are probably this species. Widespread and sometimes abundant, although one often must scan the forest canopy to see it. Sometimes comes down to flowers close to the ground. The flight is very slow for a butterfly — hinting at some sort of chemical protection, perhaps gained from the caterpillar foodplant. Flies from mid- to late summer (1 brood). ▶ White with strong black markings, but habitat and behavior are among the best clues. Black mark on the leading edge of the forewing curves around to form a *cell-end bar*. Sexes similar, with heavier black markings on the female. Female hindwing below edged with red. 🌿 **Larval foodplant:** Mainly ponderosa pine but also pinyon pine, Douglas-fir, and others.

CHIRICAHUA WHITE *Neophasia terlootii*

A specialty of a few mountain ranges in southeast Arizona and possibly southwest New Mexico. Females of this "white" are a spectacular orange and get rave reviews from all who lay eyes on them! As with the Pine White, the adults have a slow, fluttering flight, mainly staying high up in the canopy of pines. On some days, for no obvious reason, they descend in large numbers. Will feed at both mud and flowers. Flies in early summer and fall (2 broods), with fewer seen during the first flight. ▶ The forewing cell is *entirely black* on both sexes. Male white with black markings, female marked similarly but bright orange above, rarely yellow. From below, female hindwing shows red at base and outer edge. 🌿 **Larval foodplant:** Ponderosa pine and Englemann spruce.

MEXICAN DARTWHITE *Catasticta nimbice*

Rare, west Texas only, recorded from March to May from the Chisos Mountains of Big Bend National Park. The northernmost member of a large tropical group. Normally found in mountain woodlands throughout Mexico and Central America, where multiple broods occur. Males patrol back and forth along linear pathways and deep canyons. Flight is usually well above the ground. ▶ Blackish with broad pale yellow bands. 🌿 **Larval foodplant:** Mistletoe growing on trees.

WHITES OF WESTERN FORESTS

Pine White

actual size

male

female

male

males

Chiricahua White

females

Mexican Dartwhite

GREAT SOUTHERN WHITE   *Ascia monuste*

Common most of year in southern coastal Florida and Texas. More widespread than Florida White, moving northward along most of Gulf Coast, most of Florida, and along the Georgia coast in summer and fall. These movements often consist of thousands of individuals, with some reaching the northern plains and far up the Atlantic seaboard. Flight when not migrating is slow and investigative, while migratory flight is direct, fast, and often in small groups. Mostly coastal, but does establish inland colonies. Flies most of year where resident (multiple broods). ▶ *Antennal clubs usually pale blue-green.* Above black border of forewing may *follow the veins inward.* Males are white; females may be white or smoky gray, with a spot in the cell (smoky-gray form unique among North American whites). Below varies from white to gray to tan. 🌿 **Larval foodplant:** Saltwort and sea rocket in coastal areas, nasturtiums and mustards inland.

FLORIDA WHITE   *Appias drusilla*

A tropical species, mainly restricted to coastal areas in extreme southern Florida and Texas. Prefers shaded hammocks and woods to open areas. Flies most of year where resident (3–4 broods). Rare strays are known from far north of normal haunts. ▶ Both surfaces satiny white. Above the black forewing border (when present) does not follow veins inward. Below shows some *yellow-orange near wing bases.* Antennal clubs pale, but not bluish. 🌿 **Larval foodplant:** Capers.

GIANT WHITE   *Ganyra josephina*

Our largest white is an occasional resident of south Texas, mainly in fall, rarely straying farther north. Very common south of Texas in desert scrub areas of Tamaulipas, Mexico. ▶ *Very large* (usually larger than Cloudless Sulphur). Male white above, forewing cell with a conspicuous black spot. Female white or cream, sometimes brownish, often with marginal and submarginal black markings. 🌿 **Larval foodplant:** Capers.

HOWARTH'S WHITE   *Ganyra howarthi*

Rare stray to southeast Arizona, and regular around the wild capers at Quitobaquito Spring in Organ Pipe Cactus National Park, southwest Arizona. In Sonora, Mexico, it flies well above the ground in desert scrub areas with the foodplant. ▶ *Large* (but not as large as Giant White). Above white with conspicuous black cell spot. Female often has marginal and submarginal black markings on forewing. 🌿 **Larval foodplant:** Capers.

TROPICAL WHITES

male

female

actual size

male

Great Southern White

females

Florida White

female

male

male

male

Giant White

female

Howarth's White

53

and orangetips (next two pages) are beautiful butterflies, mostly on the wing quite early in the season.

LARGE MARBLE   *Euchloe ausonides*

Ranges widely in the mountain west, but not found in very dry country. Flies in spring at low elevations (1 or 2 broods), summer at high elevations (1 brood). ► Difficult to separate from Pearly Marble where they fly together. Above leading edge of forewing *lightly marked*, and forewing cell bar *usually narrow.* Some females have *buff-yellow hindwings* above. Marbling below is extensive and yellow-green, with veins usually yellower. 🌱 **Larval foodplant:** Tower mustard and other rock cresses.

PEARLY MARBLE   *Euchloe hyantis*

A marble seen in southwestern deserts is most likely this one. Wings have a pearly luster. Flies in early spring in most areas, early summer at higher elevations (1 brood). Flight is fast, erratic. Males hilltop and rarely pause except briefly at flowers. ► Similar to Large Marble, averaging smaller. Above leading edge of forewing is checkered, and forewing cell bar varies from narrow (mountains) to wide (deserts). Marbling below is extensive, with veins rarely yellower. Varies by region; may be more than one species. 🌱 **Larval foodplant:** Tansy mustard, rock cress, other native and exotic mustards.

NORTHERN MARBLE   *Euchloe creusa*

Only from Alaska to Saskatchewan and northwest Montana, in forest edges, clearings, tundra. Flies in late spring and early summer (1 brood), notably early in northernmost areas. ► Usually smaller than Large Marble, more heavily patterned below, with dense gray-green marbling *broken up by white lines.* 🌱 **Larval foodplant:** Mustards, including whitlow grass and rock cress.

GREEN MARBLE   *Euchloe naina*   *(not illustrated)*

A small marble with a limited range in the far northwest. Found above timberline and gravelly spots in lowlands. Flies in summer (1 brood). ► Below more *heavily and solidly marbled* than Northern Marble. Resembles Large Marble, but has forewing tips squared off and small black spots at ends of veins above. 🌱 **Larval foodplant:** Probably mustards such as rock cress.

SONORAN MARBLE   *Euchloe guaymasensis*   *(not illustrated)*

Very rare (found once in Bisbee, Arizona). Check hilltops in southern Arizona in early spring. ► Pale yellow above; marbling sparse below. 🌱 **Larval foodplant:** Tansy mustard and perhaps other mustards.

MARBLES

actual size

female

male

Large Marble

Pearly Marble

widespread form

desert form

Northern Marble

Two eastern species and one from the West Coast. Like most members of these two groups, these fly early in the season.

FALCATE ORANGETIP   *Anthocharis midea*

In the southeast this butterfly is a true springtime delicacy, easily overlooked because of its small size and early flight season. Colonies are rather local. Flight style is wavering from side to side, close to the ground, and not extremely fast. It flies in early spring (1 brood); most females emerge a week or so following the first males. ▶ Named for the distinctly *curved and pointed* (or "falcate") *tip of the forewing*, a good field mark. White above with a black spot in the forewing cell. Male has a patch of orange in the wingtip area, while female is white there, occasionally with a hint of yellow. Below hindwing is almost completely marbled brown, often two-toned. 🐛 **Larval foodplant:** Rock cress, bitter cress, and other mustards.

OLYMPIA MARBLE   *Euchloe olympia*

Look for this springtime beauty from the eastern edge of the Rockies eastward. Absent from the southeast and New England. Inhabits lakeshore dunes, shale grasslands, and open cedar glades; tends to occur in localized colonies. A really good glimpse of a fresh, perched adult with its rosy tinted wings will not soon be forgotten. Flies in spring (1 brood). Males fly directly, fast, and close to the ground when seeking females. ▶ White above with narrow forewing cell bar. Yellow-green marbling below is *rather sparse*, and absent from lower angle of hindwing. Along western edge of range, compare to Large Marble (previous page). 🐛 **Larval foodplant:** Mainly rock cress.

GRAY MARBLE   *Anthocharis lanceolata*

West Coast only, barely extending into southern Oregon. This very pale species (essentially an orangetip without orange in the wingtips) lives in rocky canyons or meadows where its foodplant occurs. It flies early spring to summer, depending on elevation (1 brood). Flight is relatively fast, direct, and erratic, a style typical of most whites. Always a delightful beast to encounter. ▶ Above white with narrow black cell bar often reduced to a spot. The tip of the forewing is pointed and has some gray markings. Hindwing below is striated brownish gray, with a *white intrusion just below the leading edge.* 🐛 **Larval foodplant:** Tower mustard and other species of rock cress.

ORANGETIP AND MARBLES

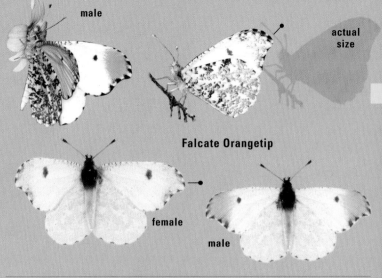

male

actual size

Falcate Orangetip

female

male

Olympia Marble

Gray Marble

SARA ORANGETIP   *Anthocharis sara*

Few butterflies match the elegance of this western species. Popular for its beauty and because, for some, the Sara Orangetip signals the first days of spring and the beginning of another butterfly season. Best observed patroling foothill canyon slopes, stream bottoms, washes, or mountain meadows. Stops at flowers, but usually briefly. Males do not congregate on hilltops. Flight is direct and side to side, but orange wingtips are visible on fly-bys. Flies in early spring at low elevations, late spring to early summer at higher elevations (1 brood). Some lowland populations have a small second brood in late spring following wet winters. ▶ Variable, with many regional forms; more than one species may be involved. Above male is usually white, female white or pale yellow. Male forewing tip is black with red-orange patch. Female's orange patch is usually lighter, often set off from wing edge by paler area. Hindwing below with brown or brownish-green marbling, varying by region, usually broken by *lengthwise white stripe.* Compare to next species. Second-brood adults larger and much less strongly marked. 🦋 **Larval foodplant:** Rock cress; also other native and exotic mustards.

DESERT ORANGETIP   *Anthocharis cethura*

A brightly colored species of arid western regions. Male Desert Orangetips flitting about a desert hilltop provide one of springtime's most dazzling rituals. Females are best encountered on slopes in the afternoon. May be absent following dry winters; can stay in pupal stage for four or more years before emerging. Flies with rapid wingbeats, but orange wingtips are visible in flight. Flies early to late spring depending on region (1 brood). Isolated population on Santa Catalina Island off California coast. ▶ Overall color varies, yellow in east half of range (also known as Pima Orangetip), usually white farther west. Bright yellow forms distinctive, but others similar to Sara Orangetip. Note that Desert has *wide pale edge* on wingtip above, more pointed wingtip shape, and usually *lacks* the white stripe through green marbling below. Female's orange forewing patch is duller, often reduced. Females from some western populations lack orange patch and can be confused with Pearly Marble (p. 54); note blue-gray eyes, not green. 🦋 **Larval foodplant:** Tansy mustard, rock cress, lace pod, London rocket, and other mustards.

WESTERN ORANGETIPS

actual size

female

variant female
lightly marked, yellow

male

Sara
Orangetip

Desert Orangetip

females

male

"Pima"
Desert
Orangetip

are usually some shade of yellow, orange, or white. Those on the next four pages, in the genus *Colias,* can be very confusing. Their uppersides feature black borders (usually solid in males, often with pale spots in females); they always perch with wings closed, but upperside pattern may be seen faintly through the wing, or glimpsed in flight. Note overall color above and below, and details of the central spot on the hindwing below.

CLOUDED SULPHUR   *Colias philodice*

This is a familiar, bright yellow species (often called Common Sulphur) that ranges across most of the continent. Often very common in fields and along roadsides. Adults come to both mud and flowers. Flight is slightly erratic and direct. Flies spring to fall (multiple broods). ▶ Male yellow above, female either yellow or greenish white. Below both sexes yellow with little or no black overscaling, hindwing spot (often double) trimmed with red, and some black postmedian markings. Some Orange Sulphurs show very little orange and can be hard to separate from this species. 🌿 **Larval foodplant:** White clover, alfalfa, and other legumes.

ORANGE SULPHUR   *Colias eurytheme*

Our most widespread orange sulphur butterfly. Often seen by the hundreds fluttering over alfalfa fields, but also found in most other habitats. Less tolerant of cold regions than Clouded Sulphur. Avidly visits flowers. Slightly erratic flight like that of Clouded Sulphur. Flies spring to fall (multiple broods). ▶ Very similar to Clouded Sulphur except for orange on upperside. (Some females of both species are greenish white and almost identical.) In early spring, may have reduced orange above and some black overscaling below. Clouded and Orange Sulphurs sometimes hybridize, so not all individuals can be identified. 🌿 **Larval foodplant:** Alfalfa, native and exotic clovers, and other legumes.

HARFORD'S SULPHUR   *Colias harfordii*

Southern California only. Prefers chaparral, foothill canyons, and openings in lower montane woodlands. Flies in spring and summer (2 broods). ▶ Like Clouded Sulphur, but different range. Bright yellow above, with no orange (compare to Orange Sulphur). No white female form. One of two bright yellow sulphurs in most of its habitats. (California Dogface females, p. 68, are larger with a pointed forewing tip.) Below mostly yellow, sometimes with postmedian spots. Early spring individuals have some black overscaling. 🌿 **Larval foodplant:** Rattleweed.

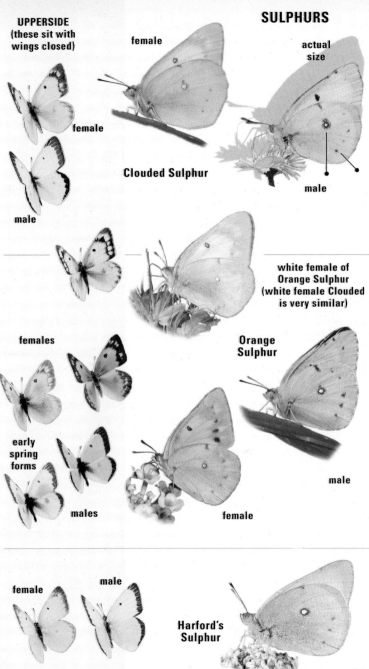

UPPERSIDE
(these sit with
wings closed)

female

actual
size

female

male

Clouded Sulphur

white female of
Orange Sulphur
(white female Clouded
is very similar)

females

**Orange
Sulphur**

early
spring
forms

males

male

female

female

male

**Harford's
Sulphur**

PINK-EDGED SULPHUR   *Colias interior*

A bright yellow species, more restricted in range than Clouded Sulphur. Associated with burns, clearings, woodlands, other habitats where blueberry abounds. Flies in summer (1 brood). ▶ Clear yellow below. Resembles Clouded Sulphur (previous page), but has no dark postmedian spots and center spot on hindwing is single, not double. *Pink fringes obvious* except when worn. Females rarely white. ❧ **Larval foodplant:** Blueberry.

PELIDNE SULPHUR   *Colias pelidne*

A sulphur of tundra and subalpine forest, with disjunct range in Arctic and Rockies. Flies in summer (1 brood). ▶ Male yellow above; female usually white, especially in northern areas. Pink wing fringes. Heavy pink rim around hindwing spot. *More black overscaling* below than Pink-edged or Clouded Sulphurs, especially near leading edge of forewing. Also compare to Palaeno Sulphur (p. 64). ❧ **Larval foodplant:** Blueberry.

QUEEN ALEXANDRA'S SULPHUR   *Colias alexandra*

A large, bright sulphur of sagebrush flats, prairie grassland, mountain meadows. Adults are attracted to flowers or mud. Flies in summer (1–2 broods). ▶ Hindwing below *smooth gray-green*, the central spot with *little or no red rim.* Wing fringes yellow or only faintly pink. Above male bright yellow; female yellow (usually) or whitish, with black margin reduced or absent. ❧ **Larval foodplant:** Golden banner, vetches, other legumes.

CHRISTINA'S SULPHUR   *Colias christina*

Spectacular if seen well, a sulphur of forest openings and slopes. Long summer flight (1 brood). ▶ Known by rather large size, orange flush on male above. Female white, orange, or in between. Hindwing below yellow or greenish yellow, central spot rimmed with red. Wing fringes pink. Some males have postmedian spots below. ❧ **Larval foodplant:** Sweet vetch, other legumes.

WESTERN SULPHUR   *Colias occidentalis*

This rather variable species roams a variety of habitats, coastal areas to high elevations. Taxonomy of Western and Christina's Sulphurs still debated. Flies late spring through summer (1 brood). ▶ Hindwing below with *light but extensive black overscaling,* postmedian spots sometimes present, central spot *strongly rimmed red.* Wing fringes pink. Above male bright yellow or lightly flushed orange, female yellow or white. ❧ **Larval foodplant:** Milk vetch, golden banner, other legumes.

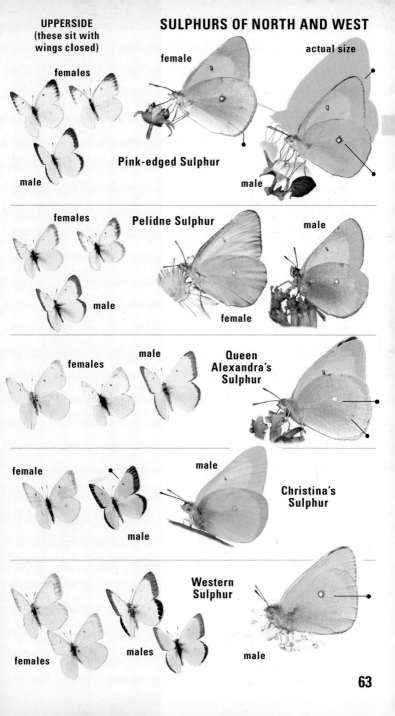

SULPHURS OF NORTH AND WEST

UPPERSIDE
(these sit with
wings closed)

actual size

Pink-edged Sulphur

females

male

female

male

Pelidne Sulphur

females

male

male

female

Queen Alexandra's Sulphur

females

male

Christina's Sulphur

female

male

male

Western Sulphur

females

males

male

63

GIANT SULPHUR *Colias gigantea*

A large, bright sulphur, closely tied to willow bogs in northern boreal and mixed forests. Closely related to Scudder's Sulphur. Flies in summer (1 brood). ▶ Often the *largest* sulphur in its habitat. Male bright yellow above, female yellow or white with black border reduced or absent. Hindwing below yellow, with central spot (double or not) rimmed with red. Fringes yellowish in male, pink in female. Lacks submarginal spots of Clouded Sulphur (p. 60). 🌿 **Larval foodplant**: Willows.

SCUDDER'S SULPHUR *Colias scudderi*

Central Rocky Mountains only, where restricted to willow bogs in alpine regions. Flies in summer (1 brood). ▶ Similar in all aspects to the closely related Giant Sulphur, only smaller, and male has somewhat wider black borders above; best identified by *range*. Hindwing below yellow-green with some black overscaling. Male yellow above; female white (usually) or yellow, with very little black at wingtip. 🌿 **Larval foodplant**: Willows.

PALAENO SULPHUR *Colias palaeno*

A sulphur of remote Arctic tundra and boggy taiga. Not often found near human haunts. Flight is fairly fast, darting, and very close to the ground. Flies in summer (1 brood). ▶ Below yellowish green with pink fringes. Hindwing central spot is small, *not* rimmed with red (compare to Pelidne Sulphur, previous page). Male yellow above, female greenish white or yellow. 🌿 **Larval foodplant**: Arctic bilberry.

LABRADOR SULPHUR *Colias nastes*

A butterfly of arctic or alpine tundra in the far north, above timberline at its southern limits. Flight is fast, difficult to follow over rugged terrain. Flies in summer (1 brood). ▶ Variable, greenish to dingy white above. Dusky green below with pink fringe; central spot *rimmed with red and pointed outward*. 🌿 **Larval foodplant**: Showy locoweed and other legumes.

SIERRA SULPHUR *Colias behrii*

High elevations in the central Sierra Nevada of California only. Flies fast and low. Not very conspicuous in flight, but a worthwhile butterfly to pursue. Flies in summer (1 brood). ▶ The only *green* sulphur in its range. Both sexes green above and below. Male with yellow fringe; female paler, with pink fringe. 🌿 **Larval foodplant**: Dwarf bilberry.

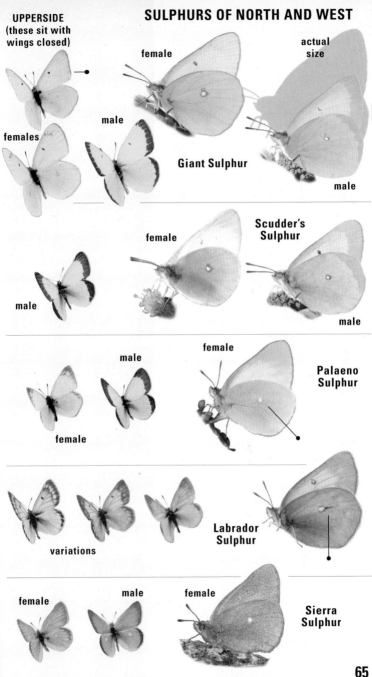

SULPHURS OF NORTH AND WEST

UPPERSIDE
(these sit with
wings closed)

female

actual
size

females

male

Giant Sulphur

male

Scudder's Sulphur

female

male

male

male

Palaeno Sulphur

female

female

male

variations

Labrador Sulphur

female

male

female

Sierra Sulphur

65

These five richly colored species of the *Colias* group are found only in the far north or in high mountains of the west.

MEAD'S SULPHUR   *Colias meadii*

A lovely creature of high Rocky Mountain habitats. On the wing, it lends a bright splash of orange to flower-strewn alpine meadows. Flight is deceivingly fast, with quick wingbeats, making adults difficult to follow over steep terrain. Flies in summer (1 brood). ▶ No other sulphur in its range shows such *deep orange above, green below*. Female is somewhat duskier. White females are rare. 🌱 **Larval foodplant:** Clovers.

CANADIAN SULPHUR   *Colias canadensis*

Known only from eastern Alaska to northern edge of Canadian Rockies. Only recently separated from Hecla Sulphur. Flight is low and moderately fast, with rapid wingbeats. Flies in early summer (1 brood). ▶ Male is orange above, paler than Mead's or Hecla Sulphurs. Female usually white, rarely orange or yellow. Below mostly yellow or white. Central spot is *red rimmed and pointed outward*. 🌱 **Larval foodplant:** Legumes.

HECLA SULPHUR   *Colias hecla*

One of our most northerly occurring butterflies, a hardy inhabitant of Arctic tundra. Similar to and formerly confused with the Canadian Sulphur, but flies later than that species where the two occur together. Flies in summer (1 brood). ▶ Adults are *deep orange above, green below;* Canadian Sulphur is paler. 🌱 **Larval foodplant:** Alpine milk vetch.

BOOTH'S SULPHUR   *Colias tyche*

A small sulphur of arctic habitats. Thought by some to be a hybrid between Hecla and Labrador Sulphurs. Flies in summer (1 brood). ▶ Below yellowish green. Similar to Labrador Sulphur (previous page) while perched, but forewing disk below is yellow-orange, not green. Some individuals uniquely *two-toned above*, with pale orange forewing, greenish yellow hindwing. 🌱 **Larval foodplant:** Unknown.

JOHANSEN'S ("COPPERMINE") SULPHUR   *Colias johanseni*

Extremely limited in range, rare. Recently discovered, so far known only from near Barnard Harbour, Northwest Territories. Flies in midsummer (1 brood) over hilly glacial tundra near the coast. ▶ Deep orange above, dark green below. Resembles Hecla Sulphur but may have more distinctly doubled center spot on hindwing below. 🌱 **Larval foodplant:** Unknown.

UPPERSIDE
(these sit with
wings closed)

actual
size

female   male

Mead's Sulphur

female

Canadian Sulphur

female

male

male

**Hecla
Sulphur**

male

male

**Booth's
Sulphur**

female   male

Johansen's Sulphur
(rare)

67

Dogface sulphurs show a forewing pattern above, outlined by black, that suggests the profile of a poodle's head. The oranges below begin the genus *Eurema,* more tropical than the *Colias* sulphurs on previous pages.

SOUTHERN DOGFACE   *Colias cesonia*

A dashing bright yellow and black sulphur. Common most of the year in the southwest (2 or more broods), less common northward and in the east, in open habitats. ▶ Forewing tips *pointed.* Below bright to pale yellow, with more pink markings in fall. *Dogface pattern* sometimes visible from below, especially when backlit, and may be glimpsed in flight. Female less heavily marked above. Barely overlaps with similar California Dogface. 🐛 **Larval foodplant:** Indigo bush, kidneywood, clovers, and other legumes.

CALIFORNIA DOGFACE   *Colias eurydice*

California only (the official state butterfly). Beautiful colors of upperside of male rarely seen well, because it perches with wings closed. Flies from spring to fall (2 broods). ▶ Forewing tips *pointed.* Yellow below with black forewing cell spot. Dogface pattern of male (with broader black than on Southern Dogface) sometimes visible from below, especially when backlit. Female all yellow, rarely with faint dogface outline; note wing shape. 🐛 **Larval foodplant:** False indigo and other legumes.

SLEEPY ORANGE   *Eurema nicippe*

Common in southern regions, less so to north, in all open habitats. Flight is rapid, erratic but direct. Flies most of year in warmest regions, mostly late summer and fall farther north (2–4 broods). ▶ Orange above with *wide black borders.* Below yellow-orange with brick red markings and a black spot in forewing cell. (From above, this spot looks like a closed eye, hence "sleepy.") Markings heavier in late fall and winter. Compare Orange Sulphur (p. 60), Tailed Orange (below). 🐛 **Larval foodplant:** Sennas.

TAILED ORANGE   *Eurema proterpia*

Summer immigrant to south Texas and the southwest, especially in years of good rains. Like other sulphurs, males may gather at puddles, sometimes in numbers. Flies late summer through fall (2 broods). ▶ Separated from Sleepy Orange by *pointed hindwing edge* and *lack* of forewing cell spot. Two seasonal forms: summer form unmarked below, hindwing edge slightly pointed. Winter with brown lines and blotches below, hindwing edge sharply pointed. 🐛 **Larval foodplant:** Sennas.

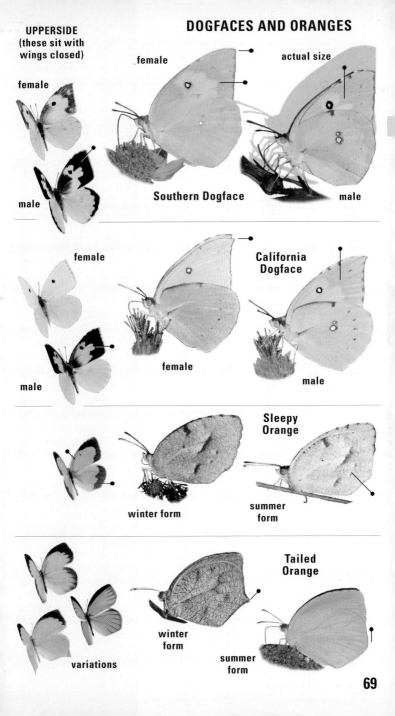

DOGFACES AND ORANGES

UPPERSIDE
(these sit with
wings closed)

female

female

male

actual size

female

male

Southern Dogface

female

male

female

male

California Dogface

female

male

Sleepy Orange

winter form

summer form

Tailed Orange

variations

winter form

summer form

69

DAINTY SULPHUR *Nathalis iole*

Common in southern areas in all open habitats, including fields, deserts, vacant lots. Usually flutters along within inches of the ground. Flies most of year in south (multiple broods), mostly summer and fall farther north. ▶ Tiny (our smallest sulphur). Hindwing below varies from pale yellow to dusky green. On forewing below, note *submarginal black spots and orange flush near base.* In flight, looks pale greenish yellow. 🦋 **Larval foodplant:** Dogweed, marigold, and other asters.

LITTLE YELLOW *Eurema lisa*

Very common in the southeast, in open areas with weedy understory, such as roadsides and fields. Moves northward in summer, colonizing much of the east. Rare stray in southwest. Flight is direct and close to the ground. Flies most of year in south (4–5 broods), mainly late summer farther north. ▶ A small, bright yellow sulphur, usually the most common in its range. Hindwing has one or two *tiny black dots at base,* lacking in Mimosa and Barred Yellows, and often a *round pink spot at hindwing upper angle* (apex). Female paler yellow or sometimes white. 🦋 **Larval foodplant:** Senna.

MIMOSA YELLOW *Eurema nise*

A Little Yellow look-alike with a much more limited range, mainly resident in south Texas and south Florida. A rare stray north of those areas and in the southwest. Prefers flying through woodland understory rather than open areas. Flies most of year where permanently established (3–4 broods). ▶ Very similar to Little Yellow, but *lacks* black dots at base of hindwing. Often with a pink spot at the hindwing apex and other light pink markings. 🦋 **Larval foodplant:** Mimosa.

BARRED YELLOW *Eurema daira*

A seasonally variable species, flying weakly through open habitats. Mainly resident in Florida and along adjacent Gulf Coast, straying farther afield. Flies most of year in south (3–4 broods). ▶ Hindwing below rather *plain,* mostly whitish or pale yellow on summer form, washed brown or reddish on winter form, *lacking* dark dots at base and pink spot at apex. Named for heavy black bar along the inner margin of the forewing (visible in flight), but this is reduced on winter forms. 🦋 **Larval foodplant:** Pencil flower, joint vetch, other legumes.

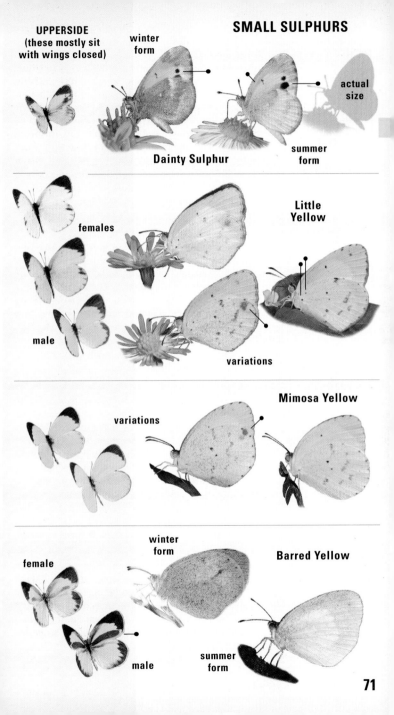

SMALL SULPHURS

UPPERSIDE
(these mostly sit
with wings closed)

winter
form

summer
form

actual
size

Dainty Sulphur

females

male

Little Yellow

variations

variations

Mimosa Yellow

female

male

winter
form

summer
form

Barred Yellow

71

MEXICAN YELLOW · *Eurema mexicana*

A pale yellow species common from Arizona to south Texas. Wanders well northward, rarely even reaching Canada. Easily observed at mud in fall in the southwest, also attracted to flowers. Flies most of year in southern regions (3–4 broods), mostly late summer and fall to north. ▶ *Pale yellow ground color* is obvious in flight. Hindwing *sharply angled.* Below pale yellow with some reddish markings, heavier on winter individuals. Black markings outline a "dogface" pattern on upperside of forewing. Male has brighter yellow patch along leading edge of hindwing above. 🐛 **Larval foodplant:** Fern acacia, locust, and other legumes.

BOISDUVAL'S YELLOW · *Eurema boisduvaliana*

Mainly a stray (but sometimes in good numbers) to Arizona, New Mexico, and southern Texas, rarely farther north; extremely rare in Florida. Tends to fly in undergrowth rather than open areas. Strays recorded spring to fall (1 or 2 broods in some years). ▶ Similar to Mexican Yellow but smaller and much brighter yellow above. Hindwing angled, less sharply than Mexican Yellow. Black markings form a weak "dogface" pattern on upperside in male only. Female paler with reduced black above. 🐛 **Larval foodplant:** Sennas.

DINA YELLOW · *Eurema dina*

Mainly southern Florida, although scarce and local there. A rare stray to southern Texas and Arizona. Best observed along brushy edges of hammocks. Flight is relatively weak and close to the ground. Florida individuals average smaller than those farther west. Flies all year in Florida (3 broods). ▶ Below note small spot in hindwing cell (some western individuals are unmarked below) and pinkish patches near wingtips. Above black border very narrow. In Florida, male orange above, females yellow with variable orange flush. In southwest, females are yellow or orange above. 🐛 **Larval foodplant:** Mexican alvaradoa tree in Florida.

SALOME YELLOW · *Eurema salome*

Extreme south Texas only, a rare stray there. Flies all year in Mexico (multiple broods). ▶ Similar to Mexican Yellow but *much brighter yellow above,* with more limited black. Larger than Boisduval's Yellow. Hindwing sharply angled. Hindwing below pale yellow with reddish markings and a round spot near the trailing edge; on Mexican and Boisduval's Yellows this spot is not round. 🐛 **Larval foodplant:** Not reported for Texas.

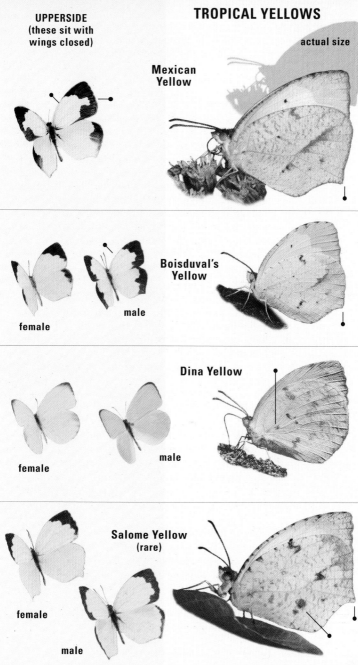

UPPERSIDE
(these sit with
wings closed)

TROPICAL YELLOWS

actual size

Mexican Yellow

Boisduval's Yellow

female

male

Dina Yellow

female

male

Salome Yellow
(rare)

female

male

Large and brightly colored, often flying high, these sulphurs are among the most conspicuous butterflies in southern regions. They perch with wings closed, usually showing their uppersides only in flight.

CLOUDLESS SULPHUR   *Phoebis sennae*

Very common in warm southern regions, capturing the attention of even casual observers. Often seen at flowers or at mud. Tends to invade northward every year, mainly in late summer (sometimes reaching Canada), although numbers vary from year to year. Flight is strong and rapid. Migrating individuals appear very direct and driven, rarely pausing. Flies most of year in deep south (3–4 broods). Temporary colonist in many areas (1–2 broods). ▶ Above male bright yellow, while female is greenish white, bright yellow, or pinkish orange. Below both sexes have cell-end spots on forewing and hindwing, often the only markings on males. Female shows a *broken* line leading to the tip of the forewing. ❧ **Larval foodplant:** Senna.

LARGE ORANGE SULPHUR   *Phoebis agarithe*

Not as common or widespread as Cloudless Sulphur. Flies all year in south Florida and south Texas (3 or more broods), irregular farther north and in southwest. May stray far to the north of known foodplant colonies. ▶ Identical in size to Cloudless Sulphur but male distinctly orange, not yellow. Females range from orange to white and can be pinkish when in worn condition. On forewing below, note the *straight line* leading to wingtip (not a broken line as on Cloudless Sulphur). Some males are almost unmarked, but known by overall color. ❧ **Larval foodplant:** Blackbead, wild tamarind, Texas ebony, and feather tree.

ORANGE-BARRED SULPHUR   *Phoebis philea*

This high-flying sulphur is best observed in southern Florida, where it might be seen any season. Occurs regularly in extreme south Texas, rare in southwest. Strays northward. Attracted to both flowers and mud. All year in southern Florida (3 or more broods), mainly late summer and fall elsewhere. ▶ Larger than Cloudless and Large Orange Sulphurs. Above male is yellow with broad orange bars. Female uppersides range from yellow to white, with reddish forewing borders, reddish suffusion along the lower hindwing, and no orange bars. Below both sexes with *broken line* leading to tip of forewing. Male much less marked than female. Some females with heavy pink to red suffusions on both wings. ❧ **Larval foodplant:** Senna.

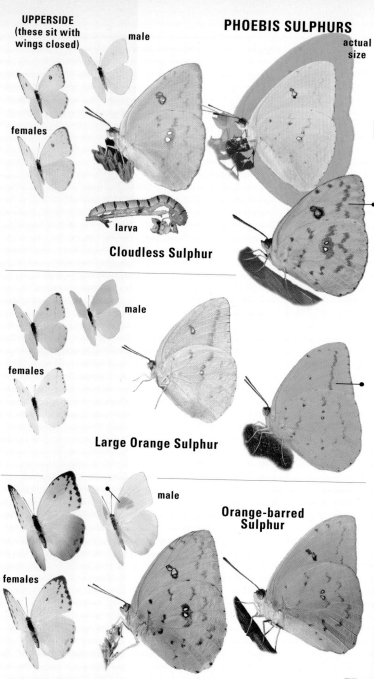

male

actual
size

females

larva

Cloudless Sulphur

male

females

Large Orange Sulphur

male

**Orange-barred
Sulphur**

females

These four occur mainly in the southernmost states and are usually not common, but all are known to stray northward at times.

LYSIDE SULPHUR *Kricogonia lyside*

A small sulphur resident in southern Texas, more temporary in Florida and the southwest. In years of heavy summer rains, thousands may move north in mass flights; such flights are frequent in Texas, less so in the southwest. Flight is swift. May breed in Florida but not known to breed in the southwest. Flies most of year in south Texas (3 or more broods). ▶ Adults variable. White male with yellow basally above and often with a *short curved black bar* on leading edge of hindwing (faintly visible from below). Female white or pale yellow, mainly unmarked. Below greenish, the hindwing usually with a *contrasting white vein.* In flight, may look like a smaller version of Cloudless Sulphur (previous page), but size and pale color might also suggest a Cabbage White (p. 46). ❦ **Larval foodplant:** Lignum vitae.

STATIRA SULPHUR *Phoebis statira*

Mostly south Florida, strays regularly to south Texas. Attracted to flowers and mud. Flies most of year in south Florida (3 broods). ▶ Similar to Cloudless Sulphur (previous page) and difficult to distinguish in flight. Above male yellow with pale outer edge, female greenish white. Below both sexes pale green to white, leading edge of forewing flushed with yellow, female with pinkish markings. ❦ **Larval foodplant:** Coinvine.

WHITE ANGLED-SULPHUR *Anteos clorinde*

A large white sulphur found mainly from southern Texas to southern Arizona, rarely straying much farther north. Flies high, with strong wingbeats. Attracted to both mud and flowers. Flies from early summer through fall in Texas (1 brood?), late summer through fall in Arizona. ▶ Very large, with curved forewing tip. White above, with an *orange-yellow forewing spot,* most pronounced on male. White upperside is usually visible in flight. Greenish below, the hindwing with numerous *swollen veins.* ❦ **Larval foodplant:** Senna.

YELLOW ANGLED-SULPHUR *Anteos maerula*

Less often seen than White Angled-Sulphur; a rare stray to Texas and the southwest, very rare in Florida and elsewhere. Adults are strong fliers. Probably does not breed north of Mexico. ▶ Very large, with curved forewing tip. Similar to White Angled-Sulphur, but *bright yellow above* (female somewhat paler); adults in flight appear green, not white. Greenish below, the hindwing with two whitened veins. ❦ **Larval foodplant:** Senna.

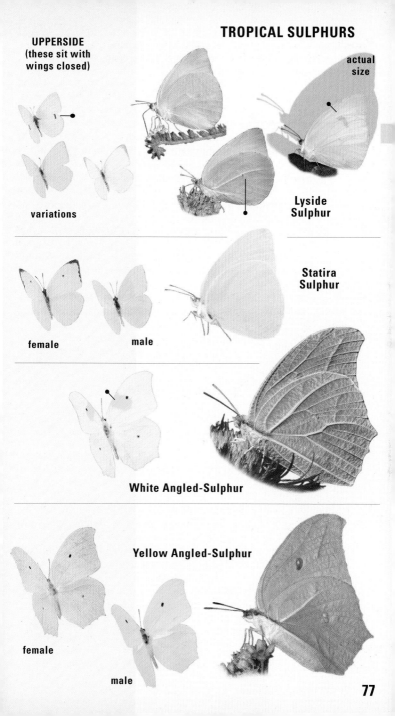

TROPICAL SULPHURS

UPPERSIDE
(these sit with
wings closed)

variations

actual
size

Lyside
Sulphur

Statira
Sulphur

female   male

White Angled-Sulphur

Yellow Angled-Sulphur

female

male

77

GOSSAMER-WINGED BUTTERFLIES

(family Lycaenidae) make up a large worldwide group of small butterflies. The four subfamilies occurring in North America are distinctive, and were formerly regarded as separate families.

Many gossamer-wings, especially among the blues and hairstreaks, have a prominent spot near the lower rear angle of the hindwing below, commonly called an "eyespot." When they also have short thin "tails" on the hindwing, the combination can suggest an eye and antennae, and this may fool birds into grabbing for this false head rather than the real head — allowing the butterfly to escape with only a nick taken out of its wings. Gossamer-wings often sit with their wings closed and rub their hindwings back and forth alternately, further drawing attention to this "wrong end" of the butterfly. This action may give us a glimpse of the color of the upperside of the wing.

Caterpillars of gossamer-wings are slug-shaped. Those of some species are tended by ants, which feed on sweet liquids secreted by the larvae.

HAIRSTREAKS (subfamily Theclinae), pp. 92–123, are widespread, with many tropical species, but mostly absent from the far north. They are mostly small, and tend to be fast and erratic in flight. Many have short narrow "tails" on the hindwings (as do a few of the coppers and a couple of blues). A few species of hairstreaks regularly bask with the wings open, but most hold the wings closed at rest. Most field marks, therefore, involve the pattern on the underside of the wings.

Some groups of hairstreaks are challenging to identify, requiring close attention to details such as the exact pattern of color around the eyespot on the hindwing, or arrangement of stripes in the median area of the wings.

Adults of most hairstreaks avidly visit flowers. Caterpillars of the Gray Hairstreak feed on a wide variety of plants, but most species (like most other butterflies) are much more choosy. Even among groups of very similar hairstreaks, the species often have different larval foodplants, and their association with these plants is often a good clue to their identity.

HARVESTERS (subfamily Miletinae), p. 80, are found mostly in the Old World tropics. The one species in North America is our only butterfly with carnivorous larvae, feeding on woolly aphids. Adults have a fast and erratic flight. They may be seen perched on leaves, but they do not visit flowers.

COPPERS (subfamily Lycaeninae), pp. 80–91, occur mostly in the north and west, especially in open meadows and marshes. Rather small butterflies, their flight can be fast but not as erratic as that of the hairstreaks. All are avid flower visitors. Coppers often bask with the wings spread, and many have beautiful colors on the upperside, but for some species the best field marks are on the underside of the wings.

BLUES (subfamily Polyomattinae), pp. 124–141, are found in most habitats from the Arctic to the tropics. They vary from small to tiny. Most species have blue on the upperside of the wings, at least in males. Their flight is mostly weak and fluttering, and they will flutter about for what seems like minutes at a time while we wait for them to stop so we can see what species they are. Blues will bask with their wings spread but usually rest with their wings closed, which is just as well for us, since the important field marks for most are on the undersides of the wings. The sexes are often colored differently above (with females tending to have less blue) but usually have the same pattern below. Like other gossamer-wings, blues will rub their hindwings back and forth while perched.

Adult blues are avid visitors to flowers, and males often gather around the edge of water in "puddle parties" that may number into the scores or even hundreds, with several species present. Their larvae often feed on flowering parts of plants in the legume or buckwheat families.

More than most groups of butterflies, blues have a tendency to form well-marked local populations, which may be vulnerable to extinction. (The Xerces Blue, whose habitat disappeared under housing developments in the San Francisco area, was one famous casualty.) These populations also add to the difficulty of classifying species and subspecies. Some of our most perplexing taxonomic problems involve blues (such as the azures, p. 130, and the buckwheat blues, pp. 138–141). The classification of blues was a particular interest of Vladimir Nabokov, who was a lepidopterist as well as a famed novelist.

Coppers **(subfamily Lycaeninae)** are found mainly in the north. Compared to other gossamer-winged butterflies, they fly more strongly than blues but not as fast as most hairstreaks. They are often seen visiting flowers. Coppers frequently bask with their wings open, but most of them are best identified by field marks on the underside of the wings. Harvesters **(subfamily Miletinae)** live mainly in Africa and Asia and are represented on this continent by only one species.

AMERICAN COPPER   *Lycaena phlaeas*

A brightly colored butterfly with separate eastern and western populations. In the east, where the larvae feed mainly on the introduced sheep sorrel, colonies are widespread in pastures, roadsides, and other disturbed land; adults are often very common. Some experts think the eastern population might have been introduced from Europe. Out west, adults fly at or above timberline in very local colonies, often below melting snowbanks. There they are generally scarce and difficult to see as they cavort above rocky slopes and trails. Flies spring to fall in the east (2–3 broods), summer in the west (1 brood). ▶ Strongly *two-toned look* both above and below, with orange forewings and gray hindwings. Above forewing shiny red-orange with bold black spots, hindwing dusky brown with an orange submarginal band; compare to female Bronze Copper (p. 88). Below hindwing gray with thin orange submarginal band and small black spots. Lustrous Copper (p. 86) similar from below but has bold black spots on hindwing. Western individuals are more golden orange above. 🐛 **Larval foodplant:** Sheep sorrel, alpine sorrel, and other species of docks.

HARVESTER   *Feniseca tarquinius*

The only carnivorous butterfly in North America! This odd little gossamer-wing is generally scarce, living in wooded or semiopen areas and usually staying close to alders along streams or swamps. It seldom or never visits flowers, but may be found basking on leaves at the edges of clearings. Flies spring to early fall (2 broods in the north, 3 broods in the south). ▶ Above orange with blotchy black edgings and spots. Below mostly red-brown with numerous *white circular markings.* 🐛 **Larval foodplant:** Not a plant! The carnivorous larvae feed on woolly aphids, especially those living on alders.

western

actual size

eastern

American Copper

Harvester

These have dark gray uppersides and whitish gray undersides. The first two of these are our largest coppers.

GRAY COPPER *Lycaena dione*

A large copper of northern prairies. Rather local, found mainly in moist areas such as meadows, low-lying pastures, and roadside ditches where docks grow. Flies in summer (1 brood). ▶ Dark gray above with orange marginal band and a hint of a tail on the hindwing. Below whitish gray with many black spots and with a *broad orange marginal band* on the hindwing. Bronze Copper (p. 88) has similar hindwing pattern below but has orange on forewing. ▲ **Larval foodplant:** Docks, both native and introduced.

GREAT COPPER *Lycaena xanthoides*

West Coast only, from Oregon to southern California. A large gray copper of chaparral and scrub habitats. Often visits flowers, and males also perch on low vegetation along gully bottoms to await females. Flies late spring or summer (1 brood). ▶ Very large, usually with a slight tail on the hindwing. Above male dark gray with few black spots and a trace of an orange hindwing band. Female above dark gray or sometimes with variable amounts of yellow, numerous black spots, and an orange hindwing marginal band. Below both sexes whitish or brownish gray with black spots and a short orange marginal line. Very similar to Gray Copper, but easily separated by range. Compare to Edith's Copper. ▲ **Larval foodplant:** Dock.

EDITH'S COPPER *Lycaena editha*

Often common around wet areas in its range, from marshes in sagebrush country to damp mountain meadows. Appears somewhat silvery in flight. Males often perch on the ground in gullies to await females. Flies in summer (1 brood). ▶ Similar to Great Copper and sometimes confused with it where their ranges meet, but Edith's is smaller and occurs at higher elevations. Edith's has stronger pattern below, with many irregularly shaped brown spots and a contrasting submarginal line of *white arrowheads* on the hindwing. Above female Edith's often shows more pale orange than female Great. ▲ **Larval foodplant:** Dock and horkelia.

DRAB COPPERS

female

actual size

Gray Copper

male

female (richly colored)

male

Great Copper

female (duller individual)

Edith's Copper

female

male

83

SMALL COPPERS

In these three species, males have beautiful purplish sheens above, while females are brown, often with varying amounts of orange.

DORCAS COPPER   *Lycaena dorcas*

Mostly boreal zones, extending south to the Great Lakes. Colonies tend to favor marshy areas, bogs, and moist open meadows, where adults stay close to the ground. An isolated and threatened population occurs in New Brunswick and Maine, while the salt-marsh population in eastern Quebec is sometimes considered a separate species. Flies in early or late summer depending on region (1 brood). ▶ Very similar to Purplish Copper; where they occur together, males are difficult to separate with certainty. Male above dark brown with a purplish sheen and numerous black spots. Female above light brown with numerous black spots and with any pale orange or yellow scaling (when present) less extensive than on female Purplish Copper. Both sexes above with a weakly developed orange submarginal line. Below pinkish brown or tan with a red-orange submarginal line. 🐛 **Larval foodplant:** Cinquefoil, dock, and knotweed.

PURPLISH COPPER   *Lycaena helloides*

Found in a wider variety of habitats than Dorcas Copper, living in moist habitats from sea level to higher mountains in the west. The purplish overlay of a fresh male sitting in the sunlight is a grand sight! Individuals from several Rocky Mountain populations resemble Dorcas Coppers quite closely, and there is controversy over their status. Flies from spring to fall at low elevations (3 broods), summer at high elevations (1 brood). ▶ Similar to Dorcas Copper, especially males, but usually has a *more obvious orange submarginal line* above. Most females have extensive orange above. 🐛 **Larval foodplant:** Dock, knotweed, and cinquefoil.

BOG COPPER   *Lycaena epixanthe*

Our smallest copper, found locally in acid bogs where cranberries grow. Its flight is weak and close to the ground, but adults are difficult to follow because of the nature of their habitat. Flies in summer (1 brood). ▶ Smaller than either Purplish or Dorcas Coppers. Male above dark brown with purplish sheen and few black spots. Female is gray-brown above with a light purplish sheen. Below both sexes whitish gray to light tan. 🐛 **Larval foodplant:** Cranberries.

SMALL COPPERS

actual
size

female

males

Dorcas
Copper

Purplish
Copper

males

female

variations

Bog Copper

male

female

These three are among our most brightly colored butterflies, especially the males.

LUSTROUS COPPER   *Lycaena cupreus*

A brilliant red-orange copper of western mountains. The first encounter with one of these little gems is an experience not soon forgotten. Generally found in open forested areas except in some Rocky Mountain regions where the colonies occur in and around steep rocky slopes, at or above treeline. Flies in summer (1 brood). ▶ Above *shiny red-orange* with relatively *wide black borders;* numerous black spots, larger on female. Strongly patterned below, with bold black spots on orange forewing and gray hindwing, and a thin red submarginal line on hindwing. Ruddy Copper is somewhat similar above but much less strongly marked below. ❦ **Larval foodplant:** Dock and sorrel.

RUDDY COPPER   *Lycaena rubidus*

A bright orange copper of the west. Lives mainly near moist areas in arid regions; often found with Blue Copper. Males are particularly fond of perching on low shrubs (often sagebrush) to await females. When they perch with wings closed, their whitish undersides make them inconspicuous until one is disturbed and shows its bright upperside. The isolated population in the White Mountains of Arizona is sometimes regarded as a separate species, Ferris's Copper. Flies in summer (1 brood). ▶ Male above bright orange, sometimes with a pinkish hue and limited spotting. Female orange-brown to brown above with bold black spots. Below both sexes whitish gray with *hindwing spots tiny or absent.* ❦ **Larval foodplant:** Dock, sorrel, and knotweed.

BLUE COPPER   *Lycaena heteronea*

Our only blue copper, found in a variety of arid habitats, from sea level to treeline. Flight is erratic and close to the ground. Flies in summer (1 brood). ▶ Male bright blue above with no spots and with black-lined veins. Female above gray-brown or lightly powdered blue with bold black spots. Below both sexes white to gray or cream with no spots, or with small spots restricted to the inner portion of the hindwing. The male is often mistaken for a species of Blue, such as Boisduval's (p. 134). Resembles Ruddy Copper below, but distinguished by upperside colors. ❦ **Larval foodplant:** Sulphur, Heermann's, California, and other buckwheats.

WESTERN COPPERS

female

variations

male
(Colorado)

actual
size

Lustrous
Copper

male
(California)

male

variations

females

Ruddy
Copper

male

variations

females

Blue Copper

Males of these three coppers are brown above with purplish sheens. All have distinctive patterns below.

BRONZE COPPER *Lycaena hyllus*

A large copper found from the northern plains eastward. Stays close to wet areas at meadow edges, streams, swamps, and rivers. Local but sometimes common in preferred habitat. Only recently found to occur in Utah and New Mexico, and may be a recent import there. Flies spring to fall (2 or 3 broods). ▶ Identified by the distinctive color combination below, with forewing mostly orange, hindwing whitish gray with *broad orange submarginal band*. Gray Copper (p. 82) also has a broad orange band on the hindwing, but its forewings are gray below. Male above dark brown with purplish sheen and a broad orange marginal hindwing band. Female forewing above orange with brown border, hindwing brown with broad orange marginal band. 🌿 **Larval foodplant:** Water dock and curled dock.

LILAC-BORDERED COPPER *Lycaena nivalis*

Western only. Widespread and often common in mountain meadows, sagebrush flats, and forest clearings. Males patrol along gully bottoms. Flies in summer (1 brood). ▶ Very similar to Purplish Copper (p. 84) but with a *two-toned hindwing below,* with yellow or yellow-green inwardly, pink outwardly. (Caution: Some individuals are not as clearly two-toned as others.) Often found in drier habitats than Purplish Copper. Male above dark brown with purplish sheen and very few black spots; male Purplish Copper has many black spots above. Female above variable, brown and orange or mostly brown with bold black spots. 🌿 **Larval foodplant:** Knotweed.

MARIPOSA COPPER *Lycaena mariposa*

A copper of open coniferous forests of the west. Common through most of its range, although quite localized in the Sierra Nevada. Males patrol forest edges for females. Flies in summer (1 brood). ▶ Hindwing below mottled gray with *strong markings,* including submarginal row of *arrowheads* pointing inward. Forewing below pale yellow with bold black spots. Above male dark brown with purplish sheen, female brown with varying amounts of orange; both sexes with *black and white checkered fringes,* unlike other coppers. 🌿 **Larval foodplant:** Blueberry.

COPPERS

female

actual size

Bronze Copper

male

variations

male

Lilac-bordered Copper

female

Mariposa Copper

female

male

89

These have distinctive patterns below; two have tails on the hindwings.

GORGON COPPER   *Lycaena gorgon*

Found mostly in California, in foothill and chaparral habitats; does not occur at high elevations. Males perch on low vegetation in gully bottoms, along canyons, and in other natural corridors. Flies in late spring or early summer (1 brood). ▶ Whitish or tan below with bold black spots. Row of *distinct red-orange spots* near margin of hindwing is clear distinction from other coppers, but compare to various blues (pp. 124–141). Male above light brown with purplish overlay, but no spots. Female above brown with varying amounts of yellow and with bold black spots. 🌿 **Larval foodplant:** Nude and elongate buckwheats.

TAILED COPPER   *Lycaena arota*

A common and distinctive western copper, most often seen along streams through meadows, woodland edges, and sagebrush flats. Flight is erratic and faster than that of other coppers. Males often sit on higher perches than other coppers while awaiting females. Although widespread, this copper is strangely absent from many areas where its foodplants are common. Flies in summer (1 brood). ▶ Both sexes with short hindwing tails. Mostly gray or brownish gray below, with *strong markings,* including a black spot just above the tail and an irregular *white submarginal band* on the hindwing. Quite unlike other coppers, but might suggest a large hairstreak (see pp. 92–123). Male above dark brown, often with purplish sheen. Female above brown and orange. 🌿 **Larval foodplant:** Gooseberry (*Ribes*).

HERMES COPPER   *Lycaena hermes*

This beautiful and highly sought after copper is limited to San Diego County, California, and adjacent northern Baja California. Sometimes locally common in chaparral near stands of redberry, its larval foodplant, but disappearing as its habitat is converted to housing developments. Flies rather slowly, looking distinctly dull yellow in flight. Avidly takes nectar, especially from the white flowers of California buckwheat. Males often perch on plants 4 to 6 feet above the ground to await females. Flies in early summer (1 brood). ▶ Distinct but short hindwing tails. Hindwing below mostly yellow, with few markings or none. Above brown with yellow on the forewing, more extensive on the female. 🌿 **Larval foodplant:** Redberry (*Rhamnus*).

WESTERN COPPERS

female

actual
size

**Gorgon
Copper**

male

Tailed Copper

female

male

female

Hermes Copper

male

HAIRSTREAKS

(subfamily Theclinae) are mainly small butterflies, many with threadlike tails on the hindwing. They fly rapidly, flitting from side to side or in circles, with movements that are difficult for human eyes to follow. Most (except for scrub-hairstreaks and a few others) perch with wings closed, revealing the upper surface only in flight. Males of many have an oval black stigma on the forewing.

GRAY HAIRSTREAK   *Strymon melinus*

The most widespread hairstreak in North America, occurring just about everywhere. Any "gray" hairstreak encountered in gardens, parks, and other urban habitats is probably this one. Unlike most hairstreaks, often basks with its wings open. Males perch on trees in flat country or shrubs and trees on hilly summits to wait for females, often remaining until sundown. Flies most of year in south, spring through fall northward (2–5 broods). ▶ Below variably gray to brownish gray. Black and white postmedian line is often *edged with orange* inwardly; no markings *between* postmedian line and base of wings. Above brownish gray, with a bold orange eyespot on the hindwing. Abdomen orange on males, gray on females. 🌿 **Larval foodplant:** Eats flowering parts of legumes, mallows, and many other types of plants.

AVALON SCRUB-HAIRSTREAK   *Strymon avalona*

Only on Santa Catalina Island, off southern California coast. Occurs in chaparral throughout the island. Flies spring to fall (2–3 broods). ▶ Gray below, somewhat darker gray inward of the postmedian line, and brownish gray above. Like a *drab, faded version* of Gray Hairstreak (a recent arrival on Santa Catalina Island), but the hindwing eyespot is rather small and indistinct, and there may be a *gap* in the *hindwing* postmedian line. 🌿 **Larval foodplant:** Deerweed and other legumes.

WHITE M HAIRSTREAK   *Parrhasius m-album*

A large eastern hairstreak, most common in the south. Perches with wings closed, hiding its brightest colors. Adults fly around and perch on large oak trees. Flies spring to fall in most areas (3 broods). ▶ Brown below. Has a *prominent white* **M** (or **W**?) mark in the submarginal line of the hindwing, but many other hairstreaks show a similar pattern; note the white spot at the center of the leading edge of the hindwing, the red spot set inward from the margin of the hindwing, and especially the *brilliant blue upperside* (visible only in flight). 🌿 **Larval foodplant:** Oaks.

HAIRSTREAKS

female

actual size

variations

Gray Hairstreak

male

Avalon Scrub-Hairstreak

female

White M Hairstreak

male

UPPERSIDE (these sit with wings closed)

93

Mainly eastern in occurrence. They perch with wings closed.

BANDED HAIRSTREAK   *Satyrium calanus*

Common throughout the east, often seen at flowers. Males frequent sunny glades where they dart out and furiously flutter around each other before returning to their perches. Flies in spring in south, summer northward (1 brood). ▶ Below dark gray, white markings variable. Postmedian band usually edged with white on outer edge, but *rarely* on inner edge. Blue hindwing spot is rarely capped with red and does not reach postmedian band. ❦ **Larval foodplant:** Oaks and hickories.

HICKORY HAIRSTREAK   *Satyrium caryaevorum*

A seldom seen inhabitant of clearings and edges of deciduous woods. Generally rare, although sporadic outbreaks are known to occur. Flies in summer (1 brood). ▶ Very similar to Banded Hairstreak, difficult to separate from it in the field. Postmedian band has white on *both outer and inner edges.* Hindwing blue spot extends *farther inward,* reaching or nearly reaching lower end of postmedian band. ❦ **Larval foodplant:** Hickories.

EDWARDS'S HAIRSTREAK   *Satyrium edwardsii*

Locally common in east. Inhabits sand and shale barrens, limestone ridges, and other open areas with scrub oak. Flies in late spring in the south, summer northward (1 brood). ▶ Below gray. Hindwing postmedian band is made up of *disconnected dark spots,* each one circled in white. Blue hindwing spot usually capped with a *thin orange crescent.* ❦ **Larval foodplant:** Scrub oak.

KING'S HAIRSTREAK   *Satyrium kingi*

A southeastern specialty. Not often seen, but can be common near young larval foodplants. Adults may be observed at flowers or perched on sweetleaf. Flies in late spring or summer (1 brood). ▶ Brownish gray below. Hindwing blue spot has *obvious red-orange cap.* Cell-end bar on hindwing set off from postmedian band. ❦ **Larval foodplant:** Common sweetleaf.

STRIPED HAIRSTREAK   *Satyrium liparops*

Widespread in forest edges and thickets, but seldom common. Flies from early to late summer depending on region (1 brood). ▶ Brownish gray below with *extensive thin white stripes* and often a violet sheen. Blue hindwing spot capped with red-orange. Cell-end bar on hindwing is lined up with upper part of postmedian band. Some populations have orange above. ❦ **Larval foodplant:** Wild cherry, blueberry, oak, and others.

HAIRSTREAKS

UPPERSIDE
(these sit with
wings closed)

actual
size

**Banded
Hairstreak**

most on
this page are
similarly
plain above

**Hickory
Hairstreak**

**Edwards's
Hairstreak**

**King's
Hairstreak**

Striped Hairstreak

variations

95

OAK (SOUTHERN) HAIRSTREAK *Satyrium favonius*

"Southern"

"Northern"

Widespread, variable. Adults perch with wings closed. Included here are two forms previously considered full species. **"Southern" Oak Hairstreak (*Satyrium favonius favonius*):** Inhabits most of Florida, blending into "Northern" Oak Hairstreak from the western panhandle west and north. Common in woodland edges, scrubby places. Flies spring to early summer (1 brood). ▶ Hindwing below gray-brown with an *extensive flare of orange* on submargin and often a white spot near center of leading edge. **"Northern" Oak Hairstreak (*S. f. ontario*):** Replaces "Southern" throughout most of range. In woodland edges, usually scarce. Flies late spring in south, summer in north (1 brood). ▶ Hindwing below gray-brown, no markings inward of postmedian line except sometimes a white spot near center of leading edge. Resembles Gray Hairstreak (p. 92) but usually browner below, and has hindwing blue spot capped with red. 🌿 **Larval foodplant:** Oaks.

ILAVIA HAIRSTREAK *Satyrium ilavia*

A close relative of Oak Hairstreak, restricted to Arizona and adjacent New Mexico. Inhabits thickets of scrub oak on arid hills. Not often encountered, although it can be locally common. Flies in May and June (1 brood). ▶ Below pale brown, the postmedian line *indistinct* with *no markings inward*. Brown above with orange or tan patches. Compare to Golden Hairstreak (p. 108). 🌿 **Larval foodplant:** Scrub oak.

POLING'S HAIRSTREAK *Satyrium polingi*

A rarely encountered hairstreak of oak woodlands in west Texas and southeastern New Mexico. Does not overlap range of Ilavia or Oak Hairstreaks. Flies in late spring and late summer (2 broods). ▶ Gray-brown below with bold white postmedian line. Hindwing with no orange cap on blue spot and no markings inward of postmedian line; submarginal white spots on hindwing *faint*. 🌿 **Larval foodplant:** Emory oak and gray oak.

SOAPBERRY HAIRSTREAK *Phaeostrymon alcestis*

Highly localized, seldom found away from soapberry trees. Adults mostly stay in host trees but will visit flowers nearby. Flies May to June (1 brood). ▶ Light to dark gray below, with *conspicuous white cell-end bars* on forewing and hindwing (lacking on Gray Hairstreak, p. 92). Note the *strong zigzag* in white postmedian line on hindwing. 🌿 **Larval foodplant:** Western soapberry.

HAIRSTREAKS

UPPERSIDE (these sit with wings closed)

"Southern" Oak Hairstreak

actual size

male

Oak Hairstreak

female

"Northern" Oak Hairstreak

male

Ilavia Hairstreak

Poling's Hairstreak

Soapberry Hairstreak

These have light gray undersides with postmedian lines composed of black spots. Adults perch with wings closed. Uppersides are brown-gray or tan to pale orange.

ACADIAN HAIRSTREAK   *Satyrium acadica*

Mainly a species of northeastern wetlands, barely reaching east edge of Rocky Mountains. Closely tied to willows around marshes and streams; can be common in such habitats. Flies in summer (1 brood). ▶ Light gray below, with postmedian band of round black spots. Orange cap on hindwing blue spot is obvious and *well connected* to orange marginal spots. California Hairstreak is very similar but mostly separated by range and habitat. 🐛 **Larval foodplant:** Willows.

CALIFORNIA HAIRSTREAK   *Satyrium californica*

Common in the west, mainly in foothill chaparral or lower mountain habitats. Often seen in large numbers at buckwheat, dogbane, and other flowers, and adults also perch on larval foodplants. Range barely overlaps that of similar Acadian Hairstreak. Flies in late spring or summer (1 brood). ▶ Below light gray to dusky gray, with postmedian band of black spots. Orange cap on hindwing blue spot is *small or absent,* rarely connected to orange leading to lower angle (compare to Acadian Hairstreak). 🐛 **Larval foodplant:** Oaks, mountain mahogany, and others.

SYLVAN HAIRSTREAK   *Satyrium sylvinus*

A species of western wetlands where willows occur. Similar to California Hairstreak and often found with it where their habitats overlap. Adults are most often found resting on willows or on nearby flowers. Flies late spring or summer (1 brood). ▶ Light gray below, sometimes tailless, with postmedian band of black spots. Hindwing blue spot *lacks orange cap.* Usually with much less orange along hindwing margin than California Hairstreak. 🐛 **Larval foodplant:** Willows.

CORAL HAIRSTREAK   *Satyrium titus*

This attractive hairstreak is widespread and often common in the east, scarcer in the west. Favors brushy places, thickets, overgrown fields. Adults are particularly fond of the flowers of butterfly weed in the east. Flies in summer in most areas (1 brood). ▶ Tailless. Brownish gray below. Hindwing has a *prominent row of red spots* along the margin, but *lacks* the blue spot shown by many hairstreaks. 🐛 **Larval foodplant:** Wild cherry and wild plum.

HAIRSTREAKS

UPPERSIDE
(these sit with
wings closed)

**Acadian
Hairstreak**

actual
size

**California
Hairstreak**

**Sylvan
Hairstreak**

**Coral
Hairstreak**

female

male

western
female

eastern
male

eastern
female

HEDGEROW HAIRSTREAK   *Satyrium saepium*

The most common brown hairstreak in the west, and a regular visitor to flowers. It is not unusual to observe more than 100 adults per day in some areas. Most common in lower foothills, but ranges from coastal dunes to lower mountains. Flies in late spring or summer (1 brood). ▶ Below brown, variable. Distinct postmedian line may or may not be edged with white. Often shows faint cell-end bars. Bright *orange-brown upperside* may be visible in flight. 🌿 **Larval foodplant:** Buckbrushes.

MOUNTAIN MAHOGANY HAIRSTREAK   *Satyrium tetra*

Fairly common in foothill chaparral habitat of far west. More local than Hedgerow and California Hairstreaks, but often found among them. Flies in late spring or early summer (1 brood). ▶ Below gray-brown. Hindwing postmedian line white but sometimes indistinct, especially toward lower angle where it is often obscured by *extensive white overscaling*. 🌿 **Larval foodplant:** Mountain mahogany.

GOLD-HUNTER'S HAIRSTREAK   *Satyrium auretorum*

California to southern Oregon only. A brown species of oak woodland in foothill habitats and at western edge of Mojave Desert. Usually uncommon, although adults may be found in numbers sitting on oaks. Flies in late spring or summer (1 brood). ▶ Mostly plain warm brown below, with postmedian band mainly *absent on forewing and indistinct on hindwing*. Tail short, especially on male. 🌿 **Larval foodplant:** Oaks.

BEHR'S HAIRSTREAK   *Satyrium behrii*

A tailless gray-brown species of arid regions in the west. Males perch on branch tips of the host or nearby trees to locate females. Often swarms to flowers. Flies in spring or summer (1 brood). ▶ Grayish brown below with numerous black submarginal spots. Hindwing postmedian band broken into *black crescents edged outwardly with white*. 🌿 **Larval foodplant:** Bitterbrush and mountain mahogany.

SOOTY HAIRSTREAK   *Satyrium fuliginosum*

Most often found around lupine on sagebrush-covered slopes. Not a flashy species and easily overlooked. Males perch on high points of low shrubs to watch for females. Flies in summer (1 brood). ▶ Gray or brown below, variable, but generally with a dingy look. Hindwing postmedian band composed of *black spots circled in white (sometimes all white)*. 🌿 **Larval foodplant:** Lupines.

WESTERN HAIRSTREAKS

UPPERSIDE
(these sit with
wings closed)

variations

actual
size

Hedgerow Hairstreak

Mountain Mahogany Hairstreak

Gold-hunter's Hairstreak

Behr's Hairstreak

variations

Sooty Hairstreak

HAIRSTREAKS

The first two below are in the groundstreak group. Very fast fliers, they spend a considerable amount of time close to the ground as adults; their caterpillars also feed on the ground, on rotting dead leaves.

RED-BANDED HAIRSTREAK   *Calycopis cecrops*

Very common in the southeast, less common north-ward, but strays well to the north. Often found sitting in the shade or close to the ground. Adults congregate in treetops in the late afternoon and early evening. Flies most of year in Florida (3–4 broods); spring to fall else-where (2–3 broods). ▶ Small. Gray-brown below. White postmedian lines below are edged inwardly with a *thick red band*; the blue spot near the hindwing lower angle has little or no red cap. Black above with varying amounts of blue. ❦ **Larval foodplant:** Rotting leaves.

DUSKY-BLUE GROUNDSTREAK   *Calycopis isobeon*

Texas only. A small species that frequents the ground but also perches well up in trees. Closely related to Red-banded Hairstreak, and intermediates may be found where their ranges converge. Flies spring to fall (2–3 broods). ▶ Similar to Red-banded Hairstreak, but red band across wings below is usually *narrower,* and the blue spot near the hindwing lower angle usually has a red cap. ❦ **Larval foodplant:** Rotting leaves.

FULVOUS HAIRSTREAK   *Electrostrymon angelia*

South Florida only. Apparently was introduced from the West Indies in the 1970s and is now fairly common. Flies all year (3 or more broods). ▶ Brown below. Post-median line on hindwing is broken, with an *isolated white spot near leading edge.* Forewing postmedian line usually lacks white. Orange-brown upperside may be glimpsed in flight. Compare to Oak Hairstreak (p. 96) and White M Hairstreak (p. 92). ❦ **Larval foodplant:** Brazil-ian pepper.

RUDDY HAIRSTREAK   *Electrostrymon sangala*

South Texas only. Uncommon, status not well known; may be resident. Flies most of year in Mexico (multiple broods). ▶ Below brown with thin white postmedian line edged with red. Above male golden-orange, female dull gray. ❦ **Larval foodplant:** Probably coral bean.

MUTED HAIRSTREAK   *Electrostrymon canus*

South Texas only. May be resident, but status not well known because of previous confusion with Ruddy Hairstreak. Common in Mexico, where it flies all year (multiple broods). ▶ Very similar to Ruddy Hairstreak, probably inseparable in the field, but male is duller above, lacking orange. ❦ **Larval foodplant:** Probably mango.

UPPERSIDE
(these sit with
wings closed)

HAIRSTREAKS

actual
size

**Red-banded
Hairstreak**

**Dusky-blue
Groundstreak**

**Fulvous
Hairstreak**

female

**Ruddy
Hairstreak**

male

male

Muted Hairstreak

103

ELFINS

Nickel-sized hairstreaks, mostly tailless, with wings patterned in brown, gray, and black. Most are on the wing early in the season, and some are among the first spring butterflies in some localities. Generally not as fast flying as other hairstreaks. Adults perch with wings closed.

BROWN ELFIN *Callophrys augustinus*

Our most widespread and commonly encountered elfin. Occurs in a wide variety of habitats but seldom encountered in large numbers. Flies spring or summer depending on locality (1 brood). ▶ Somewhat variable. Below reddish or tannish brown, usually much darker basally and richer red along hindwing margin. 🌱 **Larval foodplant:** Blueberry and other heaths in east; manzanita, buckbrush, dodder, and other plants in west.

HENRY'S ELFIN *Callophrys henrici*

A tailed elfin of mostly eastern occurrence. Quite localized, but chooses a variety of habitats. Flies early spring in south, later northward (1 brood). ▶ Below hindwing with frosted margin and *white at both ends of the postmedian line.* Forewing has postmedian line fairly straight, no frosted effect on margin. Tails mostly short and thick, longer in the extreme southeast and in northern Florida. 🌱 **Larval foodplant:** Redbud, American holly, Mexican buckeye, and many others.

FROSTED ELFIN *Callophrys irus*

Very localized and rarely common, with colonies in open areas such as clearings, burns, woodland edges. Flies in spring, or into early summer in north (1 brood). ▶ Rather large. Below hindwing with frosted margin and a *black spot near the tail area* (sometimes absent). Forewing postmedian line more jagged than that of Henry's Elfin. Tails short. Texas individuals are darker and less contrasting below. 🌱 **Larval foodplant:** Wild indigo and lupine.

HOARY ELFIN *Callophrys polios*

Primarily a northern species with scattered outposts in the west. Small and tailless. Local, with isolated colonies in low pine barrens, ridges, woodland edges. Males perch on larval foodplant to await females. Flies in spring (1 brood). ▶ Rather dark below, but has frosted margins on *both hindwing and forewing.* Hindwing postmedian band shows little or no white at either end, unlike Henry's Elfin. 🌱 **Larval foodplant:** Bearberry and trailing arbutus.

ELFINS

UPPERSIDE
(these sit with
wings closed)

variations

actual
size

Brown Elfin

Henry's Elfin

variations

Frosted Elfin

Hoary Elfin

EASTERN PINE ELFIN · *Callophrys niphon*

An eastern species of pine barrens and mixed pine woodland. Males perch on pines in clearings and along road edges to await females. Flies early or late spring (1 brood). ▶ *Strikingly banded below* with chestnut and black. Hindwing with gray along margin and blunt black arrowhead markings in submargin. ❦ **Larval food-plant**: Pitch pine, jack pine, white pine, and others.

WESTERN PINE ELFIN · *Callophrys eryphon*

Common in the west, but also found locally in northern Great Lakes region. Males perch on small trees or shrubs in forest clearings to await females. Flies late spring or early summer (1 brood). ▶ Nearly identical to Eastern Pine Elfin, and difficult to separate where their ranges overlap. Hindwing has little or no gray along the margin, and the submarginal black arrowheads are *more sharply pointed.* ❦ **Larval foodplant**: Pines.

BOG ELFIN · *Callophrys lanoraieensis*

Our smallest elfin, a specialty of black spruce and tamarack bogs in the northeast. Highly localized and not often seen. Flies late spring to early summer (1 brood). ▶ Like a small version of the Pine Elfins but with pattern reduced. Submarginal line on hindwing is *relatively smooth,* lacking arrowhead pattern. Hindwing postmedian line has little white except near leading edge of wing. ❦ **Larval foodplant**: Black spruce.

DESERT ELFIN · *Callophrys fotis*

In the southern Great Basin, this elfin inhabits rocky slopes and canyons. Adults perch on branch tips on or near cliff rose and can be locally common. Flies in spring (1 brood). ▶ Best known by overall gray look. Outer part of hindwing below always soft gray, with or without brown in submarginal area. Nothing really similar in its range. ❦ **Larval foodplant**: Cliff rose.

MOSS'S ELFIN · *Callophrys mossii*

An elusive elfin of mossy, stonecrop-covered hillsides and steep canyon walls. Extremely local, rarely seen in numbers. Some populations near San Francisco are endangered. Flies in spring (1 brood). ▶ Variable, especially near coast. Purplish or reddish brown to gray below. Hindwing postmedian line often with white. Populations without white in postmedian line very similar to Brown Elfin (previous page), but often have a *grayish patch* near bottom of hindwing postmedian line. ❦ **Larval foodplant**: Stonecrop and dudleyas.

ELFINS

UPPERSIDE (these sit with wings closed)

female

male

Eastern Pine Elfin

actual size

Western Pine Elfin

Bog Elfin

Desert Elfin

female

Moss's Elfin

variations

male

endangered "San Bruno" subspecies

HAIRSTREAKS WITH DISTINCTIVE PATTERNS

GREAT PURPLE HAIRSTREAK   *Atlides halesus*

A large and spectacular hairstreak, usually encountered singly. Not uncommon in favored habitats but tends to stay well above the ground. Males sit on trees on hill summits or flat plains to await females, mostly in afternoon. Perches with wings closed. Flies mainly spring to fall, most of year in south Florida (2–4 broods). ▶ *Black below* with red basal spots. Abdomen orange. Above brilliant blue, more so on male, but color hidden except in flight. ❦ **Larval foodplant:** Mistletoes growing on oak, ash, cottonwood, juniper, mesquite, etc.

ATALA   *Eumaeus atala*

Southeastern Florida only. Formerly rare there, but has thrived recently as foodplants have become popular ornamentals in suburbs and parks. Slow on the wing, and usually close to foodplant. Flies most of year (3 or more broods). ▶ Unmistakable. Below black with iridescent blue-green spots. Abdomen orange. Above black with varying amounts of iridescent blue. ❦ **Larval foodplant:** Coontie and other cycads, native and ornamental.

COLORADO HAIRSTREAK   *Hypaurotis crysalus*

A large hairstreak found locally near thickets of Gambel oak. Adults tend to remain in trees, not visiting flowers. May bask with wings open, revealing a stunning upperside. Active in cloudy weather and until dark. Flies in summer in most areas (1 brood), summer and fall in southern Arizona (partial second). ▶ Below light to dark gray. Hindwing with *white stripe near base.* Above purple with orange spots near lower margins (orange spots reduced or absent in most of Utah). ❦ **Larval foodplant:** Gambel oak, probably silverleaf oak.

GOLDEN HAIRSTREAK   *Habrodais grunus*

Mainly California and Oregon. Adults may congregate in large numbers on host trees, but shun flowers. May bask with wings open. On the wing until dusk. Flies in summer (1 brood). ▶ Below golden brown, lightly marked. Hindwing with pale blue metallic crescents near margin. Brown to orange-brown above. ❦ **Larval foodplant:** Canyon live oak, chinquapin, and others.

CREAMY STRIPE-STREAK   *Arawacus jada*

A rare stray to south Texas and the southwest. Adults may open wings while perched. Flies most of year in Mexico. ▶ Below creamy yellow with many light stripes. Above dark gray with powder blue basally. ❦ **Larval foodplant:** Potato tree and other nightshades.

COOL HAIRSTREAKS

UPPERSIDE
(these sit with
wings closed)

female

male

female

actual
size

male

**Great Purple
Hairstreak**

female

male

Atala

typical
male

Utah
male

Colorado Hairstreak

**Golden
Hairstreak**

**Creamy
Stripe-Streak**

109

THE JUNIPER HAIRSTREAK COMPLEX

JUNIPER HAIRSTREAK   *Callophrys gryneus*

"Olive" and "Sweadner's"

Widespread, variable, always close to (or on) junipers or other evergreens. May go unnoticed until branches shake, causing it to fly. Perches with wings closed. Some forms listed here are probably separate species. **"Olive" Juniper Hairstreak (*Callophrys gryneus gryneus*):** eastern, not uncommon near red cedar, the larval foodplant. Flies spring and summer (2 broods). ▶ Below green with jagged white postmedian line. Hindwing with two white basal spots and orange eyespot near lower angle. **"Sweadner's" Juniper Hairstreak (*C. g. sweadneri*):** Florida. Local and uncommon near redcedar. Flies spring and fall (2 broods). ▶ Similar to "Olive" form, but lacks orange in eyespot, and the two basal spots are reduced. **"Siva" Juniper Hairstreak (*C. g. siva and others*):** Widespread in west near junipers, its larval foodplant. Flies spring and summer (2–3 broods). ▶ Similar to "Olive" but lacks two basal hindwing spots; some populations are brown. Intermediates between "Olive" and "Siva" in west Texas and New Mexico. **"Nelson's" Juniper Hairstreak (*C. g. nelsoni and others*):** British Columbia to California near incense-cedar or western red cedar, its larval foodplants. Common. Flies in summer (1 brood). ▶ Brown with purplish sheen; white postmedian line partial or absent. **"Muir's" Juniper Hairstreak (*C. g. muiri*):** Coast ranges of northern and central California, mainly near Sargeant's cypress, the larval foodplant. Flies in late spring (1 brood). ▶ Brown with purplish or greenish sheen, postmedian line partial to complete. **"Loki" Juniper Hairstreak (*C. g. loki*):** Southern California only. Often common near junipers, its larval foodplant. Flies spring and early summer (1–2 broods). ▶ Green to purplish brown. Hindwing often with darker band inward of postmedian line. **"Thorne's" Juniper Hairstreak (*C. g. thornei*):** Local and scarce in San Diego County, California, around rare Tecate cypress, its larval foodplant. Flies in spring (1 brood). ▶ Very similar to "Loki"; usually lacks green; identify by foodplant association.

"Siva" and subspecies of far west

"Nelson's"

HESSEL'S HAIRSTREAK   *Callophrys hesseli*

A very local denizen of eastern white cedar swamps, often overlooked because of its difficult habitat. Flies spring and summer (1 brood north, 2 broods south). ▶ Similar to "Olive" Juniper Hairstreak, but often more blue-green below, and with top white spot of forewing postmedian line *shifted outward*. Habitat is the best clue. ❧ **Larval foodplant:** Atlantic white cedar.

EVERGREEN HAIRSTREAKS

UPPERSIDE
(these sit with
wings closed)

"Olive"

"Olive"

actual
size

"Olive"

Juniper Hairstreak
(various populations)

"Nelson's"

"Siva"

"Siva"

"Muir's"

"Siva"

"Thorne's"

"Loki"

**Hessel's
Hairstreak**

Tailless, nickel-sized hairstreaks of the west, with green undersides. They fly relatively slowly. Males perch in gully bottoms or on hill summits to await females. Larval foodplants are mostly buckwheats. Classification of this group is very complex and controversial. Here we treat them all as composing two species, but some experts split them into seven or more.

BRAMBLE HAIRSTREAK   *Callophrys dumetorum/perplexa*

Includes several distinct populations with separate ranges. Compared to Sheridan's, Bramble usually has more brown below, especially near trailing edge of forewing. **"Bramble" Bramble Hairstreak (Callophrys perplexa perplexa):** From southern California to Washington. Flies in early spring (1 brood). ▶ Hindwing below green, often with one, two, or more white spots in postmedian area, rarely forming postmedian line. **"Coastal" Bramble Hairstreak (C. p. viridis):** Central to northern California along immediate coast, also locally in western Oregon. Flies in spring (1 brood). ▶ Hindwing below green or blue-green. Postmedian white spots may be few, or often may form a complete curved line. **"Immaculate" Bramble Hairstreak (C. p. affinis):** Higher elevations of the intermountain west, often in sagebrush habitat. Flies in early summer (1 brood). ▶ Green below, rarely with a trace of a white postmedian line or spots. **"Canyon" Bramble Hairstreak (C. p. apama):** Eastern edge of Rocky Mountains to southern Utah and south into Arizona. Flies in summer (1 brood). ▶ Hindwing green below with white postmedian line complete, edged inwardly by brown in Arizona/New Mexico, reduced to spots or absent in Colorado/Utah.

SHERIDAN'S HAIRSTREAK   *Callophrys sheridanii*

Several distinct populations, including **"White-lined" Sheridan's Hairstreak (Callophrys sheridanii sheridanii):** An attractive hairstreak often found at high elevation near melting snow in Rocky Mountain region. Flies in early spring (1 brood). ▶ Below green with fairly straight white postmedian line. **"Desert" Sheridan's Hairstreak (C. s. comstocki):** Great Basin and Mojave Desert, mainly Nevada and southern Utah. Small and seldom encountered. Adults are fast fliers. Flies mainly in spring, rarely summer and fall (1–3 broods). ▶ Hindwing green with white postmedian line well developed in southwestern part of range, less so to east and north. **"Alpine" Sheridan's Hairstreak (C. s. lemberti):** Found at mid- to high elevation from the Sierra Nevada northward. Flies in late spring or early summer (1 brood). ▶ Hindwing green with little or no trace of white postmedian line.

HAIRSTREAKS

UPPERSIDE
(these sit with
wings closed)

actual
size

"Bramble"

"Bramble"

"Immaculate"

"Coastal"

"Immaculate"

Bramble Hairstreak

"Canyon"

"Desert"

"White-lined"

"White-lined"

"Desert"

Sheridan's Hairstreak

"Alpine"

THICKET HAIRSTREAK　　*Callophrys spinetorum*

A large species of western foothills and mountains. Often encountered singly. Males come to mud and sit on hilltop trees to seek mates. Both sexes are fond of flowers. Flies spring to fall in lower foothills (2 broods), summer at high elevations (1 brood). ▶ Below dark red-brown with *bold white postmedian line* forming a W near the outer angle. Forewing below often with white cell-end bar. Steel blue above. Smaller individuals occur along the eastern Rockies. 🐛 **Larval foodplant:** Dwarf mistletoe growing on pine and other conifers.

JOHNSON'S HAIRSTREAK　　*Callophrys johnsoni*

Resident in conifer forest of the far west, but not often seen. May be found with Thicket Hairstreak where their ranges overlap. Males come to mud and sit on hilltop trees to seek females. Both sexes come to flowers. Flies spring to fall in lower foothills (1 brood, partial second?), summer at high elevations (1 brood). ▶ Similar to Thicket Hairstreak, but postmedian white line is usually less bold and does not form a distinct W; forewing below *lacks* cell-end bar. Dark brown to orange-brown above (visible in flight). 🐛 **Larval foodplant:** Dwarf mistletoe growing on pine and other conifers.

ARIZONA HAIRSTREAK　　*Erora quaderna*

A small gem of southwestern oak woodlands. Both sexes regularly visit flowers or mud, frequently basking with wings open. Males perch in treetops on mountain summits to locate females. Flies mainly spring to summer (2–3 broods). ▶ Tailless. Below pale green with numerous orange markings and with orange fringe. Above dark gray with some bright blue, especially on female. 🐛 **Larval foodplant:** Oak, buckbrush, and possibly manzanita.

EARLY HAIRSTREAK　　*Erora laeta*

A small hairstreak of eastern woodlands. Perhaps not rare, but seldom seen, and always an exciting find. Adults frequent the canopy of tall trees, rarely descending to the forest floor, but may sometimes be found at flowers or sitting on dirt roads. Males perch in treetops on open hilly summits to await females. Flies spring to early fall (2 broods, 3 in the south). ▶ Tailless. Pale green below with orange markings and fringe, dark gray above with some bright blue, especially on female. Similar to Arizona Hairstreak, but no overlap in range. 🐛 **Larval foodplant:** Beech and beaked hazelnut.

HAIRSTREAKS

UPPERSIDE
(these sit with
wings closed)

**Thicket
Hairstreak**

actual
size

**Johnson's
Hairstreak**

**Arizona
Hairstreak**

male

females

**Early
Hairstreak**

female

SANDIA HAIRSTREAK   *Callophrys mcfarlandi*

This southwestern specialty is very closely tied to Texas beargrass, its larval foodplant. Flies mainly early spring to early summer (1 brood), sometimes a second brood in late summer. ► Yellow-green below. White postmedian line *very prominent, unbroken, and relatively straight.* Separated from other green hairstreaks by shape of this line, relative lack of other markings, and lack of hindwing tails. ✿ **Larval foodplant:** Texas beargrass.

XAMI HAIRSTREAK   *Callophrys xami*

Rare and local in the southwest, usually seen singly. Adults fly more slowly than most other hairstreaks. Flies spring to fall (2–3 broods). ► Below a distinctive shade of yellowish or brownish green. Hindwing postmedian line white with two *sharp outward projections* forming a W. Above light to dark golden brown. ✿ **Larval foodplant:** *Graptopetalum* and other succulents.

SILVER-BANDED HAIRSTREAK   *Chlorostrymon simaethis*

A flashy resident of southern Florida and Texas. Strays into the southwest and southern California, sometimes in numbers. May open wings while perched. Flies most of year where resident (2–3 broods). ► Below bright green with a *straight* silver-white postmedian line. Note maroon marginal patch and outward jutting of postmedian line on hindwing. Male above deep purple, female gray. ✿ **Larval foodplant:** Balloon-vine.

AMETHYST HAIRSTREAK   *Chlorostymon maesites*

South Florida only. Extremely rare, perhaps extirpated from our area. Flies most of year (3 or more broods). ► Resembles Silver-banded but lacks white on forewing, has *less extensive maroon* on hindwing. Male above brilliant purple, female light blue. ✿ **Larval foodplant:** Not known.

CLENCH'S GREENSTREAK   *Cyanophrys miserabilis*

South Texas only. Local, occasionally common. ► Hindwing margin with several maroon spots. Postmedian line on hindwing white, often incomplete. Male above steel blue, female light blue. ✿ **Larval foodplant:** Retama.

GOODSON'S GREENSTREAK   *Cyanophrys goodsoni*

South Texas only. Uncommon. ► Tailless. Hindwing with single maroon spot at outer angle. Above powder blue. ✿ **Larval foodplant:** Pigeon-berry.

TROPICAL GREENSTREAK   *Cyanophrys herodotus*

Rare stray to south Texas. ► Hindwing below green with single maroon spot at outer angle and a small orange spot along the margin (sometimes absent). Similar to Goodson's but with tails. Above steel blue. ✿ **Larval foodplant:** Lantana and other tropical plants.

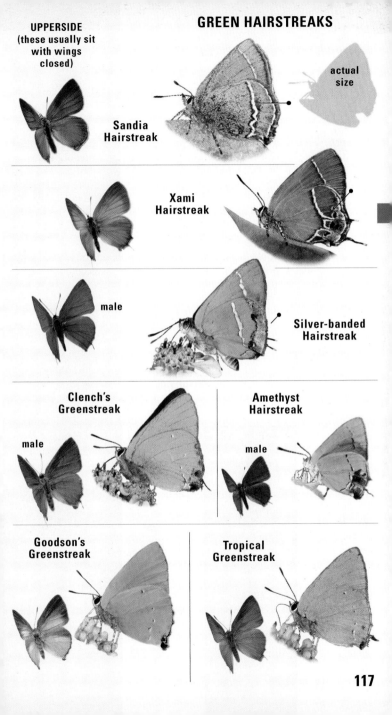

GREEN HAIRSTREAKS

UPPERSIDE
(these usually sit
with wings
closed)

actual
size

**Sandia
Hairstreak**

**Xami
Hairstreak**

male

**Silver-banded
Hairstreak**

**Clench's
Greenstreak**

male

**Amethyst
Hairstreak**

male

**Goodson's
Greenstreak**

**Tropical
Greenstreak**

MINISTREAKS AND TWO RARE STRAYS

Ministreaks are very small, fast-flying hairstreaks with gray-green eyes. They rarely perch with open wings.

LEDA MINISTREAK   *Ministrymon leda*

A small common hairstreak of the southwest. Best seen around stands of mesquite trees. Often found in large numbers at flowers or sitting in shady spots on hot summer afternoons. Flies late spring to late fall (2–3 broods). ▶ Below *pebbled gray* with postmedian line edged with red and a short line near center of hindwing leading margin. Forewing below with thin cell-end bar. Most in fall and winter (form *ines*) are darker gray with red reduced or absent below. Smaller than Gray Hairstreak (p. 92) with more mottled look; eyes *gray,* not black. 🌿 **Larval foodplant:** Mesquites.

CLYTIE MINISTREAK   *Ministrymon clytie*

South Texas only. Not uncommon, but small and easily overlooked. Flies most of year (2–3 broods). ▶ Light gray below with red-orange markings, including basal marks on hindwing and cell-end bar on forewing. Winter individuals can be darker gray with reduced red markings; best told from Leda Ministreak by range. 🌿 **Larval foodplant:** Creeping mesquite and other legumes.

GRAY MINISTREAK   *Ministrymon azia*

South Texas and Florida only; colonized southern Florida in the 1970s. Our smallest hairstreak. Flies most of year in Florida (3 or more broods), March to October in Texas (3 broods?). Rarely strays north. ▶ Below light to dark pebbly gray with *red marginal lines.* Hindwing with red postmedian line, lacks basal markings shown by Clytie Ministreak. 🌿 **Larval foodplant:** Vine mimosa in Texas, lead tree in Florida.

SONORAN HAIRSTREAK   *Hypostrymon critola*

Extremely rare stray to Arizona, reported May and October. ▶ Larger than Leda Ministreak, hindwing with orange postmedian line *offset near leading edge.* Forewing below lacks cell-end bar. Odd *striated look* below, especially on forewing. Winter individuals more heavily striated with red reduced or absent. Male above brilliant blue-purple, female light blue to gray. 🌿 **Larval foodplant:** Possibly mangle dulce in coastal northwestern Mexico, unknown inland.

RED-SPOTTED HAIRSTREAK   *Tmolus echion*

Rare stray to south Texas. ▶ Similar to Clytie Ministreak, but larger, and forewing below lacks cell-end bar. Light gray below, with hindwing postmedian line broken into several red spots and with red spots basally. Male above deep blue, female bluish gray. 🌿 **Larval foodplant:** Lantana and others.

MINISTREAKS AND RARITIES

UPPERSIDE
(these usually sit
with wings closed)

male

summer
form

actual
size

winter form

**Leda
Ministreak**

**Clytie
Ministreak**

female

male

winter
form

summer form

**Gray
Ministreak**

Sonoran Hairstreak

male

winter
form

summer
form

female

**Red-spotted
Hairstreak**

male

119

SCRUB-HAIRSTREAKS

(genus *Strymon*) are small fast-flying species with distinctive undersides. Unlike most hairstreaks, will perch with wings open. Mainly inhabitants of weedy openings and edges of tropical scrub forests. Most members of this group have very limited ranges in North America, with the striking exception of the common and widespread Gray Hairstreak (p. 92).

MALLOW SCRUB-HAIRSTREAK   *Strymon istapa*

Of the scrub-hairstreaks on this page and the next, this is the most commonly encountered. Resident in southern Texas and Florida, sometimes also moving northward into the southwest and California. Males hilltop in late afternoon to locate females. Flies most of year in Florida and Texas (3 or 4 broods), mainly fall in southwest and California (1–3 broods?). ► Gray below, hindwing with *two black basal spots* (lacking on other hairstreaks), prominent postmedian band, and short tails. Brownish gray above, female with some grayish blue on hindwing. Florida individuals are more boldly marked. 🌱 **Larval foodplant**: Mallows.

MARTIAL SCRUB-HAIRSTREAK   *Strymon martialis*

Extreme southern Florida only, mainly on the Florida Keys and in Everglades National Park. An attractive but local species, best found near stands of its larval foodplants. Flies most of the year (3 or more broods). Also found in the West Indies. ► Below gray with bold white postmedian line. Not quite as contrastingly marked as next species, and hindwing *lacks basal spots*. Above brownish gray with patches of powder blue. 🌱 **Larval foodplant**: Bay cedar and Florida trema.

BARTRAM'S SCRUB-HAIRSTREAK   *Strymon acis*

Extreme southern Florida only, mainly on the Florida Keys and in Everglades National Park. Local around colonies of narrow-leaved croton growing in open pine areas on rocky soil. Flies most of year (3 or more broods). Also found in the West Indies. ► Below gray with *very bold white postmedian line*. Hindwing has two distinct white basal spots. Brownish gray above. 🌱 **Larval foodplant**: Narrow-leaved croton.

RED-LINED SCRUB-HAIRSTREAK   *Strymon bebrycia*

A rare stray to south Texas and the southwest only. Easy to overlook because of its similarity to Gray Hairstreak. Flies most of year in south Texas, spring or late summer elsewhere (1–3 broods?). ► Below light gray, with hindwing postmedian line red, edged outwardly with white. Resembles Gray Hairstreak (p. 92), but has *extensive whitish markings* near the hindwing margin. Above brownish gray, female with extensive grayish white on the hindwing. 🌱 **Larval foodplant**: Balloon-vine.

SCRUB-HAIRSTREAKS

male

female

Florida

actual size

Mallow Scrub-Hairstreak

Texas

Martial Scrub-Hairstreak

Bartram's Scrub-Hairstreak

Red-lined Scrub-Hairstreak

121

These Mexican species reach our area mainly in extreme southern Texas, although two of them have also been recorded in Arizona.

LACEY'S SCRUB-HAIRSTREAK   *Strymon alea*

Rare and local, from central to south Texas only. Stays close to larval foodplant. Flies most of year (3 or more broods). ▶ Below mottled gray, hindwing with irregular postmedian line and large black marginal spot. Underside has a blotchier look than on most similar species. Above dark gray-brown. 🌿 **Larval foodplant:** Southwestern bernardia.

RED-CRESCENT SCRUB-HAIRSTREAK   *Strymon rufofusca*

Extreme southern Texas only, rare. In late afternoon, males perch on low shrubs in open areas near mallows to await females. Found sparingly from spring to late fall (1–3 broods). ▶ Below gray, hindwing with a postmedian line of *red crescents edged outwardly with white*. No basal spots. Suggests Red-lined Scrub-Hairstreak (previous page), but is smaller and has the hindwing postmedian line more broken up. Above brown, the red hindwing spot visible but smaller than that of Gray Hairstreak (p. 92). 🌿 **Larval foodplant**: Mallows.

TAILLESS SCRUB-HAIRSTREAK   *Strymon cestri*

Rare stray to southern Texas and Arizona, recorded sparingly from spring to fall. Males may occur on hilltops. ▶ Tailless. Below *boldly mottled* white, gray, and brown. Hindwing has brown postmedian band, often a round brown spot on leading margin (compare to next species). Above dark gray-brown, females with blue on hindwing. 🌿 **Larval foodplant**: Unknown.

LANTANA SCRUB-HAIRSTREAK   *Strymon bazochii*

South Texas only, uncommon there, recorded February to December (3 broods). Widespread in American tropics. Also introduced into Hawaii to control weedy lantana. ▶ Hindwing sharply angled, lacks tails, and often crossed by a white ray. Note the light brown postmedian band and *brown spot in middle of leading margin* of hindwing. Less contrast than Tailless Scrub-Hairstreak and has gray eyes, not black. Above dark gray-brown with blue on hindwing. 🌿 **Larval foodplant**: Lantana and frogfruit.

YOJOA SCRUB-HAIRSTREAK   *Strymon yojoa*

Rare stray to southern Texas and Arizona, recorded mainly in fall. ▶ Below light gray. Hindwing with faint postmedian line (straighter than that of Lacey's Scrub-Hairstreak) and whitish submarginal band. Above dark gray-brown. 🌿 **Larval foodplant**: Hibiscus and other tropical plants.

WHITE SCRUB-HAIRSTREAK   *Strymon albata*

Very rare tropical stray to south Texas. Apparently resident only where the larval foodplant maintains a continuous bloom, thus absent from many seemingly suitable areas. ▶ Paler below than other hairstreaks, mostly gray or white. Hindwing with faint brown postmedian line. Mostly white above with black markings. 🌿 **Larval foodplant**: Indian mallow.

RARE SCRUB-HAIRSTREAKS

actual size

Lacey's Scrub-Hairstreak

Red-crescent Scrub-Hairstreak

Tailless Scrub-Hairstreak

Lantana Scrub-Hairstreak

White Scrub-Hairstreak

Yojoa Scrub-Hairstreak

123

BLUES

(subfamily Polyommatinae) are very small butterflies, mostly blue above, although females of many are browner. Adults often bask with wings open, but their field marks are mainly on the undersides of the wings. Blues tend to fly more slowly than most hairstreaks, with more up-and-down fluttering. Like hairstreaks, they may rub their hindwings together while perched. Males often gather in "puddle parties" around wet soil.

EASTERN TAILED-BLUE *Everes comyntas*

Very common in the east, visiting flowers in gardens, parks, and meadows. Scarcer and more localized in the west. Flies spring to fall (3 broods). ▶ The only *tailed* blue in the east (tails may be short or missing on worn individuals). Hindwing below has one to three orange spots near base of tail. Above male bright blue, female mostly blackish brown with blue basally in spring. Both have one or two orange spots near tail above. ❀ **Larval foodplant:** Flowers and seeds of many legumes.

WESTERN TAILED-BLUE *Everes amyntula*

Common in the west, from sea level to high elevations. Flies spring to fall (2–3 broods). ▶ Nearly identical to Eastern Tailed-Blue. Where they overlap, Western is generally at higher elevations. Below Western usually has less orange near tail. Above male Easterns usually have some orange near tail, male Westerns usually lack it. Female Easterns usually lack blue above, except in spring, while female Westerns usually have some blue basally. ❀ **Larval foodplant:** Milk vetches, other legumes.

SILVERY BLUE *Glaucopsyche lygdamus*

Often one of the first blues of spring. Widespread and variable. Males readily attracted to mud. Flies in spring or early summer depending on elevation (1 brood). The extinct Xerces Blue (San Francisco) was a close relative. ▶ Gray below with postmedian line of r*ound black spots.* Size of hindwing spots varies by region; margins below unmarked. Compare Reakirt's Blue (p. 128), Boisduval's Blue (p. 134). Male above bright blue; female varies from mostly brown to mostly blue. ❀ **Larval foodplant:** Lupines, vetches, and other legumes.

ARROWHEAD BLUE *Glaucopsyche piasus*

An attractive blue usually found close to lupines. Not as widespread as Silvery Blue and less commonly seen. Flies late spring to early summer (1 brood). ▶ Below light to dark gray. Best known by the prominent *postmedian band of white arrowheads* pointing inward on the hindwing. Above blue with brown margins, fringes checkered black and white. ❀ **Larval foodplant:** Lupines.

124 BLUES

BLUES

summer female

male

actual size

Eastern Tailed-Blue

female

male

Western Tailed-Blue

variations

western female

eastern male

Silvery Blue

variations

female

male

Arrowhead Blue

variations

125

MARINE BLUE   *Leptotes marina*

Common from Texas west to southern California, regularly straying well northward. Flight is faster and more erratic than that of most blues. Flies most of year in southernmost regions (multiple broods). ► Strongly *striped* gray-brown and white below (in Texas, compare to Cassius Blue). Above male is brown with strong purple overlay, female brown with blue basally. 🌿 **Larval foodplant:** Flowering parts of many legumes.

CASSIUS BLUE   *Leptotes cassius*

Florida and Texas only. Common. Flight is fast and erratic. Flies most of year (multiple broods). ► Striped gray-brown and white below. Very similar to Marine Blue (with which it overlaps in Texas), but usually whiter overall, with *white patchy area on lower part of forewing*. Above male is brown with strong purple overlay, female brown with white and blue basally. 🌿 **Larval foodplant:** Flowering parts of many legumes.

EASTERN PYGMY-BLUE   *Brephidium isophthalma*

Living at the edges of coastal salt marshes and flats in the southeast, this blue is tiny and easily overlooked, but common. Adults stay close to the ground. Flies all year in south Florida, spring to fall in other areas (3–4 broods). ► Brown below with narrow white stripes and with four bold marginal spots on hindwing. Above mostly brown. 🌿 **Larval foodplant:** Glassworts.

WESTERN PYGMY-BLUE   *Brephidium exile*

Tiny but often abundant in salt marshes, desert salt flats, disturbed alkaline areas. Flight is weak and low, but adults stray northward and high into mountains. Flies all year in south, otherwise spring to fall (2–4 broods). ► Similar to Eastern Pygmy-Blue, but underside of wings strongly *two-toned*, with *gray* at base. Above some blue at wing bases. 🌿 **Larval foodplant:** Saltbush, Russian thistle, lambsquarters, and others.

CYNA BLUE   *Zizula cyna*

Uncommon in southern Texas; rare stray to southern Arizona. Very small and easily overlooked. Adults sway hypnotically from side to side while perched. Recorded from spring to fall (2 broods?). ► Below gray with many small spots and dashes. Margin lacks bold black spots, unlike Ceraunus Blue (next page). More strongly marked than Spring Azure (p. 130). Above brown with blue basally. 🌿 **Larval foodplant:** Not well known.

BLUES

pale variant

male

actual size

female

Marine Blue

female

male

Cassius Blue

Cyna Blue

Eastern Pygmy-Blue

Western Pygmy-Blue

CERAUNUS BLUE   *Hemiargus ceraunus*

Common in southern regions, straying northward. Best found in hot areas where legumes bloom continuously. Flies most of year at southern limits, spring to fall elsewhere (3 or more broods). ► Most markings below *not very prominent,* except black spots near lower angle and near leading edge of hindwing. Male above lavender-blue, female brown with blue basally. 🌿 **Larval foodplant:** Flowers and buds of many legumes.

REAKIRT'S BLUE   *Hemiargus isola*

A common blue of many southwestern habitats, establishing temporary colonies far to the north and east. In the southwest, more at home at higher elevations than Ceraunus Blue. Flies all year in south, spring to fall elsewhere (3 or more broods). ► Forewing below with *conspicuous row of white-ringed black spots* (compare to Silvery and Arrowhead Blues, p. 124). Male above lavender-blue, female brown with blue basally. 🌿 **Larval foodplant:** Flowers and buds of many legumes.

NICKERBEAN BLUE   *Cyclargus ammon*

Extreme south Florida only. Recently established (1990s) on Big Pine Key, but still uncommon. Flies all year (3 or more broods). ► Easily confused with Miami Blue. Below with broad white postmedian band. Hindwing below like that of Miami Blue but with more white in center, *bullet-shaped orange cap* on bold black marginal spot, and three, not four, black basal spots. Above male lilac-blue, female bright iridescent blue with brown margins. 🌿 **Larval foodplant:** Nickerbean *(Caesalpinia).*

MIAMI BLUE   *Cyclargus thomasi*

Extreme south Florida only. Formerly common, now rare and local, only in the Florida Keys; a species in need of protection. Flies all year (3 or more broods). ► Below with broad white postmedian bands. Hindwing below with orange *crescent cap* on bold black marginal spot and *four* black basal spots (one often pale). Above male lilac-blue, female bright iridescent blue with brown borders. 🌿 **Larval foodplant:** Balloon-vine.

SONORAN BLUE   *Philotes sonorensis*

A spectacular little jewel of California. Localized, but can be common along sunny, steep canyon slopes where dudleyas grow in the rocks. Reaches edge of Colorado Desert in southern California. Despite the name, not found in Sonora, Mexico. Flies in early spring (1 brood), to late spring at higher elevations. ► Above shiny bright blue with black markings and *bright redorange patches* (two on male, four on female). Below dusky gray with distinct orange patch. 🌿 **Larval foodplant:** Dudleyas.

SOUTHERN BLUES

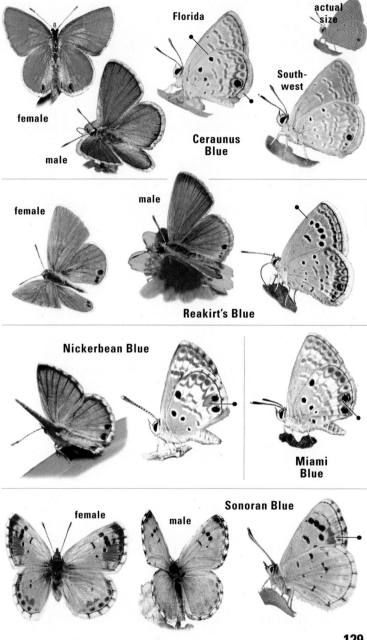

actual size

Florida

South-west

Ceraunus Blue

female

male

female

male

Reakirt's Blue

Nickerbean Blue

Miami Blue

Sonoran Blue

female

male

129

At one time, all North American azures were regarded as one abundant and variable species. It now appears certain that there are several species, all very similar. Their classification is still being studied. Unless you are a specialist on this group or have access to detailed information for your local area, it may be best to just enjoy them all as Azures — and marvel at the fact that butterflies can still keep so many secrets from us.

THE SPRING AZURE COMPLEX   *Celastrina ladon*

In many regions the emergence of this pale, delicate blue is among the first signs of spring. Common in woods, clearings, and gardens, it may fly high around flowering trees; males sometimes swarm at mud puddles. Flies in spring and summer in north, most of year in south (1–3 or more broods). ▶ Variable. Most commonly seen form is very pale and lightly marked below. Other forms have a dark brown blotch in center of hindwing (form *lucia*) or a dark brown border below (form *marginata*). Above male is bright pale blue, female has dark borders and often some white scaling, especially in late spring and summer. 🐛 **Larval foodplant:** Flowering parts of many plants. Note: This is almost certainly a complex of several species. Some forms proposed as full species include **"Summer" Azure (*Celastrina ladon neglecta*):** Widespread in the east, flying in summer. Very pale below, and usually with more white above than Spring Azures. **"Hops" Azure (*C. l. humulus*):** Eastern Colorado, flying mostly in June. Very similar to pale Spring Azures, but larvae feed on hops. **"Holly"** or **"Atlantic" Azure (*C. l. idella*):** Atlantic seaboard, flying in spring; larvae feed on hollies.

APPALACHIAN AZURE   *Celastrina neglectamajor*

Apparently local and uncommon in rich deciduous or mixed forest. Flies mid-May into June, between the spring and summer flights of Spring Azure (1 brood). ▶ Probably not safely separated from Spring Azure, but averages larger, with hindwing below very pale chalk white; lacks whitish on upperside. Might be identified by association with foodplant. 🐛 **Larval foodplant:** Bugbane or black cohosh (*Cimicifuga*).

DUSKY AZURE   *Celastrina nigra*

Local and uncommon in moist, rich deciduous forest. Visits flowers, and males may come to mud puddles. Flies in midspring (1 brood). ▶ Below very similar to some of the typical pale forms of Spring Azure. Above male is *solid dark gray;* female is very dark above, with limited blue-gray areas. 🐛 **Larval foodplant:** White goatsbeard (*Aruncus*).

male

female

female

female

male

actual size

variations

the Spring Azure complex

"Summer" Azure

"Holly" Azure

Appalachian Azure

Dusky Azure

WESTERN BLUES

Classification of the first two below is controversial. The widespread forms may be Lupine, not Acmon, or they may make up multiple species.

ACMON BLUE   *Plebejus acmon*

Widespread and common in the west, in many habitats, including gardens. Males readily gather at mud. Flies spring to fall (2–3 broods). ▶ Strongly marked below, with *orange hindwing band* capping *metallic blue spots.* "Buckwheat blues" (pp. 138–141) lack these metallic spots; also see Melissa and Northern Blues (p. 134). Male above lilac with pink or orange submarginal band on hindwing. Female above brown with orange hindwing band, and often with varying amount of blue basally. Often quite difficult to separate from Lupine Blue in areas where they overlap (see below). 🌿 **Larval foodplant:** Buckwheats and legumes.

LUPINE BLUE   *Plebejus lupinus*

As traditionally defined, only in Oregon, California, and Nevada. Flies in spring or summer depending on locality and elevation (mainly 1 brood). ▶ Very similar to Acmon Blue. In southern California, male's band on hindwing above is orange on this species, more pinkish on Acmon. Male Lupine Blue may have wider black borders above. Female varies from mostly brown to mostly greenish blue above, many not separable from female Acmon Blues. 🌿 **Larval foodplant:** Buckwheats.

VEINED BLUE   *Plebejus neurona*

Southern California, locally common. Unique among blues in that both sexes lack blue above. Males fly slowly around stands of larval foodplant, searching for females, or perch on low shrubs in gully bottoms. Flies late spring and summer (1–2 broods). ▶ Similar to Lupine and Acmon Blues but hindwing submarginal band has metallic *gold* specks. Above dark brown with *orange veining* and wide hindwing submarginal orange bands. 🌿 **Larval foodplant:** Wright's buckwheat.

SAN EMIGDIO BLUE   *Plebejus emigdionis*

Southern California, sometimes common, but extremely local; the larval foodplant is much more widespread than the butterfly. Flies in spring, occasionally in summer (1–3 broods). ▶ Below submarginal orange band on hindwing is *thin and pale,* and forewing lacks dark cell spot. Above submarginal band on hindwing of both sexes is *blurred,* not well defined. Male above lilac, female brownish orange with some blue basally. 🌿 **Larval foodplant:** Four-wing saltbush.

BLUES

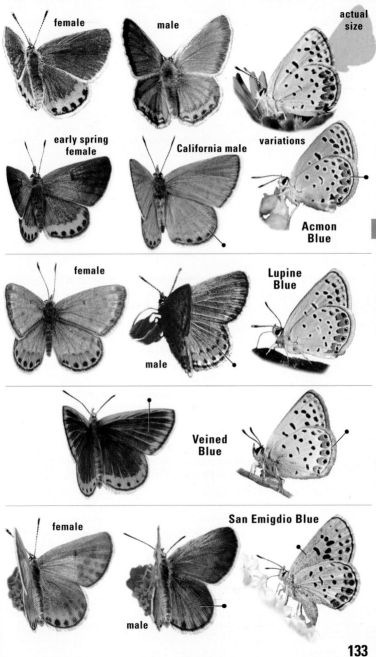

female

male

actual size

early spring female

California male

variations

Acmon Blue

female

male

Lupine Blue

Veined Blue

female

male

San Emigdio Blue

BOISDUVAL'S BLUE *Plebejus icarioides*

Widespread in west, often very common, from coastal dunes to mountain meadows. Flies in spring or summer (1 brood). ▶ Large for a blue. Quite variable. Postmedian spots on hindwing below vary from *nearly all white* to *black circled in white*. Forewing below has bold black postmedian spots, but submarginal spots are *usually faint*. Male above usually violet-blue, rarely with forewing cell-end bar. Female above all brown or with varying amounts of blue, and shows forewing cell-end bar (often a faint line). 🐛 **Larval foodplant:** Lupines.

GREENISH BLUE *Plebejus saepiolus*

A blue of clover-strewn wet meadows and forest openings. Often common to abundant. Flies in summer (1 brood). ▶ Variable. Usually smaller than Boisduval's, with more pointed forewings. Black spots on hindwing below are usually encircled with much *less white* than on Boisduval's, and submarginal spots on forewing are usually stronger. Male greenish to grayish blue above. Female dark brown above, sometimes with blue basally and a trace of orange band on the hindwing. Both sexes above with cell-end bars. 🐛 **Larval foodplant:** Clovers.

MELISSA BLUE *Lycaeides melissa*

Common and widespread in west. Some populations in Great Lakes region and northeast ("Karner" Melissa Blue) are endangered or are already extirpated. Flies spring to fall (1–3 broods). ▶ Dusky to whitish below, with orange submarginal bands on *both* wings. Separated from most blues by orange on forewing below. Spalding's Blue (p. 138) lacks metallic blue-green specks in hindwing orange band. Above male blue, female brown with some blue; orange forewing band obvious in some populations, absent in others. 🐛 **Larval foodplant:** Lupines, alfalfa, rattleweeds, and other legumes.

NORTHERN BLUE *Lycaeides idas*

Widespread in the north, somewhat more local southward along Pacific Coast and in Rockies. Flies in summer (1 brood). ▶Very similar to Melissa Blue; impossible to distinguish from it in many areas. Ground color below may be more bluish white. Orange submarginal bands often less well developed than those on Melissa Blue or can be nearly to completely absent. Above male blue, female brown with variable blue; female often has less obvious orange above than female Melissa. 🐛 **Larval foodplant:** Legumes, blueberries, and others.

BLUES

female

male

actual size

Boisduval's Blue

variations

female

males

Greenish Blue

females

male

Melissa Blue

"Karner" Melissa Blue

female

Northern Blue

females

male

135

SHASTA BLUE   *Plebejus shasta*

A small species of sagebrush flats, high prairie hills, or above timberline on rocky windswept slopes. Common but local. Flies in summer (1 brood). ▶ Gray below; orange submarginal band on hindwing caps *metallic spots.* Hindwing postmedian band below of brown or gray spots, not black. Male above dull blue, female brown with blue basally. Both sexes with cell-end bars.
🐛 **Larval foodplant:** Lupines, rattleweeds, and clovers.

ARCTIC BLUE   *Agriades glandon*

Variable; probably a complex of multiple species. Included here are **"Rustic" Arctic Blue (*Agriades glandon rustica* and other subspecies):** Rocky Mountains from Arizona to the Arctic, from openings in pine forests to prairies and tundra. Flight is fast and low. Flies in summer (1 brood). ▶ Hindwing variable but usually with *white band* just inward of submarginal spots. Above male gray-blue with cell-end bar on forewing and sometimes hindwing. Female above brown with obvious forewing cell-end bar; Alberta female brown with silver-blue overlay. 🐛 **Larval foodplant:** Rock primroses. **"Sierra" Arctic Blue (*A. g. podarce*):** High elevations from Oregon south through Sierra Nevada, in wet subalpine meadows. Flies in summer (1 brood). ▶ Below brown, female darker than male. Hindwing below with white band inward of submarginal spots, usually a postmedian band of black spots, black spot in cell. Male above silver-blue, female brown, both with frosted overscaling. 🐛 **Larval foodplant:** Shooting star.

HEATHER BLUE   *Agriades cassiope*

Recently discovered in high mountains of California. Prefers moist, rocky subalpine slopes where the larval foodplant grows. Flies in mid- to late summer (1 brood). ▶ Similar to "Sierra" Arctic Blue, but lacks frosted overscaling above; on hindwing below, black spot in cell is *very small or absent.* Habitat usually differs. 🐛 **Larval foodplant:** Mountain heather.

CRANBERRY BLUE   *Vacciniina optilete*

Truly boreal in occurrence, living in habitats where few other blues dare to tread—open bogs in taiga and tundra. Flies in summer (1 brood). ▶ Below has bold black postmedian spots and a prominent single orange spot (bordered in black) at lower angle of hindwing. Above male violet-blue, female brown with varying blue basally. 🐛 **Larval foodplant:** Cranberries and blueberries.

BLUES

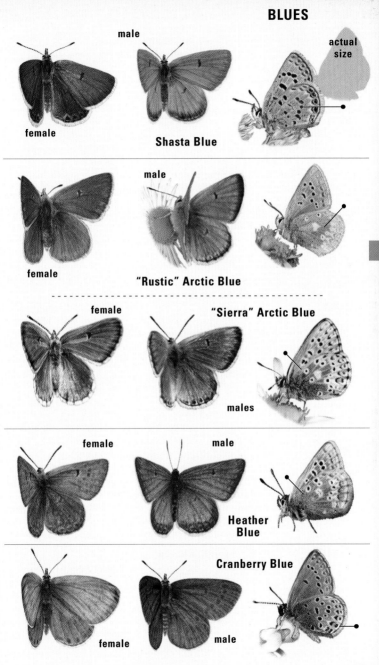

male

actual size

female

Shasta Blue

female

male

"Rustic" Arctic Blue

female

"Sierra" Arctic Blue

females

males

female

male

Heather Blue

Cranberry Blue

female

male

(genus *Euphilotes,* this page and the next) are found locally throughout the west, their larvae feeding on various species of buckwheats. Adults are sedentary, staying close to their larval foodplant. These are among our most confusing butterflies. The actual number of species is undoubtedly higher than what we indicate here, but their classification is still controversial. There are places where one of these blues may be represented by more than one form, each form feeding on a different species of buckwheat and flying at a different season. However, it remains uncertain whether these are necessarily separate species, and how they relate to forms found elsewhere. And most are so similar that they are best separated on the basis of flight period, locality, association with a particular type of buckwheat, and (for absolute certainty) dissection. The safest field identification is often just "buckwheat blue" or "*Euphilotes,* sp."

THE SQUARE-SPOTTED BLUE COMPLEX   *Euphilotes battoides*

Undoubtedly a complex of several species. Colonies occur from sea level to timberline, flying at various times in spring and summer (1 brood apiece). ► Black spots below, many of them squarish, and orange submarginal band on hindwing below. Very similar to Dotted Blue (next page), but usually has orange band more continuous (not broken into spots), and usually has a *thicker black marginal line.* Also very similar to Rita Blue (next page), but usually has checkered fringe on forewing. Separated from Acmon Blue (p. 132) by lack of metallic specks in hindwing orange band. Some of the more distinctive components of Square-spotted Blue: **"Bernardino" Blue *(Euphilotes battoides bernardino):*** Common around California buckwheat in southern California and western Arizona. Small, relatively narrow-winged. Flies in late spring. **"Bauer's" Blue *(E. b. baueri):*** Mainly eastern California and western Nevada, around oval-leafed buckwheat. Female often has extensive blue above. Flies in late spring. **"Ellis's" Blue *(E. b. ellisi):*** Mainly eastern Utah to eastern California, around Corymbose and Heermann's buckwheats. Flies in late summer. **"Central" Blue *(E. b. centralis):*** Southern Rocky Mountains south to southeastern Arizona, around Sulphur, James's, and other buckwheats. Flies in summer.

SPALDING'S BLUE   *Euphilotes spaldingi*

Localized in a range centered on the Four Corners region and western Utah. Flies in summer (1 brood). ► Below both wings with orange submarginal band. Lacks tiny metallic specks along hindwing margin (see Melissa Blue, p. 134). Female above with orange band along forewing margin. ❧ **Larval foodplant:** Red root buckwheat.

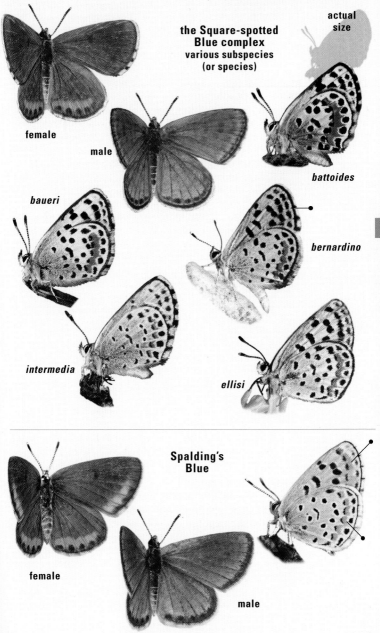

BUCKWHEAT BLUES

actual size

the Square-spotted
Blue complex
various subspecies
(or species)

female

male

battoides

baueri

bernardino

intermedia

ellisi

Spalding's
Blue

female

male

See the notes on this complex on p. 138. The classification of this group is still very uncertain, and field identification is often impossible. Although we are far from complete understanding of this group, you can find more information in *A Field Guide to Western Butterflies* by Paul Opler or in *Butterflies Through Binoculars: The West* by Jeffrey Glassberg.

THE DOTTED BLUE COMPLEX   *Euphilotes enoptes*

Found from sea level to high in the mountains. Variable, probably a complex of multiple species. Overlaps range of Square-spotted Blue (previous page), but their larvae feed on different species of buckwheats where they occur together. Flies spring, summer, or fall depending on locality (1 brood, rarely 2). ► Very similar to Square-spotted Blue, often not safely identified, but tends to have orange hindwing band narrower and more broken into disconnected spots; black marginal line is thin. Included here are **"Mojave" Dotted Blue** *(Euphilotes enoptes mojave)*: Mainly Mojave Desert of California and adjacent Nevada. Flies in spring (1 brood). Larvae feed on low-growing buckwheats. **"Ancilla" Dotted Blue** *(E. e. ancilla)*: Western edge of the Great Basin, and central Rocky Mountains. Flies late spring or summer (1 brood). Hindwing orange band tends to be more continuous. Larvae feed on sulphur buckwheat.

RITA BLUE   *Euphilotes rita*

A late-summer blue in arid regions. Flies August to September in most areas (1 brood). ► Similar to other buckwheat blues. Orange band on hindwing below is usually continuous, not broken, and forewing fringe mostly *lacks black checkering*. Included under this heading is **"Pale" Rita Blue** *(Euphilotes rita pallescens)*: Locally from Utah to eastern California in sandy desert habitats, flying July to September (1 brood). Markings below washed out and pale, hindwing orange band reduced or absent. ✿ **Larval foodplant**: Buckwheats.

SMALL BLUE   *Philotiella speciosa*

A fragile little blue of deserts, also woodlands in a few areas. Local, seldom common. Males patrol low over dry slopes near foodplant to locate females. Flies in late spring (1 brood). (Note: the population in southern Oregon was recently described as a separate species, Pumice Blue or Leona's Little Blue, *P. leona*.) ► *Very small*. Bold black spots on forewing below, but no marginal spots or orange band on hindwing. Male above blue, female brown. ✿ **Larval foodplant**: Punctured bract and reniform buckwheat.

BUCKWHEAT BLUES

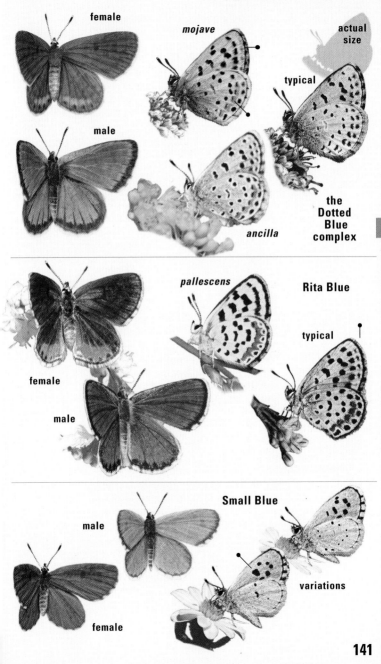

female

male

mojave

typical

actual size

ancilla

the Dotted Blue complex

pallescens

Rita Blue

typical

female

male

Small Blue

male

female

variations

141

(family Riodinidae) are so named for the small metallic markings on many. Metalmarks live mainly in the tropics, where many have dazzling colors and bizarre wing shapes; only about twenty species are resident in North America north of Mexico, and ours are mainly brown, orange, and black. Only in extreme south Texas do we see a hint of their tropical diversity. Metalmarks usually perch with their wings open; they often land underneath leaves close to the ground. Most appear to be quite sedentary, rarely straying from their place of birth. The three species on this page are the only ones found east of Texas, and they are most easily separated by range.

LITTLE METALMARK   *Calephelis virginiensis*

A tiny species of the southeast. Fairly common in some areas, in open, grassy pine flats. Less common and more localized in northern part of range. Flies spring to fall (3 or more broods). ▶ Above bright red-brown with narrow, metallic, silver-blue bands in the postmedian and submarginal areas. Below with similar pattern to upperside, but bright red-orange. No other metalmark overlaps its range. Nothing else in the southeast is really similar, but compare to other small orange butterflies, such as Pearl Crescent (p. 176). 🐛 **Larval foodplant:** Yellow thistle.

NORTHERN METALMARK   *Calephelis borealis*

Very local on shale barrens and around woodland openings with limestone soil in the east. Like other metalmarks, rather slow in flight, and perches with wings spread. Flies in summer (1 brood). ▶ Above dark red-brown to orange-brown, with a darker area through the median part of the wings. Silver-blue postmedian and marginal bands like other metalmarks. Below with similar pattern to upperside, but bright orange. Range may overlap that of Swamp Metalmark but habitats differ. 🐛 **Larval foodplant:** Round-leaved ragwort.

SWAMP METALMARK   *Calephelis mutica*

Limited to isolated areas in the upper midwest and Ozark region. Extremely local in wet meadows and other damp areas with colonies of the larval foodplant. Has disappeared from some former haunts and is probably a threatened species. Flies early to late summer (1 brood in north, 2 broods in south). ▶ Red-brown to orange-brown above, bright orange below; similar to Northern Metalmark, but lacks obvious dark median area and occurs in different habitat. 🐛 **Larval foodplant:** Swamp thistle.

METALMARKS

Little Metalmark

actual size

Northern Metalmark

Swamp Metalmark

143

SCINTILLANT METALMARKS OF THE SOUTHWEST

Scintillant metalmarks (genus *Calephelis*) are small, exquisite butterflies, seldom noticed except by the keen observer. All have narrow but stunning silver-blue metallic postmedian and submarginal bands, especially prominent on the undersides of the wings. They are among the most difficult butterflies to identify, especially when in worn condition.

FATAL METALMARK   *Calephelis nemesis*

Widespread in the southwest, common from Arizona to Texas. Most active during the heat of the day, the males often perching on shrubs in gully bottoms to await females. Flies most of year in southernmost areas, spring to fall elsewhere (3 or more broods). ▶ Variable. Male relatively plain brown above with *darker median band*. Female above brown to orange-brown, median area not always darker. Metallic bands not conspicuous above. 🌿 **Larval foodplant:** Seepwillow *(Baccharis)* and virgin's bower *(Clematis)*.

ROUNDED METALMARK   *Calephelis perditalis*

South Texas only, common in lower Rio Grande Valley, where it flies all year (multiple broods). ▶ Difficult to separate from Fatal or Rawson's Metalmarks. Forewings may look subtly more rounded, with fringes less clearly checkered. Metallic postmedian band on forewing usually obvious, bulging outward at its center. Median area of wings usually not as dark as on Fatal Metalmark. 🌿 **Larval foodplant:** Mistflower *(Eupatorium)*.

ARIZONA METALMARK   *Calephelis arizonensis*

Only in southeastern Arizona and extreme southwestern New Mexico, fairly common along streams in foothills. Flies all year (multiple broods). ▶ Similar to Fatal Metalmark, but more uniform red-brown above, lacking darkened median area; metallic postmedian band may be more obvious. 🌿 **Larval foodplant:** Beggar's ticks *(Bidens)*.

RAWSON'S METALMARK   *Calephelis rawsoni*

Rare and local in southwestern and south Texas. Flies spring to fall (3 or more broods). ▶ Median area usually not so dark as on Fatal Metalmark. Metallic postmedian band may be more obvious than on Fatal but not bulging outward as on Rounded Metalmark. 🌿 **Larval foodplant:** Mistflower.

WRIGHT'S METALMARK   *Calephelis wrighti*

Restricted to southeastern California and lower Colorado River region. A denizen of dry canyons, rocky flats, and desert washes, sometimes common. Flies from early spring to fall (2–3 broods). ▶ Above uniform red-brown. Often brighter than Fatal Metalmark, lacking dark median areas; outer margin of forewing is uneven. 🌿 **Larval foodplant:** Sweetbush *(Bebbia)*.

METALMARKS

actual
size

variations

Fatal
Metalmark

Rounded Metalmark

female

male

Arizona Metalmark

Rawson's
Metalmark

Wright's
Metalmark

145

ZELA METALMARK   *Emesis zela*

Mainly Arizona and southwestern New Mexico (one record from Big Bend, Texas). Locally common along sycamore-lined canyons in midelevation oak woodlands. Adults are easily approached at flowers but may be warier when at mud. Flies in spring and summer (2 broods). ▶ Above forewing gray-brown to brown, contrasting with orange on hindwing. On forewing, note *darker band* near center of leading edge and *lack* of obvious black spots in submarginal area (compare to Ares Metalmark). Below yellow-brown with black markings. 🌿 **Larval foodplant:** Probably oaks.

ARES METALMARK   *Emesis ares*

Southeastern Arizona only, common to uncommon in midelevation oak woodlands. Often found at flowers, where it may occur with Zela Metalmark. Flies in summer (1 brood). ▶ Similar to Zela Metalmark, but the forewing *lacks* the obvious dark band on the leading edge, and the submargin of the forewing usually has *obvious black spots.* Hindwing above is gray-brown with orange restricted to leading edge on male, more extensive on female. A few problematic metalmarks look intermediate between Zela and Ares. 🌿 **Larval foodplant**: Emory oak, possibly others.

NAIS METALMARK   *Apodemia nais*

A mid- to high-elevation species of the southern Rockies and the southwest, but sporadic in the mountains of southeastern Arizona. Often found in numbers on flowers of buckbrush or milkweed. Flies in summer (1 brood). ▶ Above orange with numerous black markings and a white spot near the forewing leading edge. Pattern might suggest a crescent or checkerspot (section beginning p. 176), but note long antennae, long forewings, and green eyes. Below has contrasting orange forewing and grayish white hindwing. 🌿 **Larval foodplant**: Fendler's buckbrush *(Ceanothus).*

"CHISOS" NAIS METALMARK   *Apodemia nais chisosensis*

A specialty of west Texas, mainly Big Bend. Considered a distinct species from Nais Metalmark by some. Adults are fond of the flowers of Texas beargrass and beebrush. Flies in late spring and sometimes again in late summer (1–2 broods). ▶ Similar to typical Nais Metalmark. Above has more limited black markings, less gray at base of wings. Below shows less orange on hindwing. 🌿 **Larval foodplant:** Havard's Plum.

SOUTHWESTERN METALMARKS

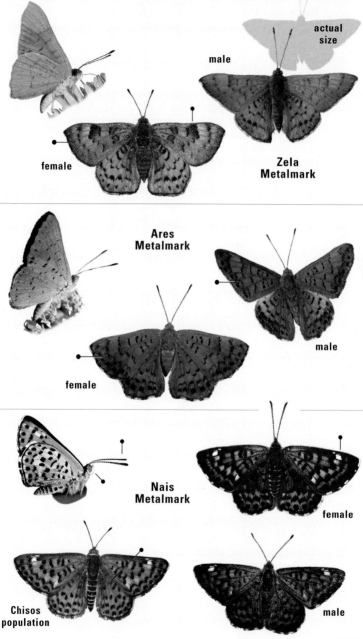

actual size

male

female

Zela Metalmark

Ares Metalmark

male

female

Nais Metalmark

female

Chisos population

male

147

THE MORMON METALMARK COMPLEX *Apodemia mormo*

Our most widespread and common western metalmark, occupying many open habitats, from deserts and sagebrush flats to open oak woodlands. Adults are fast and erratic in flight. At flowers, they walk about, opening and closing their wings with a mechanical look. Quite variable, and is almost certainly a complex of several species, but details are still being worked out. For more information (but not the final word yet) see *A Field Guide to Western Butterflies* by Paul Opler. Flies spring to fall (usually 1 or 2 broods for any one population). ▶ Above variably orange, red-orange, gray, brown, or blackish, with complex pattern of white spots, the margins usually dark gray or brown. Size of white spots also varies. Below hindwing usually silvery or brownish gray to black with white spots, forewing usually with some orange. Among the forms proposed for species status are *A. m. virgulti* (coastal southern California), *A. m. mejicanus* (desert southwest), and *A. m. duryi* (west Texas and southern New Mexico). 🦋 **Larval foodplant:** Buckwheats and ratany.

PALMER'S METALMARK *Apodemia palmeri*

A small metalmark of arid regions with mesquite. Common in most of its range, more sporadic west of the Colorado River. Adults sometimes cluster at flowers by the dozens in southeastern Arizona. Flies spring to fall (2 or 3 broods). ▶ Above pale orange-brown with orange margins (from the Colorado River westward) or gray-brown with orange restricted to lower margins (Arizona to Texas); has a *complex pattern of white spots,* including submarginal spots on the forewing. Below has a washed-out look, pale orange with white spots. 🦋 **Larval foodplant:** Mesquites.

HEPBURN'S METALMARK *Apodemia hepburni*

Sparse in the Big Bend region of west Texas, where recorded in July; rare August stray to Arizona. ▶ Similar to Palmer's Metalmark but averages darker above, with reduced white spots; *lacks submarginal white spots* on the forewing. Below pale orange, deeper orange along the margins, with white spots. 🦋 **Larval foodplant:** Unknown.

NARROW-WINGED METALMARK *Apodemia multiplaga*

Rare stray to south Texas, recorded in fall. Flies most of year in Mexico, where it is found in a variety of habitats. ▶ Note distinctive shape: forewing sharply pointed with outer margin conspicuously uneven. Above dark gray-brown with white spots. Below dark gray with white spots. 🦋 **Larval foodplant:** Unknown.

METALMARKS

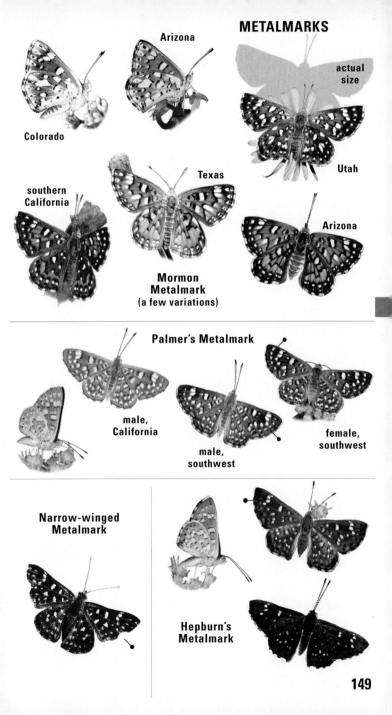

Arizona

Colorado

actual size

Utah

southern California

Texas

Arizona

Mormon Metalmark
(a few variations)

Palmer's Metalmark

male, California

male, southwest

female, southwest

Narrow-winged Metalmark

Hepburn's Metalmark

Just a hint of the brilliant diversity of metalmarks in the American tropics.

RED-BORDERED METALMARK   *Caria ino*

Southern Texas only. Localized but not uncommon in the lower Rio Grande Valley. Males perch on or around the larval foodplant to await females. Flies spring to fall (3 or more broods). ▶ Male above dark gray-brown with a wavy leading edge of the forewing, pale orange borders, and metallic submarginal line. Female mostly pale orange above, otherwise similar. Below deep red-orange with metallic submarginal markings and black spots. 🐛 **Larval foodplant:** Spiny hackberry.

BLUE METALMARK   *Lasaia sula*

Extreme south Texas only, especially in immediate vicinity of Brownsville. Flight is very fast and erratic. Adults usually open wings while perched. Flies spring to late fall (2–3 broods?). ▶ Iridescent blue-green male should be unmistakable in its range, but beware confusion with blue butterflies in other families; note pointed forewing, black bars and spots. Female checkered gray and brown with black markings, margins unevenly checkered. Below, both sexes light brown and white. 🐛 **Larval foodplant:** Unknown.

RED-BORDERED PIXIE   *Melanis pixe*

Extreme southern Texas only. The northernmost member of a large tropical genus. Highly localized in Texas, but sometimes abundant near larval foodplant. Adults shy away from direct sunlight, preferring to be active at dusk or early morning, or under heavy overcast. Flies most of year (multiple broods). ▶ Above black with orange forewing tips and red spots along lower hindwing margin. Below similar. 🐛 **Larval foodplant:** Guamuchil.

CURVE-WINGED METALMARK   *Emesis emesia*

A rare stray to extreme southern Texas, recorded in late fall. Common just south of the border around Monterrey, Mexico. Males perch on or near the larval foodplant to await females. ▶ Distinctive forewing shape, with strongly curved leading edge. Above pale brown to orange-brown with whitish spot near leading edge. Variable below, from tan to yellow or orange. 🐛 **Larval foodplant:** Mexican bird of paradise.

FALCATE METALMARK   *Emesis tenedia*

Very rare stray to southern Texas, recorded in fall. Common to the south in Mexico. ▶ Forewing slightly indented on outer margin below tip. Male above pale brown with darker brown contrasting bands. Female above similar but paler. Below male orange-brown, female yellow-brown, both with small black markings. 🐛 **Larval foodplant:** Unknown.

WALKER'S METALMARK   *Apodemia walkeri*

Extreme southern Texas only. Apparently scarce there, but small and easily overlooked. Reported in late spring and late fall. ▶ Above pale brown with dark median patch on forewing, no white submarginal spots. Below white with small tan markings. 🐛 **Larval foodplant:** Unknown.

TEXAS METALMARKS

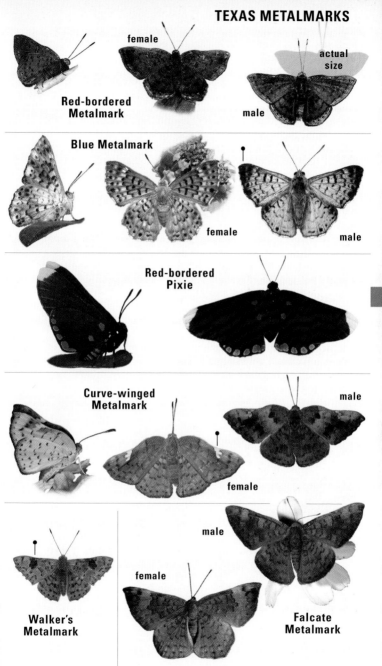

female

actual size

Red-bordered Metalmark

male

Blue Metalmark

female

male

Red-bordered Pixie

Curve-winged Metalmark

male

female

male

female

Walker's Metalmark

Falcate Metalmark

151

(family Nymphalidae) make up a very large and varied group found worldwide. Many of our most familiar and common butterflies in North America belong to this family.

The odd name "brush-footed" refers to the fact that adults have the front pair of legs greatly reduced and covered with short hairs, suggesting a tiny bottlebrush. These front legs are rarely visible in the field, so brushfoots generally appear to be four-legged. Beyond this, however, it is hard to generalize about the brushfoots. They vary from large to small, from drab to brilliantly colored. Some are avid flower visitors, while others are seldom or never seen at flowers. They are so diverse that they were formerly divided into several families. In this guide, for convenience, we have divided up the brushfoots into four sections as follows.

LONGWINGS AND FRITILLARIES

(pp. 154–175): The longwings, or heliconians, of the tropics were formerly considered a distinct family, but they are now united with the fritillaries in the **subfamily Heliconiinae.** Our few species are mostly found in the southernmost states. The true fritillaries are widespread, especially in the west and north, and are usually seen at flowers in open meadows or tundra. Despite their bright colors, many are extremely difficult to identify. The best field marks for most are on the undersides of the wings, but they tend to sit with the wings opened flat. Larvae of many longwings feed on passion vine, while those of many of the fritillaries feed on violets.

CRESCENTS AND CHECKERSPOTS (pp. 176–195): Although many of these look like tiny fritillaries, they are classified as part of a different subfamily, the **Nymphalinae.** Widespread from the tropics to the far north, mostly in open habitats, they are usually seen at flowers or visiting mud, and they usually sit with the wings opened flat. Except for the most distinctive checkerspots and patches, the best field marks are usually on the undersides of the wings. Larvae feed on many plants, especially in the sunflower family.

TYPICAL BRUSHFOOTS (pp. 196–229): This is admittedly an artificial category, and we use it as a catch-all group for a diverse set of butterflies, including part of the **subfamily Nymphalinae** and the entirety of five other subfamilies. Some of the included species, such as the ladies, regularly visit flowers, while others, such as the commas, seldom do. Various species are found in most habitats, from meadows to forests, although none occurs regularly on the tundra. Many in this group have a characteristic flight action with several rapid flaps followed by a flat-winged glide. Larvae feed on a wide variety of broad-leaved plants.

Besides the Nymphalinae, other subfamilies included are the admirals, sisters, and their relatives **(Limenitidinae)**, beginning on p. 210; the leafwings **(Charaxinae)**, p. 220; and the emperors **(Apaturinae)**, pp. 222 and 224. Also included are the odd American Snout **(Libytheinae)**, p. 222, and the milkweed butterflies **(Danainae)**, pp. 226–228, such distinctive groups that you will often see them treated as separate families in older books.

SATYRS (pp. 230–253): These butterflies **(subfamily Satyrinae)** are often found in wooded areas as well as open meadows, and several are found only in the far north or at high elevations in the mountains. Many have a rather floppy flight. They are mostly shades of brown, and many have bold spots on the wings. This combination of camouflaged colors and startling eyelike spots may suggest that satyrs are palatable to predators, perhaps because their larvae feed on grasses and sedges, so they lack the chemical defenses of some other butterflies.

LONGWINGS

(also known as Heliconians) are tropical butterflies with long forewings and bright colors. Once placed in their own family, they are now regarded as close relatives of the fritillaries. Larvae of most feed on passion vines, and chemicals from these poisonous plants make the adults noxious to predators—hence the warning colors worn by many species. Adults may live up to several months, far longer than most butterflies.

ZEBRA HELICONIAN *Heliconius charithonia*

A popular beauty of tropical gardens in Florida, also found in southern Texas, rarely straying northward to the Great Plains and the southwest. Flies slowly, with shallow, shivering wingbeats, through open woodlands and borders of tropical hammocks. Adults gather in late afternoon to spend the night in communal roosts. Flies all year in southern Florida and southern Texas, spring to fall northward (multiple broods). ▶ Unmistakable in our area. Black above with narrow yellow stripes, below similar but lighter with red spots basally. ❧ **Larval foodplant:** Passion vines.

MEXICAN SILVERSPOT *Dione moneta*

Strays to south Texas, rarely to southwest and Big Bend region. More at home in midelevation tropical woodlands but reported to breed sporadically in the lower Rio Grande Valley. Males hilltop. Recorded late spring to late fall (multiple broods in Mexico). ▶ Pattern below suggests that of the very common Gulf Fritillary (next page), but uppersides of wings a duller golden orange, *much darker toward the bases*, and *lack* the black-ringed white spots. ❧ **Larval foodplant:** Passion vines.

ERATO HELICONIAN *Heliconius erato*

Rare stray to south Texas only. Flight is slow and fluttery. Flies all year in tropics, recorded June to September in Texas. ▶ Above black with crimson patch on forewing and yellow band on hindwing. Below similar but paler. ❧ **Larval foodplant:** Passion vines.

BANDED ORANGE HELICONIAN *Dryadula phaetusa*

Rare stray to south Texas only. Flight is fast. Flies all year in tropics. ▶ Above bright orange with dark brown cross bands. Paler below. ❧ **Larval foodplant:** Passion vines.

ISABELLA'S HELICONIAN *Eueides isabella*

Rare stray to south Texas, recorded April to July. ▶ Unlike other longwings in our area, but some in tropics are quite similar; also compare to next species. ❧ **Larval foodplant:** Passion vines.

TIGER MIMIC-QUEEN *Lycorea cleobaea*

Related to the Monarch (p. 226), not to others on this page, despite its appearance. A very rare stray to Texas and Florida. ▶ Suggests previous species but black hindwing stripes make *closed loop*. ❧ **Larval foodplant:** Leaves of fig, papaya, and others.

LONGWINGS

actual size

Zebra Heliconian

larva

RARITIES (NOT TO SCALE WITH ZEBRA)

actual size

Mexican Silverspot

Erato Heliconian

Isabella's Heliconian

Tiger Mimic-Queen

Banded Orange Heliconian

155

LONGWINGS AND SOUTHERN FRITILLARIES

These thrive in warm climates. The typical fritillaries (beginning on p. 158) are more characteristic of the north and the mountains.

GULF FRITILLARY   *Agraulis vanillae*

A dazzling beauty of southern regions, straying northward. Easily attracted to gardens containing passion vine. Flight is fast and usually well above the ground. Flies most of year in frost-free areas, spring to late fall elsewhere (multiple broods). ▶ Above bright red-orange with black markings, a few *black-ringed white spots in forewing cell.* Below brown with many elongated silver spots. Longer-winged and brighter orange above than Greater Fritillaries (beginning next page). In border regions see very rare Mexican Silverspot (previous page). ❧ **Larval foodplant:** Passion vines.

JULIA HELICONIAN   *Dryas julia*

A widespread tropical longwing, reaching our area in southern Florida and south Texas around woodland edges, brushy fields, gardens. Flight is fast and direct, with shallow wingbeats. Flies most of year (3 or more broods). ▶ Above male mostly orange, female duller orange with black forewing band. Below brown to orange, no silver spots. Easily known by shape and relative lack of markings. ❧ **Larval foodplant:** Passion vines.

VARIEGATED FRITILLARY   *Euptoieta claudia*

Widespread and common in the south. Mainly a grassland species, but also found in farmland, brushy areas, roadsides, and other open habitats. Spreads northward in summer, in variable numbers, sometimes becoming common all the way to Canada. Its flight is direct and low, and it is an avid flower visitor. Flies spring to fall (2–3 broods). ▶ Above orange-brown with submarginal black spots and black median lines across both wings. Note the *black-rimmed, pale orange spot in the forewing cell.* Below brown with paler median and marginal patches and no silvering. ❧ **Larval foodplant:** Passion vines, flax, violets, and other plants.

MEXICAN FRITILLARY   *Euptoieta hegesia*

Regular only in south Texas, but also strays into the southwest and becomes a temporary resident there. Prefers open disturbed areas adjacent to tropical forests. Flies spring to fall (1–3 broods). ▶ Like Variegated Fritillary but brighter orange above, with basal part of hindwing *unmarked.* Plainer below, lacking paler median and marginal patches on hindwing. ❧ **Larval foodplant:** Passion vines, violets, and other plants.

LONGWINGS AND SOUTHERN FRITILLARIES

actual
size

female

Gulf
Fritillary

male

females

Julia

males

Variegated
Fritillary

Mexican
Fritillary

(genus *Speyeria*) are also known as silverspots because of the brilliant silvering underneath the hindwings of many. Widespread in meadows in summer, adult males are often on the wing weeks before females. Both sexes are avid visitors to thistles, milkweeds, mints, and other flowers. Despite their bright colors, some are extremely difficult to identify, especially in the west where several species may fly together.

GREAT SPANGLED FRITILLARY   *Speyeria cybele*

One of the most conspicuous and common butterflies over meadows and roadsides in parts of the east. Somewhat less common in the west and southward. Quite variable; many western individuals, especially females, hardly resemble their eastern counterparts. Flies in summer (1 brood). ► Hindwing below rich chocolate brown with silver spots and a wide cream or tan submarginal band. Above orange with black markings, conspicuously darker toward the base. In most western habitats, male is deeper orange above than in the east, female black and cream. Adults smaller in northeast and upper Great Plains. Compare to species on next four pages, especially Aphrodite Fritillary and Nokomis Fritillary. 🌱 **Larval foodplant**: Violets.

REGAL FRITILLARY   *Speyeria idalia*

This well-named regal creature is one of North America's vanishing butterflies. Favoring tall grass prairies and native meadows, it has almost disappeared from its former range east of the Mississippi River, and is now mainly restricted to the upper Great Plains. Very local, but can be common in good habitat. Adults are swift in flight, cruising close to the ground. Flies in summer (1 brood). ► Combination of *dark hindwing* (with bright white spots) and orange forewing distinctive. Some Aphrodite Fritillaries (p. 166) also have very dark hindwings, but are not so boldly marked below. 🌱 **Larval foodplant**: Violets.

DIANA FRITILLARY   *Speyeria diana*

Very large and spectacular. Restricted to openings and fields in rich moist woodlands, mainly in the southern Appalachians and southern Ozark region. The beautiful female, much sought after by butterfly watchers, apparently gains protection from predators by mimicking the distasteful Pipevine Swallowtail. Flies in summer (1 brood). ► Both sexes relatively plain below lacking silver spot pattern on hindwing. Above male orange and dark brown, female black and blue. Compare female to Pipevine Swallowtail (p. 26), Red-spotted Purple (p. 210). 🌱 **Larval foodplant**: Violets.

GREATER FRITILLARIES

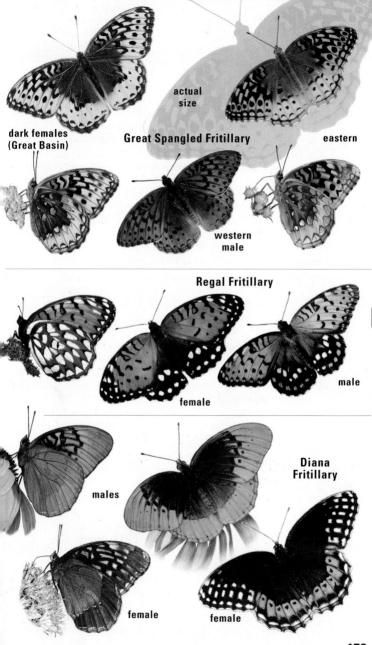

actual size

dark females (Great Basin)

Great Spangled Fritillary

eastern

western male

Regal Fritillary

female

male

males

Diana Fritillary

female

female

MORMON FRITILLARY   *Speyeria mormonia*

A small species of western mountains. Adults fly fast and close to the ground in moist alpine meadows and around nearby rocky crags and windswept ridges. Often the only member of the greater fritillary group found at or above treeline. Flies in summer (1 brood). ▶ Small and variable. Forewings short and rounded. Below variable, with hindwing pale tan or buff or sometimes yellowish, the discal area often pale reddish brown, pale brown, or olive green. Hindwing spots usually silvered, but only partially silvered or not at all in some populations. Above orange and black with little or no darkening basally. Forewing veins *black and thin,* marginal spots on females often paler, creating a *two-toned look.* Usually *smaller* than the most similar species, but can be the same as Great Basin Fritillary where they are found together in the Sierra Nevada of California. ❧ **Larval foodplant:** Violets.

GREAT BASIN FRITILLARY   *Speyeria egleis*

Widespread in western mountains, mainly in high-elevation forest opening, meadows, or adjacent rocky slopes. Fast in flight. Males patrol hilltops to find females. Flies in summer (1 brood). ▶ Medium-sized to small, and quite variable. Forewings slightly pointed. Can be quite similar to Mormon, Callippe, Zerene, Atlantis, or other fritillaries depending on region. Below buff with disk light tan to dark brown, sometimes green or yellowish. Hindwing spots may be silvered, partially silvered, or unsilvered. Above basal region darker on many populations, forewing veins *strongly edged with black* on males. ❧ **Larval foodplant:** Violets.

UNSILVERED FRITILLARY   *Speyeria adiaste*

Found only in coastal mountains of central California; range is shrinking, for unknown reasons. Local and seldom common. Adults frequent openings along fern-covered slopes in mountain forests. Flies in summer (1 brood). ▶ Below buff to tan with light purplish sheen, markings *indistinct, pale spots unsilvered.* Above male red-orange and black, forewing veins heavily edged with black. Females in northern part of range similar above but with veins not so strongly black-edged; in Monterey and San Luis Obispo counties, female pale orange to buff above. ❧ **Larval foodplant:** Violets.

WESTERN FRITILLARIES

actual size

Sierras

Rockies

male

female

Arizona

Great Basin

Mormon Fritillary

Great Basin

Sierras

Great Basin Fritillary

Rockies

Unsilvered Fritillary

male

females

CALLIPPE FRITILLARY   *Speyeria callippe*

Widespread and common in the west. Usually the first greater fritillary of the season to fly in any given habitat, and often the only one found in low-elevation foothills. Males are hilltoppers. Flies in late spring or summer depending on locality (1 brood). ▶ Variable. In most of region east of Cascades and Sierra Nevada, hindwing below has spots silvered; green or olive disk often extending into submargin. Above pale orange with veins not heavily edged with black. Coronis Fritillary usually slightly larger and not as bright green below; Mormon Fritillaries with green disks are smaller. Along West Coast from southern Oregon southward, Callippe Fritillary is extremely variable: hindwing below with brown disk, spots either silvered or unsilvered, some localities with individuals of both. Above pale to bright orange depending on locality, with veins on forewing in male heavily edged with black. Coastal California populations have more black and highly contrasting pale spots above. Hindwing marginal spots often more triangular than on other species. 🌿 **Larval foodplant:** Violets.

CORONIS FRITILLARY   *Speyeria coronis*

Wide ranging in the west in many habitats. Flies from early to late summer, with females flying well into September (1 brood). ▶ Slightly variable. Below spots always silvered. Disk olive or brown with buff submarginal band on hindwing. Above pale to bright orange with black markings. Very similar to Callippe in coastal California but with less contrasting upperside. Usually larger than Zerene Fritillary in Great Basin and Rockies with forewings more elongated near tip, black median and postmedian markings not as heavy above and larger silver spots below. 🌿 **Larval foodplant:** Violets.

EDWARDS'S FRITILLARY   *Speyeria edwardsi*

Restricted to central and northern Rocky Mountain region. Flies in summer (1 brood). ▶ Relatively little variation. Forewings pointed, indented below tip. Below always silvered with olive in disk extending into submargin. Other green-disked fritillaries within its range (Mormon, Callippe) are smaller. Coronis usually has buff submargin and is often brown below. Above orange, the silver spots below showing through as paler spots above. 🌿 **Larval foodplant:** Violets.

WESTERN FRITILLARIES

Sierras

Great Basin

actual size

Callippe Fritillary

coastal

Oregon

Coronis Fritillary

Great Basin

Edwards's Fritillary

ZERENE FRITILLARY *Speyeria zerene*

Common and widespread in west. Occurs from coastal salt spray meadows to high in the mountains. Isolated population in Spring Mountains of southwest Nevada ("Carol's" Zerene Fritillary) is considered a separate species by some. Flies in summer (1 brood). ▶ Extremely variable. From the Sierra Nevada of California westward, hindwing spots below silvered or unsilvered, disk brown to reddish or purplish brown; above red-orange with heavy median and postmedian black markings. Compare to Hydaspe Fritillary (next), Atlantis Fritillary (p. 166). From the Cascades and Sierra Nevada eastward, hindwing disk pale yellow or tan, spots silvered; above pale orange. Compare to Coronis Fritillary (p. 162). 🌱 **Larval foodplant:** Violets.

HYDASPE FRITILLARY *Speyeria hydaspe*

Mainly limited to moist woodland habitats in western mountains, absent from arid ranges. Males hilltop in some areas. Flies in summer (1 brood). ▶ Slightly variable. Below hindwing spots are pale yellow, unsilvered except on Vancouver Island. Disk below is reddish or purplish brown. Above red-orange with heavy black markings, usually darkened basally. Zerene Fritillaries west of the Sierra Nevada are similar but have hindwing postmedian spots below smaller. "Northwestern" Atlantis Fritillaries (p. 166) in Sierras and northward are smaller, paler orange with less black above, and not purplish brown below. Some "Northwestern" unsilvered forms in parts of Rockies are smaller but otherwise very similar. 🌱 **Larval foodplant:** Violets.

NOKOMIS FRITILLARY *Speyeria nokomis*

This large, attractive fritillary is extremely local but often common at springs and other boggy areas in arid country. Its flight season begins later than that of other greater fritillaries. Flies in late summer (1 brood). ▶ Similar only to western populations of Great Spangled Fritillary. Below hindwing spots always silvered, the disk yellow, orange-brown, dark brown (male), or green (female), with broad cream or yellow band. Above male orange and black, female black and cream. Populations of Great Spangled Fritillary (p. 158) that occur with this species have the disk dark or rich chocolate brown, and postmedian spots smaller. 🌱 **Larval foodplant:** Violets.

WESTERN FRITILLARIES

actual size

Zerene Fritillary

Sierras

"Carol's"

Great Basin

Hydaspe Fritillary

southwestern

Nokomis Fritillary

males

females

ATLANTIS FRITILLARY *Speyeria atlantis*
(including Northwestern Fritillary *Speyeria hesperis*)

Wide ranging across North America. Variable; traditionally treated as one species but there are probably two overlapping in central and western Canada and parts of the western U.S. Often common where found. Flies in summer (1 brood). ▶ For the complex as a whole, spots below silvered or unsilvered, disk usually brown or reddish brown (pale tan or brown in east-central Nevada and central Utah). Above red-orange, orange, or pale orange, often darkened basally with extra black along forewing veins. Northern and eastern individuals usually separated from other fritillaries by black wing margins above. Eyes blue-gray, except yellow-green in southwest (where Aphrodite Fritillary also has yellow-green eyes). In Sierra Nevada of California resembles Zerene and Hydaspe Fritillaries

(p. 164) but is smaller with larger postmedian spots below. Rocky Mountain populations are especially difficult to identify reliably, with unsilvered and silvered forms often flying together. If this complex is treated as two species, the **Atlantis Fritillary** (in the restricted sense) has the hindwing below with the disk dark reddish brown or chocolate brown, the spots always silvered, and the postmedian spots small. **Northwestern Fritillary** has the hindwing below with the disk reddish brown to pale brown, the spots silvered or unsilvered, and the postmedian spots small in Rockies but progressively larger westward. 🌿 **Larval foodplant:** Violets.

APHRODITE FRITILLARY *Speyeria aphrodite*

Fairly common across northern North America from the Rockies eastward, with an isolated population in eastern Arizona. Flies in summer (1 brood). ▶ Variable. Large in east, smaller progressively westward. Eyes yellow-green. Below hindwing spots always silvered, and the red-brown or brown in the disk often extends beyond postmedian spots into the submargin, especially in midwest. Above orange, the forewing veins not lined with black. Yellow-green eyes separate Aphrodite from most other fritillaries in its range except Great Spangled (p. 158) in east and Atlantis in southwest. In southwest Aphrodite differs from Atlantis by smaller size and lack of black-lined veins on male forewing above. In east Great Spangled has broad cream or buff submarginal band on hindwing below. 🌿 **Larval foodplant:** Violets.

GREATER FRITILLARIES

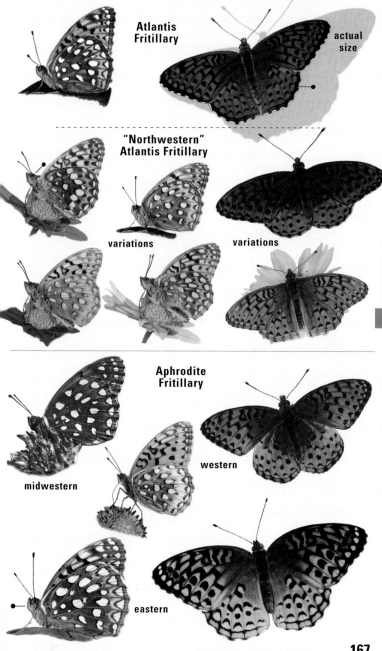

Atlantis Fritillary

actual size

"Northwestern" Atlantis Fritillary

variations

variations

Aphrodite Fritillary

midwestern

western

eastern

LESSER FRITILLARIES

(genus *Boloria*) are small orange butterflies with black markings above and exquisite patterns below. Similar to some checkerspots (beginning p. 180) but generally with forewings narrower and more pointed. Best identification marks are usually on the hindwing below, not often easy to see in the field. Most fly fast and close to the ground but avidly visit flowers. Some lesser fritillaries are among the most arctic of all butterflies, with a few species flying only every other year (biennially) in some regions. Some (Frigga, Astarte, Freija) are named for ancient goddesses.

MEADOW FRITILLARY *Boloria bellona*

Common in the east, rarer westward. Inhabits wet fields, meadows, and streamsides, but also adapts to disturbed habitats, and appears to be spreading southward in the eastern states. Flies from early to late summer (1–2 broods). ▶ Outer edge of forewing squared off near the tip. Hindwing below mottled red and brown, yellow postbasal band often obscured by red-brown scales. Above yellowish orange, brownish basally, with relatively *little black* along hindwing margin; forewing submarginal marks *do not* point outward. 🌿 **Larval foodplant:** Violets.

PACIFIC FRITILLARY *Boloria epithore*

Mainly Pacific Coast and the northwest. A slow-flying butterfly of wet meadows and clearings in mountain forest. Flies in early summer (1 brood). ▶ Resembles Meadow Fritillary (including relative lack of black along hindwing margin above, yellow postbasal band often obscured by red-brown scales), but forewing is more *rounded* near tip, not squared off. In most regions, the *submarginal markings* both above and below form *chevrons or arrowheads pointing outward;* these markings are black above, brownish below. 🌿 **Larval foodplant:** Violets.

FRIGGA FRITILLARY *Boloria frigga*

Wide-ranging from the upper Great Lakes through most of arctic Canada; rare and very local in the Rocky Mountains. An inhabitant of willow and black spruce bogs. Flies early to midsummer (1 brood). ▶ Outer edge of forewing rounded. Hindwing below shows broad pink or violet band on outer part, yellowish or reddish brown basally, with prominent basal white patch along leading edge. Above pale brownish orange, blackish basally (more so than Pacific Fritillary) and along hindwing margin. 🌿 **Larval foodplant:** Willows.

LESSER FRITILLARIES

actual size

variations

Meadow Fritillary

Pacific Fritillary

Frigga Fritillary

Rockies

northern

169

SILVER-BORDERED FRITILLARY   *Boloria selene*

Fairly common and widespread in the northeast and across northern tier of states, more sporadic in the west. Often limited to marshes and bogs southward, more generally distributed in wet meadows northward. Not particularly fast in flight. Flies in summer (1–3 broods). ▶ Hindwing below with silvered median band and marginal spots (on red-brown or pale orange background), and row of black or red-brown submarginal spots. Above, black margins enclose pale orange spots, especially on hindwing. ❧ **Larval foodplant:** Violets.

BOG FRITILLARY   *Boloria eunomia*

Wide-ranging from the upper Great Lakes and northeast through most of arctic Canada. Rare and very local in the Rockies. Males fly fast and direct, close to the ground, in seeking females. Flies in summer (1 brood). ▶ Somewhat variable. Hindwing below light or dark red-brown with postmedian band and marginal spots shiny white or cream. Note *postmedian row of small white spots outlined with black*. Above orange, blackened basally especially on hindwing. ❧ **Larval foodplant:** Willows, bistorts, and others.

POLARIS FRITILLARY   *Boloria polaris*

Found in open tundra areas of the north, from northern British Columbia to the high arctic. Flies in midsummer (1 brood). Biennial, flying in even-numbered years in most areas but in odd-numbered years in some. ▶ Hindwing below red-brown with many white marks, including white dashes cutting through dark marginal area; also note postmedian row of *round black spots set off by paler areas*. Above orange-brown with black markings, variably blackened basally. ❧ **Larval foodplant:** Mountain avens, perhaps also blueberry.

ASTARTE FRITILLARY   *Boloria astarte*

A denizen of rocky tundra ridges, extending south to areas above treeline in Glacier National Park and northern Washington. Very fast in flight. Males patrol hilltops to look for females. Flies in summer (1 brood), biennial in some regions. ▶ *Largest Boloria.* Variable. In southern areas, hindwing below with distinct white postbasal band and white postmedian band with adjacent black spots. In northern areas, hindwing below has markings less distinct, white postmedian band with adjacent spots dull red-brown. Northern populations duskier above. ❧ **Larval foodplant:** Spotted saxifrage.

LESSER FRITILLARIES

actual size

Silver-bordered
Fritillary

Bog
Fritillary

Polaris
Fritillary

northern

Astarte
Fritillary

southern

MOUNTAIN FRITILLARY *Boloria napaea*

Mostly in the far northwest, with an isolated population high in the Wind River Mountains of Wyoming. At home on lush alpine and subalpine slopes near and above treeline. Very fast in flight. Flies in summer (1 brood). ▶ Forewing *pointed*, hindwing comes to *shallow point* in middle of margin. Hindwing below rather pale orange or red-brown with white or cream-yellow bands and spots. A cream patch near the hindwing angle usually *lacks an adjacent dark chevron*. Above male orange with *relatively light* black markings, female pale brown-orange with heavier black markings, both very dark at wing bases. ✿ **Larval foodplant:** Bistorts.

DINGY FRITILLARY *Boloria improba*

A small inconspicuous species of arctic tundra, with isolated populations in Wyoming and Colorado. Flight is weak and close to the ground. Flies in midsummer (1 brood). Biennial in some areas. ▶ Forewing is narrow and quite rounded. Hindwing below red or gray-brown basally with postmedian band whitish (Colorado-Wyoming) or yellowish. Outer half of hindwing below pale gray-pink with muted markings. Above variable, pale orange to brown-orange, often dingy with black markings *smeared*. ✿ **Larval foodplant:** Willows.

ALBERTA FRITILLARY *Boloria alberta*

Canadian Rockies south to Glacier National Park, Montana. Rare on alpine tundra slopes and ridges. Adults fly slowly close to ground. Males seek females on ridges and summits. Flies in summer (1 brood), biennial in some areas. ▶ Known by *rounded wing shape* and *drab appearance*. Hindwing below dull brown-orange with paler postbasal band. Above orange-brown with black markings *muted or smudged*. Female duskier above. ✿ **Larval foodplant:** Mountain avens.

RELICT FRITILLARY *Boloria kriemhild*

Central Rocky Mountain region only. Fond of lush meadows and forest openings, mainly well below treeline. Flies early to midsummer (1 brood). ▶ Forewings rounded at tip. Note the *submarginal chevrons on the wings pointing outward* (more obvious on upperside). Hindwing below reddish brown and yellow, the yellow postbasal band *not* obscured by reddish brown scales (compare to Pacific and Meadow Fritillaries, p. 168). ✿ **Larval foodplant:** Violets.

LESSER FRITILLARIES

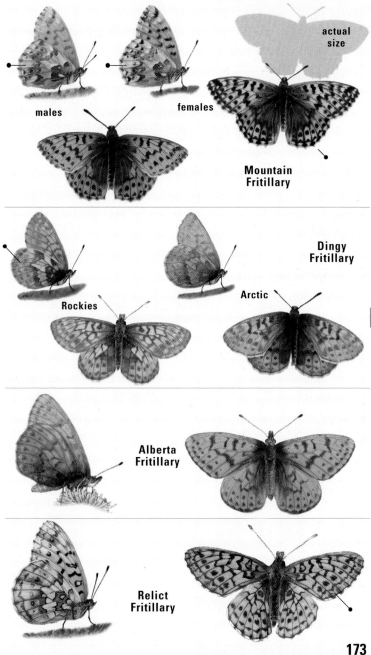

males

females

actual size

Mountain Fritillary

Dingy Fritillary

Rockies

Arctic

Alberta Fritillary

Relict Fritillary

173

FREIJA FRITILLARY *Boloria freija*

Wide-ranging across the far north on moist tundra slopes, more local south of Canada. On the wing earlier in season than similar Cryptic Fritillary where ranges overlap. Flies in early summer (1 brood). ▶ Complex pattern on hindwing below includes white patch along leading edge, central white patch *sharply pointed outward, zigzag black line at center,* and white spots in dark marginal area. Above orange or orange-brown with black markings not smeared, unlike Cryptic Fritillary. ❧ **Larval foodplant:** Blueberries, bearberries, others.

PURPLISH FRITILLARY *Boloria montinus*

Common in the Rockies and much of Canada and Alaska, with isolated population in the White Mountains of New Hampshire. Adults cruise swiftly through forest clearings and over rocky alpine slopes. Flies in summer (1 brood). ▶ Variable. Hindwing below red-brown or purple with white or cream marginal spots, creamy postmedian band often invaded by red-brown scales. Central spot in postmedian band is often *less sharply pointed* than on Arctic Fritillary. Above sometimes black basally, *submarginal black chevrons point inward.* ❧ **Larval foodplant:** Willows, bistorts, others.

ARCTIC FRITILLARY *Boloria chariclea*

Mostly Arctic regions in tundra habitats. Difficult to distinguish from Purplish Fritillary where the two occur together; some consider the two to be one species, and both were formerly confused with the Titania Fritillary of the Old World. Flies in summer (1 brood), partly biennial. ▶ Very similar to Purplish Fritillary. Hindwing below reddish brown, the postmedian band white or silvery with the central spot *sharply pointed.* Above black basally, submarginal black chevrons point inward. ❧ **Larval foodplant:** Willows, bistorts, others.

CRYPTIC FRITILLARY *Boloria natazhati*

Rarely observed owing to its limited arctic range and inaccessible habitats. Adults frequent rocky slopes and cobble beaches. Flies in summer (1 brood), possibly biennial. ▶ Below hindwing dull reddish brown or blackish with basal white patch along leading edge, central white patch sharply pointed outward. Above dull pale orange-brown with *smeared black markings and black overlay* (most areas), or pale orange with black markings slightly smeared and no black overlay (Victoria Island). ❧ **Larval foodplant:** Unknown.

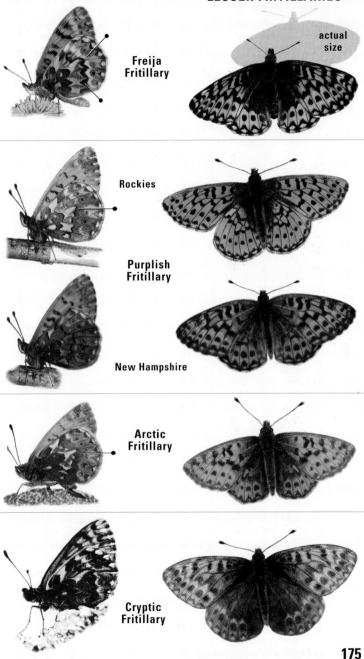

LESSER FRITILLARIES

Freija Fritillary

actual size

Rockies

Purplish Fritillary

New Hampshire

Arctic Fritillary

Cryptic Fritillary

175

The crescents, checkerspots, and patches make up our second group among the brushfoots **(family Nymphalidae)**. Crescents are small butterflies, mostly with rounded forewings and orange-and-black patterns above, named for a crescent-shaped spot near the margin of the hindwing below. They have a direct, low flight, with alternating series of flaps and flat-winged glides. Males patrol areas near larval foodplants to find females. Among the crescents there are several cases where very similar species overlap, making identification difficult or sometimes impossible.

PEARL CRESCENT   *Phyciodes tharos*

One of our most common and familiar butterflies, especially in the east, where it visits flowers in gardens, fields, roadsides, and woodland edges. More restricted to streamsides in west. Flies most of year in south, warmer months in the north (1–3 or more broods). ▶ Somewhat variable both seasonally and geographically (and may constitute more than one species). Above mostly orange with black markings. Below hindwing pale yellow with brown reticulations; a brown patch usually encloses (and often obscures) the pale crescent at center of margin. Early spring and late fall individuals are whitish or tan on the hindwing below, with heavier markings. ❧ **Larval foodplant**: Asters.

NORTHERN CRESCENT   *Phyciodes selenis   (P. cocyta)*

Some question whether this is a distinct species from Pearl Crescent. However, the two overlap broadly, apparently without much hybridization. Flies mainly in summer (1–2 broods). ▶ Like Pearl Crescent but averages a bit larger. May have fewer black markings on hindwing above, especially on males, leaving orange areas more open. Female Northerns may tend to have paler postmedian bands above, while female Pearls tend to have the orange areas more uniform. *Many are probably not identifiable in the field.* Also compare to Tawny Crescent. ❧ **Larval foodplant**: Asters.

TAWNY CRESCENT   *Phyciodes batesii*

Widespread in the north, from damp meadows to dry ridges; limited range in Appalachians and Rockies. Has disappeared from many former haunts in the east. Flies in summer (1 brood). ▶ Similar to Pearl and Northern Crescents. Tends to look *darker above,* often with the forewing postmedian band paler orange. Below hindwing *mostly yellow* with little or no brown enclosing crescent at center of margin, outer edge of forewing usually paler; these differences less apparent in west, and not all can be identified. ❧ **Larval foodplant**: Asters.

CRESCENTS

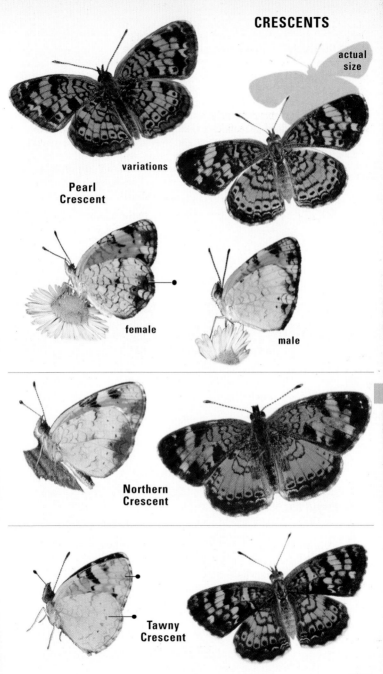

actual size

variations

Pearl Crescent

female

male

Northern Crescent

Tawny Crescent

FIELD CRESCENT *Phyciodes campestris*

The most common and widespread blackish crescent in the west, found in habitats from sea level to treeline in the mountains. Flies spring to fall, or summer only at high elevations (1–3 broods). ▶ Variable. In most areas blackish brown above with orange patches and spots, median band usually paler than submarginal orange band. In parts of the Sierra Nevada, may look more orange above. Variable below, but forewing often shows *pale bar in cell*. Antennal clubs *black or brown* (orange on some other crescents). 🐛 **Larval foodplant**: Asters.

MYLITTA CRESCENT *Phyciodes mylitta*

Widespread and common in the west in both disturbed and natural habitats, somewhat more local near wet areas in arid country. Males patrol gullies or streams to find females. Flies spring to fall (2–4 broods). ▶ Above mostly orange with fine black markings. Median band on forewing above paler on female. Black mark on lower edge of forewing is either *thin* (compare with Pale Crescent) or a black patch in southwest, where Pale Crescents do not occur. Below hindwing variable, usually yellowish or brown with fine brown lines. Antennal clubs *orange*. 🐛 **Larval foodplant**: Thistles.

PALE CRESCENT *Phyciodes pallida*

Uncommon to fairly common on dry sagebrush flats and hillsides. Flies in summer (1–2 broods). ▶ Very similar to Mylitta Crescent, averaging a bit larger. Where their ranges overlap, black spot on lower edge of forewing is *larger* on this species. Below hindwing variable, usually yellowish or brown with fine brown lines. Antennal clubs orange. Individuals from parts of Utah are large, approaching Sagebrush Checkerspot (p. 186) in size. 🐛 **Larval foodplant**: Thistles.

CALIFORNIA CRESCENT *Phyciodes orseis*

Rare and local, restricted to parts of Oregon and California. Variable, generally hard to separate from similar species. Flies in early summer (1 brood). ▶ Very similar to Mylitta Crescent in the Sierra Nevada, Field Crescent elsewhere. Hindwing slightly more angular than in similar species. Antennal clubs orange. In the Sierra Nevada, above mostly orange with fine black markings, below yellow with fine brown lines. Elsewhere in limited range, above mostly blackish brown with limited orange, below mottled tan and brown and often with a white median band. 🐛 **Larval foodplant**: Thistles.

WESTERN CRESCENTS

variations

actual size

Field Crescent

variations

Mylitta Crescent

male

female

Pale Crescent

Sierras

male

female

California Crescent

northern

VESTA CRESCENT   *Phyciodes vesta*

A small crescent of grasslands, roadsides, other open areas. Flies spring to fall (multiple broods). ▶ Above orange with black markings; female sometimes has paler median band. Forewing below has postmedian band of *orange spots circled by black.* Hindwing below variable, pale yellow marked with tan and brown. 🌱 **Larval foodplant:** Hairy tubetongue and others in acanthus family.

PHAON CRESCENT   *Phyciodes phaon*

A tropical species of the southern tier. Establishes temporary colonies northward on naturalized or planted mats of frogfruit. Flies most of year in south (multiple broods), shorter season northward. ▶ Seasonally variable. Above black and orange with *contrasting cream median band* on forewing. Below light tan with fine brown lines; winter forms with brown more extensive. 🌱 **Larval foodplant:** Frogfruits.

PAINTED CRESCENT   *Phyciodes picta*

Limited to western Great Plains and southwestern grasslands, usually in moist habitats but also found on roadsides. Flies spring to fall (2–3 broods). ▶ Best known by *very pale hindwing below,* with dark marks limited or absent; underside of forewing tip also pale. On forewing above, has contrasting creamy median band, and often creamy spots near wingtip. 🌱 **Larval foodplant:** Bindweed, slimleaf bursage, asters, and others.

TINY CHECKERSPOT   *Dymasia dymas*

A tiny butterfly of the southwest, often abundant, especially at flowers. Flight is slow and fluttery. Flies spring to fall (2–3 broods). ▶ Smaller than the crescents, with weaker flight. Above orange with fine black markings, often with a pale spot along leading edge of forewing. Below has orange and white alternating bands, with the *marginal band white.* 🌱 **Larval foodplant:** Hairy tubetongue, desert honeysuckle, and other acanthus.

ELADA CHECKERSPOT   *Texola elada*

Another tiny southwesterner, often found with Tiny Checkerspot. Flight is slow and fluttery. Flies spring to fall (2–3 broods). ▶ Resembles Tiny Checkerspot, but black markings above are *heavier,* especially in Texas, and usually lacks pale spot on forewing leading edge. Below with orange and white bands more evenly arranged, and *marginal band orange.* 🌱 **Larval foodplant:** Mexican honeysuckle and other acanthus.

CRESCENTS, SMALL CHECKERSPOTS

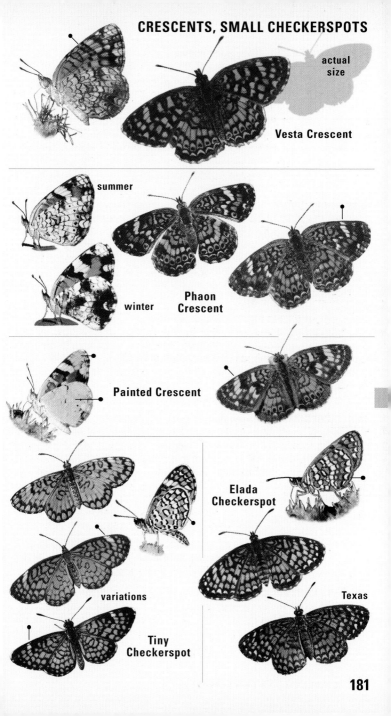

actual size

Vesta Crescent

summer

winter

Phaon Crescent

Painted Crescent

Elada Checkerspot

variations

Tiny Checkerspot

Texas

TEXAN CRESCENT *Phyciodes texana*

A black crescent of southern regions, common in open habitats, sometimes straying far north. Males patrol shaded gullies, often perching to await females. Flies most of year (multiple broods). ▶ Distinctive shape, with forewing indented below tip. Above mostly black with narrow white spot bands, reddish basally; brighter in the southeast, with larger white marks. Below forewing basal half orange, hindwing light tan with fine black lines, spots, and a *white median band*. 🐛 **Larval foodplant:** Twin-seeds and relatives in acanthus family.

CUBAN CRESCENT *Phyciodes frisia*

South Florida only, uncommon, found mostly on the edges of tropical hammocks. Flies most of year (3 or more broods). ▶ Found only with Pearl Crescent (p. 176) and Phaon Crescent (p. 180). Separated by pattern above: forewing with *large buff-orange spots* on dark outer part of wing, hindwing with pale banded pattern. 🐛 **Larval foodplant:** Shrimp plant, other acanthus.

PALE-BANDED CRESCENT *Phyciodes tulcis*

South Texas only, where it is apparently a temporary and sporadic resident. Reported spring through fall (multiple broods). ▶ Similar to Texan Crescent, with forewing less strongly indented. Above, hindwing band is *wider* and forewing spots are larger, all with a yellowish tinge. Below basal half of forewing pale yellow, hindwing brown and white with white median band. Winter individuals browner below. 🐛 **Larval foodplant:** Unknown.

BLACK CRESCENT *Phyciodes ptolyca*

Rare stray to south Texas only, reported in December. Flies all year in Mexico (multiple broods). ▶ Forewing indented below tip. Above mostly black with thin yellowish median band on hindwing and yellow forewing spots. Texan Crescent is similar but has white bands and spots. Below forewing pale orange basally, hindwing white and brown with a white median area. 🐛 **Larval foodplant:** Unknown.

ELF *Microtia elva*

Rare stray to south Texas and Arizona; may be a temporary resident in Arizona in some years. Flies slowly and low. Recorded in late summer and fall. ▶ Small and distinctive. Above black with orange bars. Below similar except the orange hindwing bar is paler. 🐛 **Larval foodplant:** *Tetramerium*.

CHESTNUT CRESCENT *Phyciodes argentea* *(not illustrated)*

Rare stray to south Texas, reported in November. ▶ Male above black with extensive chestnut basally and few white spots. Female black with pale yellow and white bands and spots, probably not separable from female Pale-banded Crescent and other Mexican species. 🐛 **Larval foodplant:** Unknown.

TROPICAL CRESCENTS

actual size

Texan
Crescent

southwest

southeast

Cuban Crescent

Pale-banded
Crescent

Black
Crescent

Elf

183

CHECKERSPOTS

Generally medium-sized, larger than the crescents (pp. 176–183), with orange and black checkered uppersides. Flight is fairly fast and direct, with rapid wingbeats followed by short glides. Adults generally stay low.

SILVERY CHECKERSPOT   *Chlosyne nycteis*

A common and widespread eastern species, found in moist woodland openings and along streams, flying low and perching close to the ground. Flies late spring to fall (1–3 broods in east, 1 brood in west). ▶ Larger than Pearl Crescent (p. 176), with wider black margins on forewing above. On hindwing above, black submarginal spots are *usually* (not always) *surrounded by orange*. Hindwing below with silvery basal band and white median band; submarginal band of whitish crescents is *invaded by brown*. 🌿 **Larval foodplant:** Black-eyed Susan, wingstem, and related plants.

HARRIS'S CHECKERSPOT   *Chlosyne harrisii*

A butterfly of wet meadows, edges of bogs, and other damp habitats in the northeast and upper midwest. Generally uncommon and local. Flies from early to midsummer (1 brood). ▶ Above like Silvery Checkerspot, but black submarginal spots on hindwing are usually *connected to black wing margin*. Below with orange bands near hindwing base. Submarginal band of whitish crescents on hindwing is *complete,* not broken by brown. 🌿 **Larval foodplant:** Flat-topped white aster.

GORGONE CHECKERSPOT   *Chlosyne gorgone*

Primarily open habitats of the midwest, but prone to establishing far-flung isolated colonies, most of which eventually disappear. Numbers vary dramatically from year to year. Flies spring to fall in most areas, summer in north (1–3 broods). ▶ Above like Silvery Checkerspot, but usually has *obvious pale chevrons* within black border of hindwing. Below more distinctive, with "busy" pattern including white arrowheads, dusky zigzag lines. 🌿 **Larval foodplant:** Sunflowers.

ROCKSLIDE CHECKERSPOT   *Chlosyne whitneyi*

A high-altitude checkerspot of the Rocky Mountains and Sierra Nevada. Local but sometimes common over rockslides and windswept rocky slopes near and above treeline. Flies in summer (1 brood). ▶ Above variable, brown-orange with black markings, paler above in Colorado. Below white with orange spotband and basal spots. Very similar to Sagebrush and Northern Checkerspots (next page); best identified by habitat. 🌿 **Larval foodplant:** Alpine fleabanes.

CHECKERSPOTS

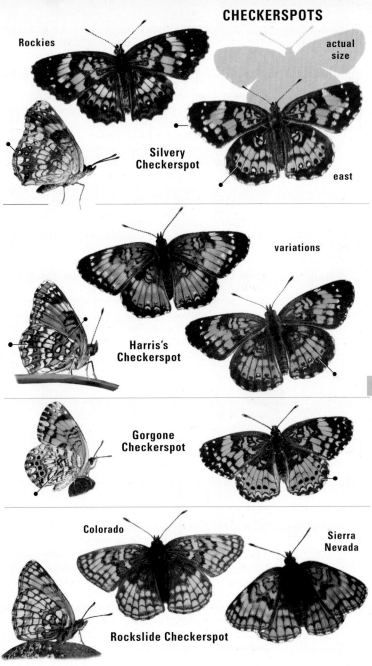

Rockies

actual size

Silvery Checkerspot

east

variations

Harris's Checkerspot

Gorgone Checkerspot

Colorado

Sierra Nevada

Rockslide Checkerspot

185

Western regions with good diversity usually contain one (sometimes two) of these. They are often best identified by flight period and habitat.

NORTHERN CHECKERSPOT   *Chlosyne palla*

Common and widespread, mainly from mountain meadows down to foothills. Males perch in gully bottoms to await females. Flies late spring and summer (1 brood). ▶ Variable, especially females. Below with pale areas usually *creamy or pale yellow* (not white), setting off red-orange or orange markings. Male above red-orange with black markings, median band often paler. Female above varies from mostly orange with black markings to mostly black with creamy bands. 🌿 **Larval foodplant**: Asters, rabbitbrush, and related plants.

SAGEBRUSH CHECKERSPOT   *Chlosyne acastus*

Common in sagebrush country. Prefers more arid habitats than Northern Checkerspot and flies earlier in the season where their ranges overlap. Males perch and patrol in gullies to seek females. Flies in spring and early summer (1 brood, partial second brood in some areas). ▶ Below with pale areas *white*, setting off orange spotbands and basal spots. Above brownish orange to bright orange with moderate to heavy black markings; reduced black markings in Mojave Desert. 🌿 **Larval foodplant**: Rabbitbrush and desert aster.

GABB'S CHECKERSPOT   *Chlosyne gabbii*

California only, common in foothills and canyons in coastal mountains. Many southern coastal populations have been eradicated by development. An extended flight from spring to early summer (1 brood, rarely partial second). ▶ Similar to Northern Checkerspot (their ranges barely touch) but has pale bands below white, not creamy. Sagebrush Checkerspot is quite similar below, but above is brighter orange with less black in nearest populations in southern California. 🌿 **Larval foodplant**: Beach aster and related plants.

HOFFMANN'S CHECKERSPOT   *Chlosyne hoffmanni*

Limited, narrow range in California and northwest, uncommon and local in openings of coniferous forests. Flies in summer (1 brood). ▶ Pale markings below usually *creamy,* not white. Best separated from Northern Checkerspot by upperside pattern in California and Oregon, by range in Washington (where Hoffmann's looks very similar but occurs in the Cascades, while Northern occurs east of those mountains). 🌿 **Larval foodplant**: Asters.

WESTERN CHECKERSPOTS

actual size

Rockies

male

Northern Checkerspot

female

Sagebrush Checkerspot

Mojave Desert

Utah

male

female

Gabb's Checkerspot

Hoffmann's Checkerspot

California and Oregon

Washington

187

belong to the checkerspot group, with typical flight alternating flaps and flat-winged glides. Most have patterns including patches of solid colors.

BORDERED PATCH   *Chlosyne lacinia*

A remarkably variable butterfly of the southwest. The most commonly encountered black checkerspot in that region, often causing confusion because individuals vary so much. Avidly visits flowers, and males hilltop. Flies spring to fall (multiple broods). ► Above forewing black with rows of white or orange spots, hindwing black with cream, white, or orange median band of variable width, sometimes obscured or absent. Below hindwing with cream median band of varying width and cream marginal spots. 🌿 **Larval foodplant:** Sunflowers, ragweed, cocklebur, and other related plants.

CALIFORNIA PATCH   *Chlosyne californica*

A fast-flying checkerspot of high desert habitats from central Arizona westward. Males avidly hilltop. Flies in spring and again in fall; summer flight dependent on rainfall (2–3 broods). ► Above dark brown to blackish with broad orange-brown median band and *orange-brown marginal spots*. Some variations on Bordered Patch can be similar, but they lack the orange marginal spots. 🌿 **Larval foodplant:** Desert sunflower.

CRIMSON PATCH   *Chlosyne janais*

Local and uncommon in dry woods of southern Texas, rarely straying farther north. Flies summer to fall (2–3 broods). ► Large with little variability. Above forewing black with white spots, hindwing black with large red-orange basal patch. Below black with white spots; yellow basal patch on hindwing has *black spots throughout*. 🌿 **Larval foodplant:** Anisacanthus and related plants.

ROSITA PATCH   *Chlosyne rosita*

Rare stray into southern Texas (reported at most seasons) and southern Arizona (reported late summer and early fall). ► Like Crimson Patch but smaller, with narrower forewings. Basal patch on hindwing above is two-toned, more yellowish inward (though Arizona strays have inner part of patch mostly black). On hindwing below, yellow basal patch *lacks black spots on outer half*. 🌿 **Larval foodplant:** Twin-seeds and related plants.

RED-SPOTTED PATCH   *Chlosyne melitaeoides*

Rare stray to south Texas from northeastern Mexico. Has been confused with a different species, Marina Patch. ► Above forewing black with white or yellow spots, hindwing black with yellow median band and red submarginal spots. Below hindwing yellow with black bands, red submarginal spotband, yellow spots along margin. 🌿 **Larval foodplant:** Unknown.

PATCHES

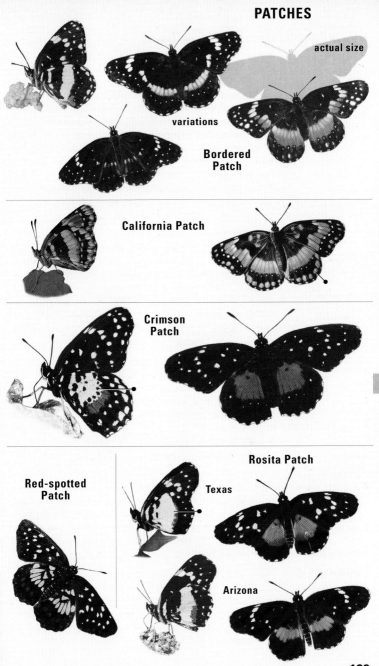

actual size

variations

Bordered Patch

California Patch

Crimson Patch

Rosita Patch

Red-spotted Patch

Texas

Arizona

LEANIRA CHECKERSPOT   *Thessalia leanira*

Local on hillsides laden with Indian paintbrush. Males are avid hilltoppers, especially in desert regions. Populations can be common one year and scarce the next. Flies spring to early summer (1 brood, except 2 broods on central California coast). ▶ Abdomen black with white rings, palps (face) *orange.* Hindwing below white or cream with *black postmedian band* enclosing white spots. Above varies by region. In deserts mostly orange with paler spots and variable black markings. West of deserts black with cream bands, red-orange spots along forewing margin. 🐛 **Larval foodplant:** Paintbrushes.

FULVIA CHECKERSPOT   *Thessalia fulvia*

Replaces Leanira Checkerspot in the southwest and western plains. Local near colonies of paintbrush on rocky hillsides. Males gather on hilltops. Flies from spring to fall (2–4 broods). ▶ Somewhat variable above. Similar to Leanira Checkerspot (apparently no overlap in range), but note that abdomen has at least some orange above, and palps (face) *black above and white below.* 🐛 **Larval foodplant:** Paintbrushes and bird's beak.

BLACK CHECKERSPOT   *Thessalia cyneas*

Southeastern Arizona only. Generally at higher elevations than Fulvia Checkerspot. Males are hilltoppers. Flies spring to fall (3–4 broods). ▶ Abdomen black with white rings, palps black above and white below. Above *mostly black* with rows of cream spots and marginal red-orange spots. Below cream with postmedian band enclosing cream spots, much like Fulvia Checkerspot. 🐛 **Larval foodplant:** Paintbrush.

DEFINITE PATCH   *Chlosyne definita*

Small, local, and rare. Flies spring to fall (2–3 broods depending on rainfall). ▶ Above red-orange with black veins and bands and red submarginal spots on hindwing. Below forewing outer half *orange,* hindwing with *white spot in center of submarginal orange spotband.* Compare to Theona Checkerspot (next page). 🐛 **Larval foodplant:** *Stenandrium.*

BANDED PATCH   *Chlosyne endeis*

Southern Texas only, rare. Flies spring to fall (3 broods). ▶ Above mostly black with white spots on forewing, pale median band and red-orange spots on hindwing. Below suggests Definite Patch, with white spot in center of submarginal orange spotband, but larger and has outer half of forewing *black.* 🐛 **Larval foodplant:** *Carlowrightia.*

CHECKERSPOTS

actual size

deserts

intermediate

Leanira Checkerspot

west of deserts

Fulvia Checkerspot

male

female

Black Checkerspot

Banded Patch

Definite Patch

ARACHNE CHECKERSPOT   *Poladryas arachne*

Locally common in the mountain west, from open grasslands to mountain meadows. Males avidly hilltop. Some consider this and Dotted Checkerspot the same species. Flies in spring, summer, and fall (1 or 2 broods depending on location). ▶ Above brownish orange (much of range) or red-orange (California) with black markings, often two-toned with a paler orange median band. Below orange with white bands, with distinct *rows of black spots* in the white median band. Also note the combination of orange rings on the black abdomen and blue-gray eyes. Compare to checkerspots on next page and p. 186. 🐛 **Larval foodplant:** Beardtongues.

DOTTED CHECKERSPOT   *Poladryas minuta*

A very close relative of Arachne Checkerspot, limited to parts of Texas and northeastern New Mexico. Uncommon, and apparently has disappeared from some areas. Males patrol high points in volcanic fields and other hilly summits to find females. Flies late spring and late summer (2 broods). ▶ Similar to Arachne Checkerspot, but above has sparse black markings, little contrast in color. Below may show wider orange bands. As with Arachne, note *distinct rows of black spots* in the white median band. 🐛 **Larval foodplant:** Beardtongues.

THEONA CHECKERSPOT   *Thessalia theona*

An attractive checkerspot of the southwest, locally common in foothills and canyons. Males are avid hilltoppers. Flies spring to fall (2–3 broods, perhaps more depending on rainfall). ▶ Above quite variable but mostly orange with black veins and margins; amount of black varies, and median band often paler. Below hindwing white with distinctive orange postmedian band lined with black, orange postbasal band *well connected* to leading edge. 🐛 **Larval foodplant:** Paintbrushes and Brachystigma in southwest, silverleafs in Texas.

CHINATI CHECKERSPOT   *Thessalia chinatiensis*

Local in western Texas, in rocky limestone habitats studded with silverleaf. Some consider this a subspecies of Theona Checkerspot; apparent intermediates or hybrids exist. Flies in spring, later flights dependent on rainfall (2–3 broods). ▶ Similar to Theona Checkerspot, but above lacks postmedian black bands, and has solid black hindwing border. On hindwing below, orange postbasal band is *weakly* connected to leading edge. 🐛 **Larval foodplant:** Silverleaf (*Leucophyllum*).

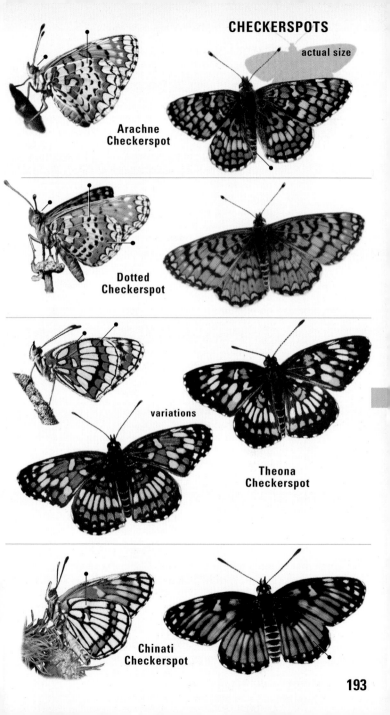

CHECKERSPOTS

actual size

Arachne Checkerspot

Dotted Checkerspot

variations

Theona Checkerspot

Chinati Checkerspot

VARIABLE CHECKERSPOT   *Euphydryas chalcedona*

This striking butterfly is widespread and common in many western habitats. To locate females, males hilltop or perch in canyon bottoms. Included here are Anicia and Colon Checkerspots, considered full species by some. Flies in spring or summer depending on elevation (1 brood, rarely 2). ▶ Above extremely variable. Along Pacific Coast and most of northwest, mostly black with pale yellow checkering and red spots especially along margin, postmedian band usually yellow or black, rarely completely red. In remainder of west, mainly orange or red with varying yellow and black bands. Abdomen usually has *white spotting*. 🦋 **Larval foodplant:** Snowberries, beardtongues, paintbrushes, monkey flowers, and related plants.

EDITH'S CHECKERSPOT   *Euphydryas editha*

A lovely reddish checkerspot of western mountains and foothills, usually local and uncommon. Males hilltop in some areas. Flies in early spring or summer depending on elevation (1 brood). ▶ Along Pacific Coast, redder overall than Variable Checkerspot. From the Sierra Nevada crest, Cascades, and central Oregon eastward, difficult to separate from Variable Checkerspot, but often flies weeks earlier where their ranges overlap. Abdomen *lacks* white spotting. 🦋 **Larval foodplant:** Paintbrushes, beardtongues, and related plants.

BALTIMORE CHECKERSPOT   *Euphydryas phaeton*

Beautiful, distinctive, unlike any other eastern butterfly. Formerly scarce and local in damp meadows with stands of turtlehead; has increased in some areas where larvae feed on introduced English plantain. Like the Baltimore Oriole, this butterfly was named for the orange and black colors of Lord Baltimore. Flies late spring or early summer (1 brood). ▶ Slightly variable, but unmistakable in its range. 🦋 **Larval foodplant:** Turtlehead, false foxglove, English plantain, and others.

GILLETT'S CHECKERSPOT   *Euphydryas gillettii*

Uncommon and local from the Canadian Rockies south to western Wyoming. Adults fly slowly near the ground in damp mountain meadows. Flies in early to midsummer (1 brood). ▶ Unlike any other species in its range. Above black with cream spots and very wide submarginal red-orange bands. Below with orange and cream bands. 🦋 **Larval foodplant:** Twinberry and others.

CHECKERSPOTS

Variable Checkerspot

actual size

variations

desert

northwest

Edith's Checkerspot

variations

Gillett's Checkerspot

Baltimore Checkerspot

195

Also known as anglewings, named for the silvery "comma" on the hind-wing below or their sharply angled wing margins. They are stunningly camouflaged in browns and grays below, and look like dead leaves when perched with wings closed. Most are woodland butterflies, preferring to feed at tree sap, rotting fruit, mud, dung, or carrion instead of flowers. Commas hibernate as adults, usually in tree crevices, logs, or cracks in buildings. Hibernating adults occasionally fly on warm winter days.

QUESTION MARK   *Polygonia interrogationis*

Wide-ranging and fairly common in woodland open-ings, streamsides, city parks, backyards, and quiz shows. Adults regularly stray far from normal breeding areas, and some are migratory, especially in the east. Seasonally variable. Flies spring to fall (2 broods); sec-ond-brood adults hibernate, fly again in spring, and then mate. ► Hindwing with longer tail than other commas. Below hindwing either uniformly purplish brown or striped tan, brown, and blue, always with centered *silvery comma and adjacent dot* forming a *question mark*. Forewing above has a black dash near tip, absent on other commas. Hindwing above orange and brown on winter brood, mostly black in summer.
🌿 **Larval foodplant:** Hops, nettles, elms, and hackberries.

EASTERN COMMA   *Polygonia comma*

Fairly common in the east in moist woods and ripar-ian edges. Adults are wary and fly exceptionally fast and erratically when disturbed. Seasonally variable. Flies spring to fall (2 broods). ► Below hindwing striped dark and light brown with silvery comma mark; me-dian line jagged, especially below comma. Above *lacks* black dash near forewing tip shown by Question Mark. Compare to other commas (below and next page). Hindwing almost entirely black in summer individuals or with reduced black enclosing orange submarginal spots. 🌿 **Larval foodplant:** Nettles, elms, and hops.

SATYR COMMA   *Polygonia satyrus*

A golden orange comma of northern woodlands and western streamside habitats. Rare in eastern portion of range, more common westward. Flies spring to fall (2 broods). ► No seasonal variation. Below similar to Eastern Comma, brownish with silvery comma; me-dian line on hindwing may be straighter. Most other commas (next page) grayer below. Above note two black spots on forewing inner margin; hindwing has black spot at center and relatively *pale tan marginal ar-eas*. 🌿 **Larval foodplant:** Nettles.

COMMAS

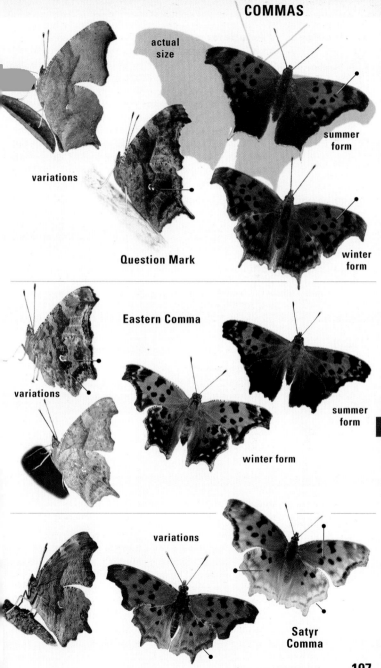

actual
size

summer
form

variations

winter
form

Question Mark

Eastern Comma

summer
form

variations

winter form

variations

**Satyr
Comma**

197

GREEN COMMA

Polygonia faunus

An attractive anglewing of coniferous woodlands. Not uncommon in east, somewhat local in west. Adults are long-lived, from mid- or late summer to following spring when they mate (1 brood). ▶ Wing edges very jagged (like those of Oreas and eastern Hoary Commas). Below varies from heavily mottled to rather uniform gray with silvery comma and often with *obvious green submarginal spots* (sometimes faint to absent in females). Above orange-brown, hindwing with black central spot and orange submarginal spotband. ❧ **Larval foodplant:** Willows, birches, alders, and others.

HOARY COMMA

Polygonia gracilis

Wide-ranging in far north and western mountains. Variable; eastern and western populations formerly considered two species. Visits flowers more than most commas. Adults live from summer to following spring when they mate (1 brood). ▶ Below variably gray, usually with *strong two-toned appearance* (darker basally in east). Above golden orange with yellow submarginal band on hindwing (in west), or orange-brown with small orange submarginal spots on hindwing (in east). Hindwing above usually *lacks* black central spot of Green and Satyr Commas. ❧ **Larval foodplant:** Currants.

GRAY COMMA

Polygonia progne

An anglewing of rich mixed or deciduous woodlands. Slower in flight than other commas. Flies spring to fall (1–2 broods). ▶ Below gray to gray-brown, often *heavily marked with white striations;* silvery comma mark very thin. Forewing below strongly two-toned, hindwing less so, especially lower part. Above hindwing margin mostly black, enclosing submarginal orange spots. Hindwing above lacks central black spot, and center of trailing edge of forewing lacks large black spot shown by some commas. ❧ **Larval foodplant:** Currants.

OREAS COMMA

Polygonia oreas

Usually rare and local in moist forests of the west. Some consider Oreas and Gray Commas to belong to same species. Flies spring to fall (1 brood). ▶ Similar to Gray Comma, separated by range. Two-toned gray below, often *heavily marked with white striations.* Above orange-brown, with hindwing border the same color on both sides of orange submarginal band, not darker outward. Central hindwing spot above (if present) is *lighter* than large basal black spot. ❧ **Larval foodplant:** Currants.

COMMAS

variations

Green Comma

actual size

east

Hoary Comma

west

Oreas Comma

Gray Comma

Close relatives of commas, with wing edges jagged but not as angular. Adults hibernate in winter and also remain inactive for lengthy periods in summer. Flight is usually fast and erratic.

COMPTON TORTOISESHELL   *Nymphalis vaualbum*

A large golden brown butterfly of openings and edges of dense northern woods. Sometimes strays far to the south, especially in years of population outbreaks. Adults are much longer-lived than most butterflies, surviving from summer to following spring (1 brood). ▶ Below hindwing striated gray and brown with tiny silvery comma mark. Gray Comma (previous page) is smaller with more extreme wing shape. Above mottled golden brown and black. *White spot on leading edge of hindwing* is diagnostic when visible. 🌿 **Larval foodplant:** Aspen, birches, and willows.

CALIFORNIA TORTOISESHELL   *Nymphalis californica*

Mainly western, but adults are prone to long-range flights, sometimes in huge numbers, and may wind up far from regular breeding areas. These large population outbreaks are often followed by years of scarcity. Adults live from early or midsummer to following spring when mating occurs (1 brood). ▶ From below, suggests Compton Tortoiseshell or commas, but has different pattern above, *mostly bright orange* with dark margin and with a few large black spots on forewing. 🌿 **Larval foodplant:** Buckbrushes.

MILBERT'S TORTOISESHELL   *Nymphalis milberti*

A distinctive butterfly of the west and north. Commonly seen at flowers in mountain meadows in summer, but also strays to parks, towns, etc. Adults sometimes breed along low-elevation watercourses in arid or coastal regions, with their offspring returning to higher elevations. Flies spring to fall (1–2 broods). ▶ Below suggests other tortoiseshells but usually smaller and *more evenly bicolored.* Compare to Mourning Cloak (next page). Unmistakable bright pattern above, dark brown with *broad yellow and orange submarginal stripes.* 🌿 **Larval foodplant:** Nettles.

SMALL TORTOISESHELL   *Nymphalis urticae*

A European butterfly reported from the New York City area in past years between August and October. The source of these individuals is uncertain, but they undoubtedly arrived with human help. ▶ Above bright orange with *leading edge of forewing banded black and yellow,* hindwing black basally. Below hindwing variably mottled dark brown to light tan, usually lighter outward of jagged median line. 🌿 **Larval foodplant:** Nettles.

Compton Tortoiseshell

actual size

feeding on sap

California Tortoiseshell

Small Tortoiseshell

Milbert's Tortoiseshell

MOURNING CLOAK *Nymphalis antiopa*

For winter-weary northerners, few sights can be as welcome as that of the first Mourning Cloak, emerged from its hibernation, gliding through leafless woods during the first spring thaw. This beautiful and familiar butterfly is seldom abundant, but it may be encountered almost anywhere, from forests and streamsides to open fields and city parks. It flies with a series of quick wingbeats interspersed with flat-winged glides; males patrol forest clearings and roads to find females. In suburban settings, the caterpillars seem to prefer to pupate under concrete or stucco overhangs rather than those made of wood. Adults live longer than most butterflies (up to 10 months or more), emerging in summer, hibernating through the winter, then flying again in spring and early summer when mating occurs (1 brood, rarely 2). ▶ Almost unmistakable, rich maroon-brown above with blue submarginal spots and broad yellow borders (borders may fade to whitish on worn individuals). Below dark striated blackish brown with paler borders; compare to species on three preceding pages. 🐛 **Larval foodplant:** Willows, cottonwoods, elms, birches, and hackberries.

RED ADMIRAL *Vanessa atalanta*

Another familiar butterfly, not likely to be confused with any other. May be seen practically anywhere (except the far north) from forest clearings, streamsides, and fields to gardens and city parks. Population numbers vary, and it sometimes migrates north in large numbers, especially in the eastern part of its range. In the southwest, adults overwinter in deserts, then move to higher elevations as the season progresses. Flight is fast and erratic. In late afternoon and early evening, males set up territories on hilltops, in clearings, or even in backyards to find females. Males are especially pugnacious, darting out at almost anything crossing their territory, even humans! On the wing most of the year in south, spring to fall northward, temporary resident at northern limits (mainly 2 broods). ▶ Almost unmistakable, dark above with fiery red-orange slashes and with white spots on outer part of forewing. Below hindwing exquisitely multicolored in browns and blues, with pale buff along margin. Forewing below has bands of red, white, and blue along leading edge. 🐛 **Larval foodplant:** Nettles, false nettles, pellitories, and related plants.

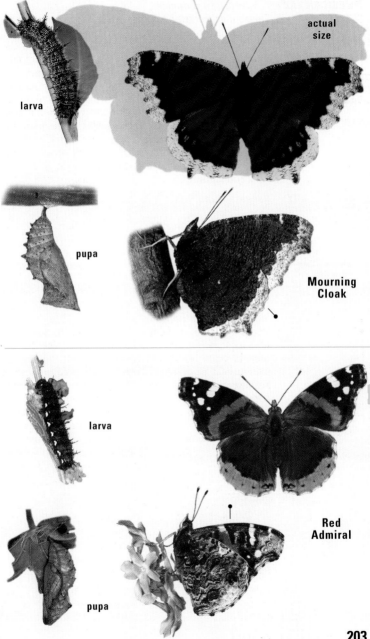

DISTINCTIVE BRUSHFOOTS

actual size

larva

pupa

Mourning Cloak

larva

pupa

Red Admiral

AMERICAN LADY   *Vanessa virginiensis*

Familiar across the North American landscape, seen in most open or semiopen habitats. Unable to survive cold winters, adults overwinter in warm southern regions before dispersing north in spring, but do not migrate in huge numbers like Painted Lady. Flies most of year in extreme south, flights are progressively shorter northward (2–3 broods). ▶ Hindwing below with *two large eyespots* on an olive background. Hindwing above has row of submarginal spots usually connected by a smeary line. On forewing above, note the *white dot on orange* and the break in the black mark on the inner part of the wing. 🌿 **Larval foodplant:** Everlastings, pussytoes, and cudweeds.

PAINTED LADY   *Vanessa cardui*

One of the most familiar butterflies in North America (and around the world). Seen in most habitats across the continent, although usually scarce in parts of the east and southeast. Adults rarely survive in areas with consistent freezing temperatures, so most overwinter in warm southern areas or in Mexico, then disperse northward in spring to recolonize the continent. Sometimes these northward flights number in the millions, attracting media attention. Males patrol hilltops in late afternoon to locate females. Flight is fast and erratic. Flies most of year in extreme south, shorter season with fewer broods northward (1–3 broods). ▶ Hindwing below with submarginal row of four small eyespots. Hindwing above has row of submarginal spots not connected. On forewing above, note heavy black mark on inner part of wing, not broken at center. 🌿 **Larval foodplant:** Thistle, mallows, and many others. Migratory individuals use fiddleneck and other spring annuals.

WEST COAST LADY   *Vanessa annabella*

Very familiar in gardens, vacant lots, and other urban areas along west coast where this lady overwinters. Migrates eastward and to higher elevations as season progresses. Flies most of year on coast (multiple broods), spring to fall elsewhere (1–2 broods). ▶ Similar to other ladies, but forewing tip extended and squared off. Hindwing below has submarginal row of small eyespots; on hindwing above, submarginal spots are separated and blue-centered. On forewing above, last large pale bar near wingtip is *orange* on this species, white on the other two ladies. 🌿 **Larval foodplant:** Mallows.

LADIES

larva

actual
size

American Lady

Painted Lady

West Coast
Lady

These brown brushfoots are named for the large colorful eyespots above. Their flight is direct, with a series of quick wingbeats followed by flat-winged glides. Only one species is widespread in our area.

COMMON BUCKEYE   *Junonia coenia*

Most common in southern regions, but a familiar sight across much of the U.S. Favors open habitats, from fields to roadsides to gardens. Often sits on open bare ground, and males can be very territorial, darting out at anything that passes. In summer, adults move northward, sometimes reaching southern Canada. In fall, southward movements can be conspicuous, especially along east coast. Flies most of year in south, summer to fall northward (2–3 broods). ▶ Unmistakable over most of its North American range, with striking pattern above including multicolored eyespots, pale forewing bar, orange bars across forewing cell and orange near wing margins. In Florida and the southwest, compare next two species. ❧ **Larval foodplant**: Plantains, snapdragons, monkey flowers, and others.

MANGROVE BUCKEYE   *Junonia evarete*

In central and southern Florida this buckeye inhabits black mangrove swamps and nearby coastal areas. Despite mingling with two other very similar buckeyes, this species appears to retain its genetic integrity. Flies all year in the Keys, most of year northward (multiple broods). ▶ Resembles Common Buckeye but forewing band above is pale to rich *orange,* not whitish; orange completely *surrounds* large forewing eyespot; eyespots on hindwing above tend to be closer to the same size. Below hindwing relatively plain, orange on forewing bar may be visible. ❧ **Larval foodplant**: Black mangrove.

TROPICAL BUCKEYE   *Junonia genoveva*

A buckeye of Mexican border regions, also locally (and irregularly?) in south Florida. Flies most of year (3–4 broods). ▶ Hindwing below often has *pale median band.* Above variable. In southwest (form *nigrosuffusa*), usually *very dark,* with pale forewing band mostly or completely obscured; however, some appear intermediate between this form and Common Buckeye. In Florida, forewing band usually flushed pink, and area just inward from large forewing eyespot is brown, not orange or white. On hindwing above, orange marginal band usually narrow, and eyespots darker and not so unequal in size as on Common Buckeye. ❧ **Larval foodplant**: Speedwells, monkey flowers, and others.

BUCKEYES

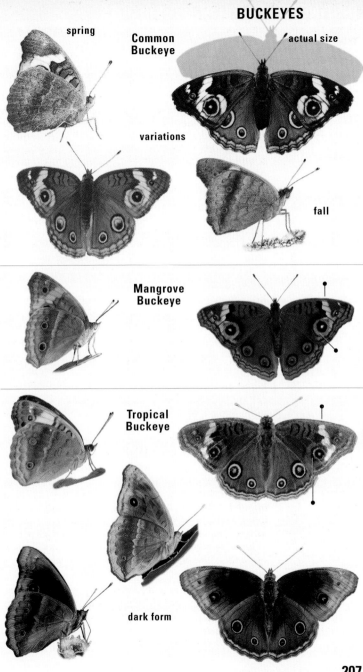

spring

Common Buckeye

actual size

variations

fall

Mangrove Buckeye

Tropical Buckeye

dark form

WHITE PEACOCK   *Anartia jatrophae*

This widespread tropical butterfly is common in Florida in open habitats, including roadsides, fields, gardens. Also found in south Texas, and strays northward, rarely as far as Nebraska, New Mexico, or North Carolina. Flight is fairly fast, direct, and low, with rapid wingbeats and short glides; often perches on lawns. Flies most of year (multiple broods). ▶ Above mostly whitish with orange to orange-brown margins and round black postmedian spots. Compare to Common Mestra (p. 214). ✤ **Larval foodplant:** Water hyssop, green shrimp plant, frogfruit, and others.

BANDED PEACOCK   *Anartia fatima*

A butterfly of forest edges, roadside, and disturbed habitats in the tropics; sometimes resident in southern Texas. Adults fly low with quick wingbeats and short glides, and avidly visit flowers. Reported at all seasons in Texas (multiple broods). ▶ Dark above with white or yellowish band crossing both wings. Several other brushfoots (admirals and sisters, next two pages) also have white wing bands, but note this species' angular hindwing, *red median band on hindwing,* and white spots on blackish tip of forewing. ✤ **Larval foodplant:** Members of acanthus family.

MALACHITE   *Siproeta stelenes*

Large, green, and spectacular best describes this tropical jewel. Unfortunately, in North America its range is quite limited, being resident only in extreme southern regions of Texas and Florida; strays north to Arizona and central Texas. Favors wooded areas such as hardwood hammocks and edges, and avidly visits flowers. Flight is strong and buoyant and often well above the ground. Massive directional movements sometimes occur in Mexico. In our area, flies most of year (multiple broods). ▶ If there is such a thing as an unmistakable butterfly, this is it: brilliant lime and dark chocolate, a feast for the eyes. Female usually paler than male below. ✤ **Larval foodplant:** Green shrimp plant in south Florida, other members of the acanthus family elsewhere.

RUSTY-TIPPED PAGE   *Siproeta epaphus*

A relative of the Malachite that has strayed very rarely to Texas and New Mexico. Widespread in the tropics, where males patrol high above linear pathways through forests. ▶ Large, distinctive. Compare to admirals and sisters on next two pages. ✤ **Larval foodplant:** Acanthus family plants.

TROPICAL BRUSHFOOTS

actual size

White Peacock

Banded Peacock

Malachite

Rusty-tipped Page

(genera *Limenitis* and *Adelpha*) are large, attractive butterflies, most with broad white bands across the wings. They fly with alternating quick wing-beats and flat-winged glides. Males often perch on trees along trails or forest clearings to await females. Adults are attracted to mud, rotting fruit, and animal dung, but also visit flowers.

WHITE ADMIRAL *Limenitis arthemis (in part)*

Widespread and common in the north, in mixed and deciduous woodlands; often along road cuts, forest edges, streams. Formerly regarded as a full species, now considered same species as Red-spotted Purple; they blend where their ranges meet, producing many intermediates. (The species as a whole may be called "Red-spotted Admiral," but it is more useful to identify individuals as White Admiral, Red-spotted Purple, or intergrade.) Flies in summer (1–2 broods). ► Black with white bands and red spots. In southwest Canada, compare to admirals on next page. Look for highly variable intergrades with Red-spotted Purple in Ontario and northeastern U.S. ☙ **Larval foodplant**: Willows, poplars, birches, and others.

RED-SPOTTED PURPLE *Limenitis arthemis (in part)*

From southern Ontario southward this butterfly replaces the conspecific White Admiral. Common across most of the eastern U.S. with an isolated subspecies in the southwest. Apparently mimics the Pipevine Swallowtail, a butterfly distasteful to birds. Flies spring to fall (2–3 broods). ► Mostly blackish with blue iridescence and with *red-orange spots* near margin and hindwing base below. Pipevine Swallowtail (p. 26) flies differently, lacks basal spots below. ☙ **Larval foodplant**: Willows, cottonwoods, poplars, and related trees.

VICEROY *Limenitis archippus*

Widespread and fairly common around streamside willows, woodland edges. Very different from its relatives, it mimics the Monarch, which is noxious to most predators. Once considered to be merely deceptive in its colors, now thought possibly to be equally distasteful to some predators. Mimics the Queen in southern areas where resident Monarchs are scarce. Flies spring to fall (2–3 broods). ► Like Monarch (p. 226) or Queen (p. 228) but smaller and usually has *black postmedian band across hindwing*. This band can be faint or lacking in southwest, occasionally elsewhere; note the flap-glide flight style (Monarch and Queen fly strongly and sail with wings in shallow V). ☙ **Larval foodplant**: Willows; sometimes poplars and others.

ADMIRALS

actual size

White Admiral

intergrade between
White Admiral and
Red-spotted Purple

Red-spotted Purple

southwest

Viceroy

widespread

Florida

211

WEIDEMEYER'S ADMIRAL   *Limenitis weidemeyerii*

A dashing admiral of Great Basin and Rocky Mountain streamside habitats and aspen woodlands. Males frequently fly out at other butterflies and insects that invade their perching territory. Flies in summer (1 brood in most areas). ► Barely overlaps with Lorquin's Admiral to the west and White Admiral (p. 210) to the north; often found with California Sister in southern regions. Mostly black and white, *lacking* orange on the forewing tip above. Below hindwing *mostly white.* White Admiral has base of hindwing below mostly dark with red spots. 🌿 **Larval foodplant:** Willows, aspen, chokecherry, serviceberry, and others.

LORQUIN'S ADMIRAL   *Limenitis lorquini*

Pacific Coast and the northwest only, replacing Weidemeyer's Admiral westward. Seen in urban habitats as well as more natural settings, almost always near willows and other larval foodplants. Common in northwest, somewhat more confined to riparian areas in arid southern regions. May interbreed with Weidemeyer's Admiral along narrow zone where ranges meet. Flies spring to fall (1–2 broods). ► Above blackish brown with broad white bands crossing both wings. Orange on forewing tip is a band *extending along margin.* Below with gray, orange-brown, and white bands. 🌿 **Larval foodplant:** Willows, poplars, and chokecherry.

CALIFORNIA SISTER   *Adelpha bredowii*

A bright denizen of western oak woodlands. Adults are strong flyers, coursing about the upper parts of oaks and other trees, alighting on the ground only to sip at mud, rotting fruit, or other nutrients. Also visits flowers on occasion. May be found with Lorquin's Admiral. Flies spring to fall (2 broods). ► Above dark brown with broken white forewing band and white hindwing band tapering toward the lower edge. Orange near forewing tip is a *squarish patch* that does *not* reach margin. Below with lilac along margins and near base with broad brown submargin and white band. Southwestern individuals are larger and more intensely colored than those farther west. 🌿 **Larval foodplant:** Oaks.

BAND-CELLED SISTER   *Adelpha fessonia*

Regular stray to south Texas, recorded in all months. ► Above brown with paler lines along submargin. White median band completely crosses both wings; small orange patch near forewing tip does not touch margin. See Pavon and Silver Emperors, p. 224. 🌿 **Larval foodplant:** Hackberries.

ADMIRALS AND SISTERS

actual size

Weidemeyer's Admiral

Lorquin's Admiral

variations

California Sister

Band-celled Sister

213

DINGY PURPLEWING   *Eunica monima*

A small brownish brushfoot of shady wooded areas, rather rare and elusive in southern Florida and Texas. Also strays to the southwest. Adults are skilled fliers, able to cease their rapid flight by suddenly alighting upside down under leaves or on tree trunks. They usually perch with wings closed. Reported most of year in Florida (multiple broods), July through September in Texas. ▶ Above mostly dark brown with purplish sheen when fresh (hard to glimpse in flight) and dingy white spots near forewing tip. Below hindwing light or dark brown, sometimes purplish; circle in postmedian area encloses a *pair of spots*, the upper spot grayish white or blue. ❦ **Larval foodplant:** Gumbo limbo.

FLORIDA PURPLEWING   *Eunica tatila*

Mainly extreme south Florida, strays to south Texas. A beautiful butterfly of shaded tropical hammocks, quite uncommon and local. Usually perches with wings closed, denying observers the pleasure of viewing its lovely upper surface. Flies all year in Florida (multiple broods). ▶ Forewing concave at tip. Above brown with basal two-thirds iridescent purple and several bold white spots on the forewing. Below variable from plain to mottled brown. Looks nondescript in the field; note size, habitat, wing shape, and white markings visible on forewing tip below. ❦ **Larval foodplant:** Crabwood.

COMMON MESTRA   *Mestra amymone*

Although it seems a weak flier, this pale brushfoot strays far north of its normal haunts in Mexico and south Texas, reaching the southwest and the central Great Plains. Might suggest the colors of a white (family Pieridae) in flight, but its frequent flat-winged glides reveal it to be otherwise. Males hilltop. Flies most of year in Texas (2–3 broods); reported June to November in southwest, mostly late summer on the Great Plains. ▶ Above pearly white with *pale orange border* on hindwing. Below mostly pale orange with thin white median spotband. ❦ **Larval foodplant:** Noseburns *(Tragia).*

RED RIM   *Biblis hyperia*

A beautiful tropical butterfly reported from various parts of Texas. Generally rare, but may breed periodically in southern areas of the state. Reported mainly July to November. ▶ Above velvety black with broad *crimson band* crossing hindwing. Below slightly paler with narrow whitish pink hindwing band. ❦ **Larval foodplant:** Noseburns.

Dingy
Purplewing

actual
size

Florida
Purplewing

Common
Mestra

Red Rim

Bluewings favor woodlands and tend to sit with wings closed. Crackers (also known as calicos) are also woodland butterflies, usually landing on tree trunks, facing downward, with wings spread. Males of some species can make a cracking sound in flight, especially when engaging in aerial disputes. Crackers are strictly tropical butterflies, and several species have occurred as very rare strays near the Mexican border.

MEXICAN BLUEWING   *Myscelia ethusa*

Mainly south Texas, uncommon but regularly seen in shaded woodlands of Rio Grande Valley. Very rare stray to west Texas. Adults habitually perch on tree trunks facing downward, only occasionally opening their wings. Flies most of year (multiple broods). ▶ Distinctive. Male above bluish purple with black crossbands and white spots near forewing tip, female similar but with white forewing spots more numerous. Below mottled in light and dark brown. 🌿 **Larval foodplant:** Adelia.

BLACKENED BLUEWING   *Myscelia cyananthe*

A rare stray to Arizona in summer and fall; reported once from California. Prefers shaded tropical woodlands. Massive directional movements occur in western Mexico. ▶ Similar to Mexican Bluewing but above shows more black on forewing, broader bands on hindwing. Female has more white spots near forewing tip above and more purplish blue on hindwing above than male. Below mottled in light and dark brown. 🌿 **Larval foodplant:** Euphorbia family plants.

GRAY CRACKER   *Hamadryas februa*

A striking butterfly regular in extreme south Texas; the cracker most likely to be seen north of the border. Found in wooded areas, flying fast in the shadows and landing on tree trunks, wings spread, head downward. Reported late summer to fall. ▶ Complex pattern above, like other crackers. For this species, note presence of some red in bar across forewing cell, red crescents in two lower eyespots of hindwing. 🌿 **Larval foodplant:** Noseburns and Dalechampia species are used by crackers in the tropics.

VARIABLE CRACKER   *Hamadryas feronia*

Rare stray to south Texas, recorded July to December. ▶ Above forewing has red bar across cell; hindwing eyespots are black with pale blue rings and white centers.

PALE CRACKER   *Hamadryas amphichloe*   *(not illustrated)*

A cracker seen in south Florida is likely to be this species, although it is a very rare stray there. ▶ Above forewing with red bar across cell, hindwing with red crescents in lower two eyespots. Often pale on outer part of forewing, especially males.

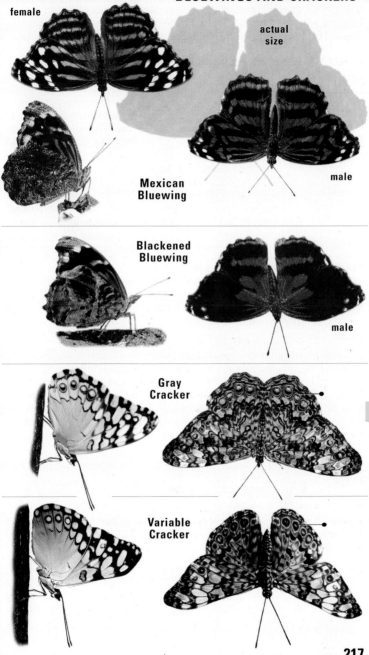

BLUEWINGS AND CRACKERS

female

actual size

Mexican Bluewing

male

Blackened Bluewing

male

Gray Cracker

Variable Cracker

A distinctive group of brushfoots with long daggerlike extensions on the hindwings. Typically fast and agile in flight. They are widespread in the American tropics, but only one species occurs regularly in our area.

RUDDY DAGGERWING   *Marpesia petreus*

Locally common in Florida, around the edges of tropical hardwood hammocks or in gardens containing fig trees. Also known to breed in southern portions of Texas and Arizona, and strays have been found as far north as Nebraska. Readily visits flowers, and also attracted to mud or to rotting fruit. Flies all year in Florida (multiple broods), late summer to fall elsewhere (1 brood). ▶ Extreme wing shape and brilliant orange color above should be diagnostic, but many are seen with damaged wings or missing hindwing tails; compare to leafwings (next page) and to Julia Heliconian (p. 156). Below pale tan to orange with light purplish sheen, sharply contrasting against the white body and wing bases. ❦ **Larval foodplant:** Leaves of fig trees.

WAITER DAGGERWING   *Marpesia coresia*

Widespread in the American tropics, mainly in forested regions; rare stray to south Texas, recorded July and October. ▶ Above dark chocolate brown with long tails. Below *sharply two-toned*, with outer half of wings brown, inner half white. ❦ **Larval foodplant:** Unknown.

MANY-BANDED DAGGERWING   *Marpesia chiron*

Resident throughout the American tropics. Strays regularly to Texas, very rarely to Arizona, Kansas, and Florida; most strays reported in late summer. May breed occasionally where figs occur naturally or as ornamentals. In the tropics, massive directional flights are sometimes seen. ▶ Distinctive with tails intact. Above striped brown with long tails. Below pale purplish brown to tan, the basal half white with orange-edged gray bands. ❦ **Larval foodplant:** Leaves of fig trees.

ANTILLEAN DAGGERWING   *Marpesia eleuchea*   (not illustrated)

A bright orange daggerwing of the northern West Indies, reported from extreme south Florida on a few occasions. ▶ Very similar to Ruddy Daggerwing, but usually somewhat smaller, tail on hindwing not as long. Black median stripe on forewing *sharply bent* at bottom of cell, not running straight across wing. From below, body and wing bases *not* contrastingly white. ❦ **Larval foodplant:** Leaves of fig trees.

DAGGERWINGS

actual size

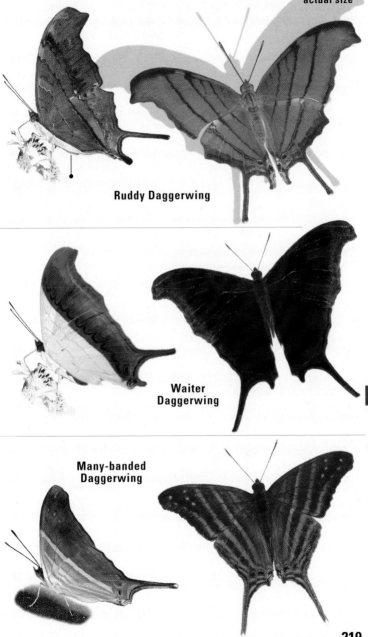

Ruddy Daggerwing

Waiter Daggerwing

Many-banded Daggerwing

(subfamily Charaxinae) have brilliant uppersides, best glimpsed during their fast and erratic flight. They usually perch with wings closed, their shape and pattern giving them an uncanny resemblance to dead leaves. They rarely visit flowers, preferring mud, rotting fruit, or tree sap.

GOATWEED LEAFWING *Anaea andria*

Widespread in southern regions where crotons grow, locally common in south-central states. Adults stray far northward, breeding where larval foodplants exist. Adults resting on twigs or branches will, if approached, move with a jerky motion to opposite side to avoid detection. Flies spring to fall (1–2 broods). ▶ Seasonally variable. Forewing tip pointed (more so on overwintering individuals), wing edges smooth, hindwing with short tail. Above male mostly red-orange, female orange with paler orange band along submargin. Below varying from glossy brown to red-brown. More uniformly colored than commas (pp. 196–199). 🌿 **Larval foodplant:** Goatweed and other crotons.

TROPICAL LEAFWING *Anaea aidea*

Regular stray to south Texas and the southwest (where occasional breeding is suspected), rarely straying farther north. Encountered at all seasons (2 broods). ▶ Very similar to Goatweed Leafwing, but wing edges slightly uneven, with a tooth between tail and lower angle on hindwing (shorter or absent on Goatweed Leafwing). Above male mostly red-brown, female mostly orange-brown, with paler spots along submargin. 🌿 **Larval foodplant:** Crotons.

FLORIDA LEAFWING *Anaea floridalis*

Extreme southern Florida only, uncommon in pine-palmetto scrub habitats. May be seen perched on pine trunks or twigs. Flies most of year (2–3 broods). ▶ Similar to Goatweed Leafwing but usually grayer below, more reddish orange above, with wing edges slightly more uneven. Hindwing below often shows a slightly darker submarginal line. 🌿 **Larval foodplant:** Narrow-leaved croton.

PALE-SPOTTED LEAFWING *Anaea pithyusa*

An uncommon periodic resident in south Texas, recorded March to December. ▶ Above black with blue-green iridescence basally and white or blue forewing spots. The only bluish leafwing known to occur in North America (there are numerous others in the tropics). Below mottled light and dark gray-brown. 🌿 **Larval foodplant:** Crotons.

LEAFWINGS

male

female

actual size

Goatweed Leafwing

female

male

Tropical Leafwing

Florida Leafwing

male

male

Pale-spotted Leafwing

Closely associated with hackberries. Emperors **(subfamily Apaturinae)** fly swiftly, alternating quick wingbeats with flat-winged glides. Males are pugnacious, darting out at other butterflies and insects invading their territory. Adults prefer sap and rotting fruit, rarely visiting flowers. American Snout is our only representative of an odd subfamily **(Libytheinae)**.

HACKBERRY EMPEROR   *Asterocampa celtis*

Widespread in east, more local in southwest, usually common. Adults mainly perch on trees or other objects well off the ground. Flies spring to fall (1–3 broods). ▶ Variable. Above grayish brown (east) to orange-brown (southwest). *One forewing cell bar is broken* or nearly so. Forewing has *one or two bold eyespots* in submargin. Below forewing marks may be visible, hindwing tan to gray-brown with row of yellow eyespots centered in blue. ꙮ **Larval foodplant:** Hackberry trees.

EMPRESS LEILIA   *Asterocampa leilia*

A specialty of southwestern lowlands. Behaves like other emperors but perches on the ground more often. Flies most of year (3 broods). ▶ Above orange-brown, forewing with *two solid cell bars* and *two submarginal eyespots.* Below forewing bars are clearly visible, hindwing purplish brown with row of blue-centered eyespots. ꙮ **Larval foodplant:** Spiny (desert) hackberry.

TAWNY EMPEROR   *Asterocampa clyton*

Less widespread than Hackberry Emperor but often found with it. Locally common. Usually perches high. Flies spring to fall (1–3 broods). ▶ Variable. Above yellow-brown (most of range) to orange-brown (southwest), hindwing dark or pale. Forewing has *two solid bars* in cell and *lacks* black submarginal spots. Below forewing marks may be visible, hindwing row of spots often indistinct. ꙮ **Larval foodplant:** Hackberry trees.

AMERICAN SNOUT   *Libytheana carinenta*

Often common in south, less so northward. In Texas and Arizona, massive flights of huge numbers are legendary but unpredictable. Visits flowers as well as sap and mud. Snouts are masters of deception in flight, bouncing like satyrs one moment, gliding like checkerspots the next. Flies all year in south, spring to fall northward (2–3 broods). ▶ Head with *long snoutlike palpi,* forewing tips extended and squared off. Above brown with orange basally and white forewing spots. Quite variable below; hindwing can be plain or mottled gray. Southeastern population sometimes considered a separate species. ꙮ **Larval foodplant:** Hackberries.

EMPERORS AND SNOUT

Hackberry Emperor

actual size

variations

Empress Leilia

Tawny Emperor

variations

American Snout

variations

223

BLUE-EYED SAILOR   *Dynamine dyonis*

Distinctive vagrant to south Texas, reported May to November. ▶ Sexes very different above: male golden green, female banded brown and white. Below with rust-red lines and two blue-centered eyespots mostly enclosed by white. ✤ **Larval foodplant:** Noseburns *(Tragia)*.

COMMON BANNER   *Epiphile adrasta*

A flashy tropical brushfoot, encountered rarely in south Texas in October. ▶ Forewing tip extended and squared off. Above male blackish brown with broad orange bands. Female similar but with buff forewing band. Below both sexes mottled brown. ✤ **Larval foodplant:** Soapberry family vines.

MIMIC   *Hypolimnas misippus*

Rare stray to Florida and the southeast. Resident of Asia and Africa; also the West Indies, where it may have been introduced by humans. ▶ Sexes are startlingly different. Male above mostly black with white patches edged with blue iridescence. Female mostly orange-brown, usually with broken white band crossing black forewing tip. ✤ **Larval foodplant:** Morning glory, purslane, mallows, and others.

BLOMFILD'S BEAUTY   *Smyrna blomfildia*

Rare stray to south Texas, recorded in late fall and winter. A strong flier. ▶ Above male golden orange with three white spots near black forewing tip. Female similar but brown with pale yellow diagonal band on forewing below tip. Below *complex pattern of wavy lines* with two submarginal eyespots. ✤ **Larval foodplant:** Plants in the nettle family.

"CREAM-BANDED" DUSKY EMPEROR   *Asterocampa idyja argus*

Rare stray to Arizona. Males seek out hilltops, unlike closely related emperors (p. 222). ▶ Above brownish red, outer half of forewing black with *buff diagonal band*. Below purplish tan with submarginal row of blue-centered spots on hindwing. ✤ **Larval foodplant:** Hackberries.

PAVON EMPEROR   *Doxocopa pavon*

Regular stray to south Texas. ▶ Both sexes with orange patch near squared-off forewing tip. Male above brown with iridescent purple overlay. Female above brown with white median band that does not touch leading edge of forewing (compare to Band-celled Sister, p. 212). Below brown, female with whitish band; lacks hindwing angle of Silver Emperor. ✤ **Larval foodplant:** Hackberries.

SILVER EMPEROR   *Doxocopa laure*

Regular stray to south Texas. ▶ Immediately recognizable with a glimpse of the *silvery underside*. Both sexes brown with white median band, pointed lower hindwing angle, and squared-off tip of forewing. Male with more extensive orange on forewing and iridescent blue sheen. Compare female to Band-celled Sister (p. 212) and Pavon Emperor. ✤ **Larval foodplant:** Hackberries.

RARE TROPICAL STRAYS

male

Blue-eyed Sailor

Common Banner

male

Mimic

male

Blomfild's Beauty

Dusky Emperor

male

Pavon Emperor

female

male

Silver Emperor

female

male

225

MILKWEED BUTTERFLIES

were formerly treated as a separate family, now considered a subfamily (**Danaiinae**) of the brushfoots. Their larvae mostly feed on milkweeds; chemicals derived from those plants make even the adult butterflies extremely distasteful to most predators. Studies have shown that birds can learn to avoid Monarchs after one taste, and will then even avoid the Viceroy, an unrelated mimic.

MONARCH   *Danaus plexippus*

The most famous butterfly in North America, perhaps in the world. Likely to be seen in any open habitat from southern Canada southward. Literally millions of Monarchs from eastern and central North America migrate to spend the winter in mountain forests of central Mexico. In early spring they begin to move north, pausing to breed where they find milkweeds. Their offspring continue north and also pause to breed, and by summer the next generation has populated much of the continent. The last brood of the summer begins to move south, forming big concentrations at some coastal and lakeside points, eventually arriving in central Mexico. The migration is all the more remarkable in that no one individual is likely to make the complete round trip, so that the Monarchs that "return" to the wintering grounds have never been there before, and they are somehow able to find these traditional sites by pure instinct. In western North America, a similar cycle of migration brings large concentrations to winter at various points on the California coast. Nonmigratory populations may be found breeding year-round in areas such as southern Florida and Texas. Has colonized various island groups, including Hawaii, where many are pale or whitish. ► Rich cinnamon-orange with black veins, with *white dots* on the black wing borders and on the body. Male has a small black spot along one vein on hindwing above, which female lacks. Queen and Soldier (next page) are similar below, but have less black near tip of forewing; above, they lack the obvious black veining. Viceroy (p. 210) usually has narrow black bar crossing hindwing, and its flight pattern is different, with quick flaps and flat-winged glides. **Note**: people sometimes apply the name "Monarch" to any butterfly that is orange and black (or yellow and black, such as Canadian Tiger Swallowtail, p. 20, in the far north), but once learned, the real Monarch is distinctive. 🌿 **Larval foodplant**: Milkweeds.

THE MONARCH

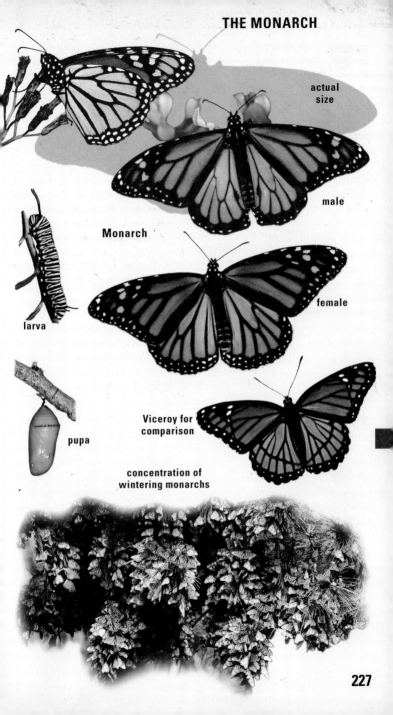

actual
size

male

Monarch

larva

female

pupa

Viceroy for
comparison

concentration of
wintering monarchs

QUEEN *Danaus gilippus*

Common in southern areas, often outnumbering the Monarch in Florida and the dry southwest; sometimes strays northward. Found in any open habitat, avidly visiting flowers. As with other milkweed butterflies, male Queens seek out particular types of flowers (such as ageratum, eupatorium, and heliotrope) to obtain certain alkaloids that they require for breeding. Adults may gather in groups to roost overnight. In some regions, such as south Texas, they appear to be migratory, although these movements are not as well understood as those of the Monarch. Flies all year in southernmost areas, spring to fall northward (3 or more broods). ▶ Mostly rich dark brown, with white spots on the black body and in the black wing margins. Below similar to the Monarch (previous page) but darker, and lacks the black bar across the forewing tip. Above obviously darker and much more uniform, lacking the Monarch's black veining. Note the distinct white spots in the forewing submarginal area. Male has small black patch along one hindwing vein, lacking in female. On hindwing above, southwestern individuals usually show pale edging along veins, lacking on those in Florida. Occasional very small individuals are seen, especially in winter. In the southwest and even more so in Florida, Viceroys (p. 210) are very dark, apparently mimicking the Queen instead of the Monarch. 🌿 **Larval foodplant:** Milkweeds.

SOLDIER *Danaus eresimus*

Uncommon to locally common in Florida and Texas; a rare but regular visitor to southern Arizona and central Texas, mostly in late summer and fall. Generally occurs where Queens are common, thus easily overlooked. Flies all year in southern Florida (3 or more broods), more limited season elsewhere. ▶ Very similar to Queen. On forewing, usually *lacks* white spots in submarginal area (may have faint yellow spots). Forewing above shows more obvious dark veining, although less defined than on Monarch. Hindwing below often has a vague dark central area contrasting with a paler postmedian area. 🌿 **Larval foodplant:** Milkweeds.

TIGER MIMIC-QUEEN *Lycorea cleobaea*

This rare tropical stray belongs to the milkweed butterfly group, but appears to mimic the looks of a heliconian. See p. 154 for illustration.

MILKWEED BUTTERFLIES

actual size

southwestern male

larva

Queen

southwestern female

pupa

Florida male

Texas

male

Soldier

female

Florida

229

SATYRS

make up a subfamily **(Satyrinae)** of the brushfoot family. Most are medium-sized and brown; on many, the wings are adorned with striking round spots, called eyespots.

LITTLE WOOD-SATYR   *Megisto cymela*

Very common in woodland edges and clearings in early summer, bouncing along perkily close to the ground, even on cloudy days when most butterflies are out of sight. Taxonomy is controversial. In many regions there are 2 flights, the second one following too closely after the first to be its offspring, and some have suggested that these may be two almost identical species. Brightly marked southern populations have been treated as a separate species, Viola's Wood-Satyr *(M. viola),* but they seem to blend broadly with other populations, and many in the southeast look intermediate. For now it may be best to call them all Little Wood-Satyrs, while recognizing that the real situation is probably more complicated. Flies mostly in late spring and early summer, sometimes late summer (1–3 broods). ▶ Two very prominent eyespots on each wing, especially on underside. "Viola's" form has larger eyespots, often with more silvery marks below. 🌿 **Larval foodplant:** Grasses.

CAROLINA SATYR   *Hermeuptychia sosybius*

Very common in the south, scarcer northward, around forested areas; often deeper in the woods than Little Wood-Satyr. Also very widespread in the tropics. Flies spring to fall, or all year in south Texas and Florida (3 or more broods). ▶ Resembles Little Wood-Satyr but slightly smaller. From below, eyespots usually look smaller and more numerous, but lower large eyespot on forewing is *lacking.* Above plain brown, *without eyespots.* 🌿 **Larval foodplant:** Grasses.

RED SATYR   *Megisto rubricata*

A small brown species of southwestern canyons and woodlands. At times can be identified by its habit of immediately opening its wings upon landing and then closing them again, often repeating this in rapid succession and allowing glimpses of the orange wing patches. Males hilltop in midmorning. Flies spring to fall (1–2 broods). ▶ Below shows one eyespot on forewing and two on hindwing; *orange flush on forewing* contrasts with brown hindwing. Above has red-orange flush and a single eyespot on each wing. Range closely approaches that of Little Wood-Satyr in Texas and Oklahoma. 🌿 **Larval foodplant:** Grasses.

SATYRS

actual size

Little Wood-Satyr

"Viola's" form

Carolina Satyr

variations

Red Satyr

GEORGIA SATYR   *Neonympha areolata*
HELICTA SATYR   *Neonympha helicta*

These were only recently shown to be separate species. Their status is still controversial and poorly known, and our range map encompasses both; most older records are simply called Georgia Satyr. Generally local and uncommon. ▶ Separated from other satyrs by dull *orange band* surrounding eyespots on hindwing, and *lack of strong eyespots on forewing below.* Separating these two from each other is more subtle. Georgia tends to have hindwing eyespots more elongated and often with some yellow at centers; the bands on the forewing below are orange and often faint. Helicta tends to have hindwing spots more rounded or oval, usually without yellow centers; bands on forewing below are brown and usually strong. Georgia Satyr occurs at least from North Carolina to Florida to Alabama and Mississippi, around wet boggy areas. Helicta lives around bogs in New Jersey, perhaps marshes south of Miami, Florida, but mainly in dry upland woods from the Carolinas to Mississippi. The two may hybridize, and many individuals are probably unidentifiable in the field. 🌱 **Larval foodplant:** Probably only sedges for both species.

MITCHELL'S SATYR   *Neonympha mitchellii*

An endangered species, very rare and local in shady bogs. Apparently extirpated from former localities in New Jersey, Maryland, and Ohio, now known mainly from Michigan and North Carolina, with a recent report from northern Alabama. ▶ Small, delicate, with wings somewhat translucent. Suggests Georgia or Helicta Satyr, with dull orange bands surrounding eyespots on hindwing, but has *three or four eyespots on forewing below,* at least two of them prominent. Hindwing eyespots are rather rounded, more like Helicta than Georgia Satyr. 🌱 **Larval foodplant:** Sedges.

PINE SATYR   *Paramacera allyni*

An Arizona specialty, limited to pine forests high in the Chiricahua and Huachuca Mountains. Males perch on tall shrubs or ferns in clearings to await females. Flies in summer (1 brood). ▶ Below tan to pinkish brown with pale median band and row of *well-developed eyespots on hindwing;* large *yellow-ringed eyespot near forewing tip* stands out. Above olive-brown with black spots along margin. No similar species occur in its restricted range. 🌱 **Larval foodplant:** Unknown, grasses suspected.

SATYRS

actual size

Georgia Satyr

Helicta Satyr

Mitchell's Satyr

Pine Satyr

SATYRS

Instead of eyespots, the first three below have gray patches with metallic gemlike markings on their hindwings below. Their wings remain closed after landing. Adults walk with jerky motions.

GEMMED SATYR *Cyllopsis gemma*

Close to the ground is where one normally finds this small gem, often around wet grassy areas in open woodlands. Not known to visit flowers. Flies all year in south Texas, mainly spring to fall elsewhere (3 broods). ▶ Below grayish brown with *soft violet patch* along hindwing margin containing s*mall, metallic silvery blue speckles.* Above light brown. All other satyrs in its range have eyespots. 🌱 **Larval foodplant:** Grasses.

CANYONLAND SATYR *Cyllopsis pertepida*

As its name suggests, most at home in rocky canyons and ravines of the southwest, but also found on wooded hillsides. Flies in summer (1–2 broods). ▶ The "gemmed" hindwing pattern identifies it in most of its U.S. range. In southern Arizona, where it overlaps with the very similar Nabokov's Satyr, some have an *orange flush* on the forewing. On hindwing below, the reddish postmedian line *curves outward* above the gray marginal patch, not reaching the leading margin of the wing. 🌱 **Larval foodplant:** Grasses.

NABOKOV'S SATYR *Cyllopsis pyracmon*

A borderland specialty of shaded midelevation woodlands and well-watered canyons, sometimes found with Red and Canyonland Satyrs. Attracted to mud. Flies in late spring and again late summer to fall (2 broods); spring and fall broods were formerly considered separate species. ▶ Below tan to grayish brown (spring) or tan to reddish brown (fall) with no orange flush on forewing. On hindwing below, postmedian line *runs toward leading margin.* (This may require a close look, as line is often sharply bent between gray marginal patch and leading margin.) 🌱 **Larval foodplant:** Bullgrass, Pinyon ricegrass, bulb panic grass, and others.

RED-BORDERED SATYR *Gyrocheilus patrobas*

This big dark satyr appears during the last days of summer, flopping along through mountain woodlands of the southwest. Adults feed at both mud and flowers. Flies early fall (1 brood). ▶ Mostly rich, velvety, blackish brown, with a broad marginal band of maroon, violet, and yellow on hindwing below and reddish brown along hindwing margin above. No similar species in its range. 🌱 **Larval foodplant:** Bullgrass.

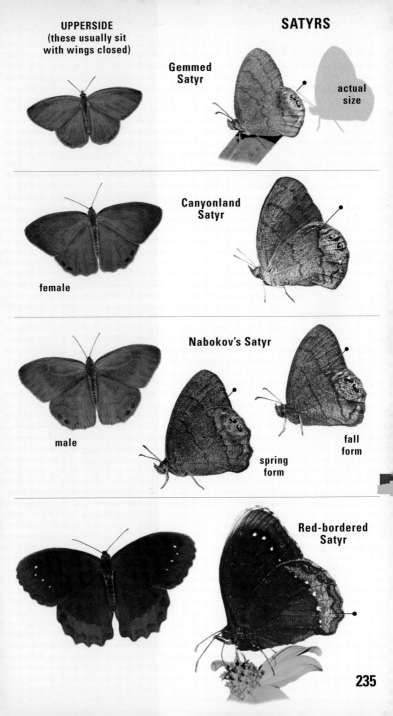

UPPERSIDE
(these usually sit
with wings closed)

SATYRS

Gemmed Satyr

actual size

Canyonland Satyr

female

Nabokov's Satyr

male

spring form

fall form

Red-bordered Satyr

235

WOOD-NYMPHS

These satyrs have a rather weak, erratic flight with a bouncing or floppy motion. Adults visit mud, rotting fruit, and dung, but they are also more fond of flowers than most satyrs.

COMMON WOOD-NYMPH   *Cercyonis pegala*

A big brown satyr, very common in woodland edges and fields of the east, more local in arid west. Flies in summer (1 brood). ▶ Geographically variable. Some populations easily known by *forewing patch of yellow-orange* (much of the east) or pale yellow (females in parts of the west). In northeast and most of west, pale patch is lacking. Usually has two yellow-ringed black eyespots on forewing, *the lower one often larger*, unlike next species in west (but some in southeast have lower spot small or absent). Hindwing below with or without small eyespots. ❧ **Larval foodplant:** Grasses.

GREAT BASIN WOOD-NYMPH   *Cercyonis sthenele*

A western species, locally common. Generally found in more arid habitats than other wood-nymphs. Flies late spring through summer (1 brood). ▶ Similar to forms of Common Wood-Nymph in its range, but smaller. On forewing below, lower eyespot is the *same size as* or *smaller than* upper eyespot. Forewing postmedian band is often fainter and extends only about *halfway up the upper eyespot* (extends to top of eyespot on Common Wood-Nymph). Hindwing below with or without eyespots. ❧ **Larval foodplant:** Grasses.

MEAD'S WOOD-NYMPH   *Cercyonis meadii*

Replaces the Great Basin Wood-Nymph to the east and south, in sagebrush flats, open woodlands, canyons. Usually uncommon. Flies in late summer (1 brood). ▶ Similar to Great Basin Wood-Nymph but forewing below has a *strong red-orange flush*. Hindwing below has a variable number of small eyespots. Above evenly brown with variable red-orange on forewing. ❧ **Larval foodplant:** Grasses.

SMALL WOOD-NYMPH   *Cercyonis oetus*

A smaller wood-nymph of sagebrush hillsides and flats, open woodlands, prairies. Common. Usually at higher elevations than Great Basin Wood-Nymph. Flies in summer (1 brood). ▶ On forewing below, lower eyespot is *smaller* than upper one and *closer to the wing margin*; postmedian line usually faint, extending only to bottom of upper eyespot. Hindwing postmedian line below (often hard to see) usually has two outward points. ❧ **Larval foodplant:** Grasses.

WOOD-NYMPHS

UPPERSIDE
(these sit with
wings closed)

actual
size

southeast

west

variations

**Common
Wood-Nymph**

**Great Basin
Wood-Nymph**

**Mead's
Wood-Nymph**

**Small
Wood-Nymph**

237

EYED BROWN   *Satyrodes eurydice*

A satyr of marshes and wet meadows, sometimes common, staying low in open areas. Flies in midsummer (1 brood). ▶ Strong eyespots on forewing and hindwing, both above and below. (Some midwestern populations, "Smoky" Eyed Browns, are darker and have five, not four, eyespots on forewing below.) Larger than Little Wood-Satyr (p. 230) with different eyespot pattern. 🌿 **Larval foodplant:** Sedges.

APPALACHIAN BROWN   *Satyrodes appalachia*

Uncommon and local in wet wooded areas. Flies spring to fall in south (2–3 broods), summer in north (1 brood). ▶ Similar to Eyed Brown but usually has postmedian and basal lines below *less jagged;* usually has spots on forewing below much more uneven and somewhat more isolated, *not* connected by a single surrounding pale line. Habitat is a clue, but the two sometimes fly together. 🌿 **Larval foodplant:** Sedges.

NORTHERN PEARLY-EYE   *Enodia anthedon*

Locally common near rocky creeks and clearings in deciduous woods. Pearly-eyes fly fast in the shadows, perch on tree trunks. They visit mud, sap, even carrion, but not flowers. Flies in midsummer (1 brood) in north, late spring to early fall (2 broods) farther south. ▶ Usually longer-winged, more boldly marked than browns. Can be very similar to next species, but antennal clubs black at base; eyespots on forewing below may form straighter line. 🌿 **Larval foodplant:** Grasses.

SOUTHERN PEARLY-EYE   *Enodia portlandia*

Locally common around canebrakes in moist southern woods. Flies spring to fall (2–3 broods). ▶ Very similar to Northern Pearly-eye, but often shows *more white* below; antennal clubs *rich yellow,* not black at base. Row of eyespots on forewing below may appear to curve toward wingtip. Note range and habitat. 🌿 **Larval foodplant:** Giant cane (*Arundinaria*).

CREOLE PEARLY-EYE   *Enodia creola*

Rare and local around canebrakes in deep woods of the south. Flies spring to fall (2 broods). ▶ Resembles other pearly-eyes but has eyespots on hindwing below more isolated, not connected; postmedian line on forewing *bulges outward* near leading edge; usually has *five* eyespots on forewing, not four. Male has more pointed forewing, dark scaling above. 🌿 **Larval foodplant:** Giant cane.

BROWNS, PEARLY-EYES

"smoky" form

typical form

actual size

Eyed Brown

Appalachian Brown

Northern Pearly-eye

Southern Pearly-eye

Creole Pearly-eye

male

male

male

COMMON RINGLET   *Coenonympha tullia*

Widespread and common in the west and north. Adults fly weakly close to the ground in grassy areas, commonly stopping at flowers, unlike many satyrs. In recent decades, has expanded its range southward in the northeastern U.S., and is now common there. Flies from spring to fall (2 broods) or in summer (1 brood). ▶ Remarkably variable geographically, and may constitute more than one species. Overall color varies: creamy white (California and southwest Oregon), yellow-cream (most of west), yellow-orange (most of Canada) blending to orange-brown (eastern Canada) and two-toned white and yellow-cream (northwest Canada and Alaska). Hindwing below has a *pale median band* (often discontinuous), thickened near the center, and a row of black submarginal eyespots (or pale spots) present or absent. Most populations have some individuals with a black spot near tip of forewing below. Populations from Great Basin southward to Arizona/New Mexico generally have well-developed row of spots along submargin below. Populations elsewhere have submarginal spots faint or lacking altogether. 🌿 **Larval foodplant:** Grasses.

HAYDEN'S RINGLET   *Coenonympha haydenii*

A brownish ringlet with a restricted range, locally common. Adults fly weakly over flower-laden meadows, grassy slopes, other openings in coniferous forest. Flies in midsummer (1 brood). ▶ Below gray-brown with *bold marginal eyespots* on hindwing, black narrowly ringed with orange. Above unmarked gray-brown. Females are paler above and below. Compare to Common Alpine (next page). 🌿 **Larval foodplant:** Grasses.

RIDINGS'S SATYR   *Neominois ridingsii*

A grayish, mothlike satyr, marked to blend with soil, rocks, or dry grass in western grasslands. Adults usually remain invisible on the ground until disturbed, then fly a short distance before disappearing again into the substrate. Flies in summer (normally 1 brood). ▶ Below speckled and striated grayish tan. Above grayish tan with dirty white or pale yellow *oblong spots* forming a submarginal band with two or more black eyespots on forewing. (**Note:** recently claimed as a separate species is the Swale Satyr, *N. wyomingo,* from isolated pockets in the central Rockies. Identical to Ridings's, it flies later in the season, usually perches in gullies.) 🌿 **Larval foodplant:** Blue grama grass.

actual size

northeast

Colorado variations

California

Common Ringlet

Alaska

Arizona

Great Basin

northwest

Hayden's Ringlet

Ridings's Satyr

These dusky satyrs live in alpine and arctic habitats. They tend to hug the ground in weak, fluttery flight. Some are common visitors to flowers.

COMMON ALPINE *Erebia epipsodea*

The most frequently encountered alpine in the west in a variety of habitats, including mountain meadows and parklands, mainly below treeline. Flies in summer (1 brood). ► Eyespots on hindwing below usually separate this alpine from others. Below mostly dark reddish brown, grayish on outer third of hindwing. Above dark reddish brown with orange submarginal patches containing eyespots. 🦋 **Larval foodplant:** Grasses.

VIDLER'S ALPINE *Erebia vidleri*

In limited range, often common in lush alpine meadows. Flies in summer (1 brood). ► Below hindwing reddish brown with obvious pale postmedian band. Above dark red-brown with orange patches containing eyespots on both wings. Most similar to Common Alpine but has checkered fringes, *lacks* eyespots on hindwing below. 🦋 **Larval foodplant:** Grasses.

TAIGA ALPINE *Erebia mancinus*

Locally common in wet, open spruce forest, tamarack bogs. Recently shown to be a separate species from Disa Alpine. Flies early to midsummer (1 brood), biennial in some areas. ► Below hindwing grayish brown with s*mall white spot near center,* dark gray median band. Above reddish brown; forewing submarginal pale orange patch contains black spots, and some orange flush extends inward. 🦋 **Larval foodplant:** Unknown.

DISA ALPINE *Erebia disa*

Restricted to wet boggy tundra along the Arctic coast, locally common. Flies in midsummer (1 brood), biennial. ► Very similar to Taiga Alpine, but hindwing below has more distinct bands and more obvious white spot near center. Forewing above has orange more restricted to submarginal patch containing black spots, not extending inward. 🦋 **Larval foodplant:** Unknown.

COLORADO ALPINE *Erebia callias*

Central Rockies only, where common near and above timberline. Adults occasionally bask with wings open. Flies in mid- to late summer (1 brood). ► Below hindwing rather smoothly mottled *gray,* forewing *reddish brown,* a distinctive color combination in its range. Above dark brown with reddish flush containing a pair of spots on the forewing. Spots on hindwing faint or absent. 🦋 **Larval foodplant:** Unknown.

ALPINES

actual size

Common Alpine

Vidler's Alpine

Taiga Alpine

Disa Alpine

Colorado Alpine

ROSS'S ALPINE *Erebia rossii*

Mainly the far north, in boggy areas in arctic tundra. Flight is slow and bouncy. Flies in summer (1 brood). ▶ Variable. Below hindwing dark brown (lighter on female) with pale postmedian band. Forewing flushed red, with one to three white-centered black spots (small or large, often fused together) near forewing tip circled in orange or red. 🐛 **Larval foodplant**: Sedges.

YOUNG'S (FOUR-DOTTED) ALPINE *Erebia (dabanensis) youngi*

A small Siberian species, common in dry, short grass tundra. Flies in summer (1 brood). ▶ Below hindwing gray-brown (lighter on female) with irregular dark median band. Forewing below with orange submarginal band enclosing three or four black dots. Above dark brown with four black spots encircled by orange on forewing, sometimes with row of spots on hindwing circled with pale orange. 🐛 **Larval foodplant**: Unknown.

ESKIMO ALPINE *Erebia occulta*

Restricted to dry gravelly areas in rocky habitats in Yukon and Alaska. Some consider this to belong to the same species as Scree Alpine of Siberia. Flies in summer (1 brood). ▶ Below hindwing gray-brown with relatively little contrast, forewing with orange spots along submargin containing small black points. Above submarginal row of orange spots with or without tiny black centers. 🐛 **Larval foodplant**: Unknown.

REDDISH ALPINE *Erebia kozhantshikovi*

A Siberian alpine also known from Alaska, Yukon, and Northwest Territories. Apt to be found in low shrub tundra near sedges. Flies in summer (1 brood). ▶ Below hindwing gray-brown overlaid by red hairs, with contrasting dark and pale bands. Very similar to Four-dotted Alpine but has redder hindwing below, and habitat often differs. Forewing below with orange submarginal band enclosing three or four black dots. 🐛 **Larval foodplant**: Unknown.

BANDED ALPINE *Erebia fasciata*

Widespread in the Canadian and Alaskan Arctic. Adults can often be seen slowly fluttering in and around wet cotton-grass swales. Flies in summer (1 brood). ▶ No eyespots on either wing above or below. Below with very strong pattern of contrasting gray and brown bands. Above dark brown with variable amounts of red flush on forewing. 🐛 **Larval foodplant**: Unknown.

UPPERSIDE
(these usually sit
with wings closed)

ALPINES

Ross's
Alpine

actual
size

variations

Young's
Alpine

Eskimo
Alpine

Reddish
Alpine

variations

Banded
Alpine

245

Three distinctive species, usually not difficult to identify.

MAGDALENA ALPINE   *Erebia magdalena*

A big, dark alpine, locally common on barren rock-slides near or above treeline. Flight may appear weak, but adults are able to sail up and over huge boulders with the greatest of ease, eluding humans who desire a closer look. Flies in summer (1 brood). ▶ Above and below essentially *unmarked black* with a greenish tinge. Best identified by shape and habitat. Adults from northwestern Canada and Alaska have a red-orange flush on the forewing and are sometimes considered a separate species, Mt. McKinley Alpine *(E. mackinleyensis)*. 🌿 **Larval foodplant:** Grasses.

RED-DISKED ALPINE   *Erebia discoidalis*

Wide-ranging from Quebec and the upper Great Lakes region across Canada to Alaska. A rather plain alpine of bog edges, wet or dry grassy forest openings, and moist prairie areas. Flies late spring or summer (1 brood). ▶ No eyespots above or below on either wing. Below hindwing dark gray, progressively lighter and more striated toward outer edge. Forewing below *flushed with red,* variable. Above unmarked dark brown with red flush on forewing, variable. Compare to Mt. McKinley form of Magdalena Alpine, above. 🌿 **Larval foodplant:** Bluegrass, possibly sedges.

THEANO ALPINE   *Erebia theano*

Very localized within its scattered and isolated populations. Adults fly weakly about moist or dry alpine habitats, often visiting flowers. Flies in midsummer (1 brood), biennial. ▶ Small and dark although often adorned with cream and orange spots forming bands. Above dark brown, both wings with postmedian red-orange dashes not centered with black dots. Below dark brown with faint orange postmedian dashes on forewing and postmedian cream spots on hindwing. *Bicolored effect* of spots is distinctive, but spots on both surfaces may be reduced or absent on individuals from northwestern Canada and Alaska. 🌿 **Larval foodplant:** Unknown.

UPPERSIDE
(these usually sit
with wings closed)

ALPINES

actual size

Magdalena Alpine

Alaska and northwest Canada

Red-disked Alpine

Theano Alpine

variations

variations

247

ARCTICS

These satyrs are strikingly marked below to match the ground, rocks, trees, and other substrates on which they rest with wings closed. Stronger fliers than alpines but, when disturbed, fly only short distances before resettling. Most are biennial, requiring two years for their caterpillars to develop, but most fly every year somewhere in their range.

CHRYXUS ARCTIC   *Oeneis chryxus*

Widely distributed from the far north through higher mountains of the west, usually common where found. Flies in summer (1 brood). ▶ Variable. Below striated brown and gray, often (but not always) with submarginal eyespots on forewing (zero to four) and hindwing (zero to two). Forewing below with median line pointing outward below upper eyespot. Above light to rich orange-brown (cream in parts of Sierra Nevada of California), with eyespots from below repeated above.
🐛 **Larval foodplant:** Grasses and sedges.

UHLER'S ARCTIC   *Oeneis uhleri*

This small arctic thrives in dry prairies but is also found on grassy subalpine slopes and tundra. Males may hover a few feet above the ground, presumably seeking females. Flies late spring to early summer on prairies, summer in mountains (1 brood). ▶ Below variably striated brown and buff, both wings almost always with submarginal eyespots (sometimes reduced or nearly absent). Forewing below *lacks* median line. Above pale to rich orange-brown. 🐛 **Larval foodplant:** Grasses.

ALBERTA ARCTIC   *Oeneis alberta*

Mainly in Canadian prairie provinces; isolated populations farther south, often on rocky volcanic soils. Flies late spring to early summer (1 brood). ▶ Below variably striated brown and buff, often (not always) with submarginal eyespots on forewing (zero to four) and hindwing (zero to two). Forewing below with *median line pointing outward* below upper eyespot. Hindwing with median band well defined. Duller than Uhler's Arctic, usually flies earlier.🐛 **Larval foodplant:** Grasses.

SENTINEL ARCTIC   *Oeneis alpina*

A Siberian species, also found locally in the North American Arctic. Inhabits rocky areas in tundra where males hilltop to await females. Flies in summer (1 brood). ▶ Below variably striated brown and gray, with one to three submarginal eyespots on forewing and usually two on hindwing. Above orange-brown with basal two-thirds darker, especially on male. Forewings relatively *short*. 🐛 **Larval foodplant:** Unknown.

UPPERSIDE
(these usually sit
with wings closed)

ARCTICS

actual
size

typical

Chryxus
Arctic

variations

pale Sierran subspecies

Uhler's Arctic

variations

Alberta Arctic

variations

**Sentinel
Arctic**

249

These species usually lack eyespots.

WHITE-VEINED ARCTIC   *Oeneis taygete*

Widespread in Canadian and Alaskan Arctic regions with isolated populations in central Rockies. Common in wet, grassy tundra habitats of far north, scarcer in southern outposts. Flies in summer (1 brood). ▶ Below variably striated brown and buff, median band on hindwing *well defined* by lighter edges, *veins lined with white*. Above gray-brown, female browner, slightly translucent. No eyespots. Some arctics on previous page can have whitened veins below also, but those have eyespots near tip of forewing. ❧ **Larval foodplant:** Sedges.

MELISSA ARCTIC   *Oeneis melissa*

Widespread in the far north and British Columbia, with isolated populations in the central Rockies and New Hampshire's White Mountains. A grayish arctic of dry gravelly slopes in tundra, taiga, and alpine areas. Flies in summer (1 brood), biennial. ▶ Variable. Below mottled gray-brown; similar to White-veined Arctic, but median band *faint* or not defined at all. Above gray-brown, slightly translucent. Sometimes has faint eyespot on forewing. ❧ **Larval foodplant:** Sedges.

POLIXENES ARCTIC   *Oeneis polixenes*

Widespread in the far north, with scarce populations southward in Rockies, Quebec, and on Mt. Katahdin, Maine. Inhabits moist or dry alpine and arctic tundra and rocky slopes above treeline. Flies in summer (1 brood). ▶ Below mottled gray-brown, median band on hindwing defined by lighter areas on either side, veins without white. Usually grayer than White-veined Arctic. Rarely with eyespot near forewing tip. Above gray or gray-brown, some populations more translucent than others. ❧ **Larval foodplant:** Sedges and grasses.

PHILIP'S (EARLY) ARCTIC   *Oeneis rosovi*   *(not illustrated)*

A Siberian species limited to areas in Alaska and north-western Canada. Occurs with similar Polixenes Arctic in some areas but prefers spruce bogs to dry tundra. Flies in summer (1 brood). ▶ Below mottled gray-brown, with median band on hindwing well defined by lighter areas on either side, veins without white. Difficult to separate from Polixenes Arctic, but Early Arctic is usually larger and grayer where the two fly together. Above gray or gray-brown. ❧ **Larval foodplant:** Grasses.

ARCTICS

UPPERSIDE
(these usually sit
with wings closed)

actual
size

variations

**White-veined
Arctic**

Melissa Arctic

variations

variations

**Polixenes
Arctic**

variations

251

LARGE ARCTICS

These have prominent eyespots, and are often found in forested areas.

GREAT ARCTIC   *Oeneis nevadensis*

A large species of Pacific Coast woodlands. Usually not found in the company of other arctics. Adults commonly land on the trunks of trees, both living and dead. Flies in summer (1 brood). Biennial, flying mainly in even-numbered years. ▶ Orange-brown overall, with scalloped wing edges. Below hindwing variably striated brown and gray, often with a single eyespot along lower submargin, and *whitish* along leading edge. Below forewing with one to three submarginal eyespots, and *lacks* median line. Above orange-brown, the eyespots from below repeated above. Much paler in north coastal California. Male above has a dark patch of specialized scales along leading margin of forewing. ❧ **Larval foodplant:** Suspected to be grasses.

MACOUN'S ARCTIC   *Oeneis macounii*

Replaces the Great Arctic eastward across Canada. Inhabits jack pine forests, where males perch to await females in forest openings. Flies in summer (1 brood), biennial. ▶ Below hindwing variably striated brown and gray, often with a single eyespot along lower submargin. Below forewing with one to three submarginal eyespots, and lacks median line. Above orange-brown. Similar to Great Arctic but leading edge of hindwing below *grayish*, not white, and male lacks dark scale patch on forewing above. Chryxus Arctic (p. 248) similar but much smaller. ❧ **Larval foodplant:** Unknown, presumably grasses and sedges.

JUTTA ARCTIC   *Oeneis jutta*

A large gray-brown species mainly of wet tundra or black spruce and tamarack bogs, widespread across Canada to Alaska. In the Rockies, more at home in lodgepole pine forests. Adults tend to stick close to forest edges in treed habitats. Flies in summer (1 brood), biennial in some areas. ▶ The only arctic with *pale orange submarginal bands or circles usually containing black spots.* Variable. Below hindwing uniformly mottled brown and gray, sometimes with an eyespot near lower submargin. Forewing below with one to three submarginal eyespots resting on a pale orange band. Above gray-brown, forewing with pale orange bands or circles containing black spots (one to four), hindwing submarginal orange band usually with one or two black spots. ❧ **Larval foodplant:** Sedges.

UPPERSIDE
(these usually sit
with wings closed)

LARGE ARCTICS

actual
size

male

female

male,
northern coastal
California

Great
Arctic

Macoun's
Arctic

Jutta Arctic

variations

SKIPPERS

(family Hesperiidae) make up a very large worldwide group of mostly small and confusing creatures. Roughly one-third of all the butterfly species in North America belong to this family. Sometimes regarded as distinct from the true butterflies, they differ in having the club of the antenna bent, with a narrow extension (called the apiculus) in most species, and in details of the wing veins. Most skippers have stout bodies, wide heads, and relatively small wings, and many of them are very fast flyers.

Beginners are often driven to despair by the skippers because there are so many of them and because they are so subtle, so challenging to identify. Experienced butterfly watchers may love the skippers for exactly the same reasons. Although skippers are undeniably frustrating at first, a real sense of accomplishment grows as we learn to recognize our local species.

In identifying skippers, even more than with most butterflies, it is essential to study the range maps. This should be one of your first steps when you try to identify a new species. There are several groups of skippers, such as the duskywings (starting on p. 280) or the Hesperia skippers (starting on p. 312), that contain numerous very similar species, and they may be almost impossible to figure out unless you begin by narrowing down the choices to those found in your own area. With luck, you will only have to choose among four or five possibilities, rather than fifteen or twenty! Even so, until you have a lot of experience, you should expect to leave many skippers unidentified. Not even experts can recognize them all in the field.

The skippers in North America are classified in five subfamilies.

SPREAD-WING SKIPPERS (subfamily Pyrginae), pp. 256–299, include many species that sit with their wings spread open flat, although there are some that usually keep the wings folded above the back, and a few (such as the cloudywings, pp. 260–265) that characteristically sit with the wings partly open. Some spread-wings in the tropics have bright colors, but in North America most are patterned in gray, black, and white. Their larvae feed on plants from a variety of families, especially legumes, but also mallows, oaks, and others.

FIRETIPS (subfamily Pyrrhopyginae) are tropical, with only one in our area, Dull Firetip (p. 256). They suggest big spread-wing skippers, and we include them in that section, but most have bright-colored ("fiery") abdomen tips. Our "dull" species lacks this feature. It usually sits with wings partly or mostly spread. Its larvae feed on oak leaves.

SKIPPERLINGS (subfamily Heteropterinae), p. 300, include a handful of small species in the north and west. Unlike most skippers, they lack the narrow extension (apiculus) of the antennal club. They often sit with their wings spread open flat, like the spread-wings, but otherwise they look more similar to the next group, grass skippers, and we include them in that section. Their larvae feed on grasses. **Note:** a few of the true grass skippers are named "skipperlings" even though they do not belong to this subfamily.

GRASS SKIPPERS (subfamily Hesperiinae), pp. 302–357, make up the most diverse and perhaps the most challenging group of skippers. They tend to be smaller than the spread-wings on average, and many are patterned with orange or yellow. They do not sit with the wings spread open flat, but instead have a characteristic posture—sometimes called the "jet-plane position"—in which the hindwings are opened farther than the forewings. This gives us an opportunity to see the pattern of both the forewing and the hindwing, but it takes some practice to understand what we are seeing. In the illustration here, the skipper's left forewing is edge-on to us, so it is hardly visible, but we can see the hindwing on the left side and the forewing on the right side, while the right hindwing is mostly hidden. Males of many grass skippers have a patch of specialized scent scales, called the stigma, on the upperside of the forewing. Larvae of most species feed on grasses.

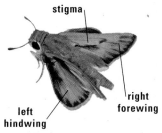

stigma

right forewing

left hindwing

GIANT-SKIPPERS (subfamily Megathyminae), pp. 358–363, include our largest skippers. Their larvae bore into the fleshy leaves and roots of yuccas, agaves, and related plants; adults of the yucca-feeding species are rather seldom seen, even where these plants are common. Like the grass skippers, they may sit with the hindwings opened farther than the forewings, but more often they sit with the wings closed. In flight they are very fast and powerful.

SHARP-LOOKING SPREAD-WINGS

SILVER-SPOTTED SKIPPER   *Epargyreus clarus*

The most easily recognized skipper across North America, in forest edges, fields, and gardens. Adults usually perch with wings closed, but may bask with wings open in early morning sun. Males patrol forest openings, often perching on low shrubs to await females. Common in east, more restricted to mountain regions in west. Flies spring through summer (1–2 broods). ▶ Note the large irregular *silver-white patch* on the hindwing below. Forewings pointed, lower hindwing angle lobed. Above brown with glassy yellow-orange band on forewing. In east, compare to Hoary Edge (next page).
🌱 **Larval foodplant:** Locusts, wisteria, and other legumes.

GOLDEN BANDED-SKIPPER   *Autochton cellus*

Usually uncommon to fairly common in southwestern woodlands, rare and local in the east. Males perch along shaded ravines, canyons, or trails to await females. Adults usually perch with wings partially open. Flies in summer (1–2 broods). ▶ Broad *golden yellow crossband on forewing* often visible even in flight. Hindwing fringe *checkered*. (Note: Sonoran Banded-Skipper (*A. pseudocellus*), not found in Arizona since 1936, is very similar but smaller, with a prominent white ring on the antenna.) 🌱 **Larval foodplant:** Hog peanut (east), wild beans, butterfly pea, and other legumes (west).

CHISOS BANDED-SKIPPER   *Autochton cincta*

Rare, found in our area only in oak woodlands of Big Bend National Park, Texas. Adults usually perch on the ground or on low branches with wings open. Flies spring to fall (2 broods). ▶ Similar to the much more common Golden Banded-Skipper but has broad *white hindwing fringes (not checkered)*; pale yellow forewing band is usually *narrower*. Below brown with two darker bands on hindwing. 🌱 **Larval foodplant:** Clovers, beggar ticks.

DULL FIRETIP   *Pyrrhopyge araxes*

A common, heavy-bodied skipper of southwestern oak woodlands. Our only representative of a tropical subfamily (**Pyrrhopyginae**), most of which show a bright tip to the abdomen — which our "dull" species lacks. Adults often perch with wings fully or partially open. Strongly attracted to flowers. Flight is direct and moderately fast, often bombing along high in the trees. Flies in late summer and early fall (1 brood). ▶ Above brown with several glassy white spots on forewing. Below brown, the body and basal region *heavily dusted yellow-orange*. 🌱 **Larval foodplant:** Emory, Toumey, Arizona white, and other oaks.

DISTINCTIVE SPREAD-WINGS

Silver-spotted Skipper

actual size

Golden Banded-Skipper

Chisos Banded-Skipper

Dull Firetip

257

LARGE SKIPPERS

HOARY EDGE   *Achalarus lyciades*

A skipper of clearings and edges of open sandy woodlands, common at times. Adults sit with wings closed or partially opened. Males perch in clearings to await females. Flies spring to fall (1–2 broods). ▶ Hindwing below has *large smeary white patch along margin,* unlike any other eastern skipper. Above brown with glassy yellow-orange patch on forewing (compare Silver-spotted Skipper, previous page). 🐛 **Larval foodplant:** Tick trefoils.

DESERT CLOUDYWING   *Achalarus casica*

Uncommon, mainly in oak-juniper woodland. Adults typically perch with wings closed. Often seen along cliffs or visiting flowers. Flies spring to fall (2 broods). ▶ Below hindwing brown with steel blue bands and bold *white patch along margin.* Above dark brown with glassy white forewing spots. Compare next three species. 🐛 **Larval foodplant:** Tick trefoils, butterfly pea.

ARIZONA SKIPPER   *Codatractus arizonensis*

A flashy skipper of arid southwestern canyons. Males perch with wings closed on cliffs or overhanging branches above canyon bottoms to find females. Flies late spring and summer (mainly 1 brood). ▶ Note contrasting pattern, wing shape, large forewing spots. Fringes checkered, hindwing slightly elongated at lower angle, variable amount of white along hindwing margin below. Above brown; glassy white forewing spots flash blue in sunlight. 🐛 **Larval foodplant:** Kidneywoods.

ACACIA SKIPPER   *Cogia hippalus*

Common brown skipper of grasslands and arid canyons in the southwest. Adults perch with wings closed. Fond of both mud and flowers. Flies spring to fall (2 broods). ▶ Below hindwing banded gray-brown, fringe white, uncheckered. White frosting along marginal line *punctuated by black dots.* Cloudywings (pp. 260–265) are somewhat similar, but usually perch with wings partly open. 🐛 **Larval foodplant:** Fern acacia.

GOLD-COSTA SKIPPER   *Cogia caicus*

Uncommon in the southwest, in same habitats as Acacia Skipper. Males perch in canyon bottoms to find females, often darting out at other insects and returning to same perch. Flies spring to fall (2 broods). ▶ Suggests Acacia Skipper (including black dots on hindwing marginal line) but smaller. Leading edge of forewing (the costa) is *contrastingly gold.* 🐛 **Larval foodplant:** Fern acacia.

SPREAD-WING SKIPPERS

BIG DARK SKIPPERS

UPPERSIDE
(most of these tend
to sit with wings closed)

actual
size

Hoary Edge

**Desert
Cloudywing**

**Arizona
Skipper**

**Acacia
Skipper**

**Gold-costa
Skipper**

259

CLOUDYWINGS

(genus *Thorybes*) make up a small group of dark skippers that can be difficult to distinguish in the field. As a group, they are often recognized by their perching posture, with wings held partly open (but they do sit in other postures as well). Adults are fast and erratic fliers.

SOUTHERN CLOUDYWING   *Thorybes bathyllus*

One of three very similar cloudywings in the east. A species of dry scrubby fields, roadsides, and other open areas. Males perch on low plants to await females and may use the same area for several days. Flies late spring and summer (mostly 2 broods, only 1 in northern areas). ► Fringes checkered tan or whitish. Above dark brown with glassy white spotband on forewing *broad and aligned*. Row of small white spots near tip of forewing forms a straight line (summer) or has the bottom spot slightly offset outward (spring). Below brown with darker brown bands. Face is often *pale*, and antennal clubs may have *white spot at bend*. Male lacks costal fold on forewing above. 🌱 **Larval foodplant:** Tick trefoils, wild beans, hog peanut, and other legumes.

NORTHERN CLOUDYWING   *Thorybes pylades*

Widespread, and often more common than other cloudywings where they occur together. Fond of both flowers and mud. Males hilltop to a degree. Flies late spring and summer (mainly 1 brood, 2 in the south). ► Fringes checkered brown. Above dark brown with tiny triangular white spots on forewing reduced and *not* aligned with each other. Face is often *dark*, and antennal clubs lack white spot at bend. Male has costal fold. Some individuals in west Texas have hindwing with white fringe and white frosting extending inward from margin below. 🌱 **Larval foodplant:** Tick trefoils, wild beans, *Cologania*, and other legumes.

CONFUSED CLOUDYWING   *Thorybes confusis*

Mainly in dry habitats in the southeast, straying northward. Generally less common than Northern and Southern Cloudywings but often found with them. Flies late spring and summer (2 broods). ► Tricky to identify because the forewing spot pattern above is so variable. These spots may be aligned and reduced (spring) or bold (summer). Row of small white spots near tip of forewing usually has bottom spot strongly *offset outward*. Fringes checkered tan or whitish. Face varies but is often *pale*, and antennal clubs lack white spot at bend. Male lacks costal fold. 🌱 **Larval foodplant:** Probably legumes.

actual size

Southern Cloudywing

Northern Cloudywing

west Texas

Confused Cloudywing

261

In addition to these three, see Northern Cloudywing (previous page), which is usually the most common member of the group in the west.

MEXICAN CLOUDYWING   *Thorybes mexicana*

A small cloudywing of western mountains. Often found on flowers or near mud in forest openings but also on rocky subalpine terrain. Males are avid hilltop-pers. Flies late spring and early summer in southern areas, summer farther north (1 brood). ▶ Above golden brown with glassy white forewing spots varying from large to small, depending on region, these spots some-times with darker outlines. Below hindwing brown with two darker bands, the outer edge often *pale gray or pinkish with fine striations*. Male has costal fold on forewing above. Smaller than Northern Cloudywing and usually occurs at higher elevations. More likely to be seen than Western Cloudywing where their ranges overlap. 🌿 **Larval foodplant**: Clovers.

DRUSIUS CLOUDYWING   *Thorybes drusius*

Mainly extreme southeastern Arizona and adjacent New Mexico, usually uncommon; rare in west Texas. A cloudywing of openings in oak woodlands, avidly visit-ing flowers. Like other cloudywings, often perches with wings partially open. Flies in mid- to late summer (1 brood), possibly earlier in the season in Texas. ▶ Dark brown with tiny white spots on forewing and *conspicu-ous white fringe on hindwing*. Note that fringe may be obscure on individuals in very worn condition. In west Texas, compare to rare white-fringed population of Northern Cloudywing, which has white frosting ex-tending farther inward on hindwing below. 🌿 **Larval foodplant**: *Cologania*.

WESTERN CLOUDYWING   *Thorybes diversus*

A rare and localized cloudywing with a restricted range, found only along western slope of the Sierra Nevada of California and limited areas of northwestern California and southwestern Oregon. Prefers wet mea-dows, streamsides, and clearings in moist coniferous forests. Flies in early summer (1 brood). ▶ Easily con-fused with both Northern and Mexican Cloudywings. Dark bands on hindwing below tend to be less distinct, and forewing may appear more pointed. Above dark brown with small narrow forewing spots, one of these spots usually *crossing the forewing cell*. Male lacks costal fold on forewing above. Fringes brown. 🌿 **Larval food-plant**: Clovers.

**Mexican
Cloudywing**

actual
size

**Drusius
Cloudywing**

less typical
posture
(not to scale)

**Western
Cloudywing**

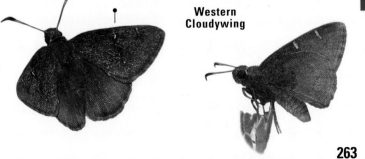

MIMOSA SKIPPER *Cogia calchas*

Extreme south Texas only. Locally common around dry lake beds, resacas, other seasonally flooded habitats. Often found perched on ground or flowers with wings closed. Flies spring to fall (3 broods). ► Forewings narrow and pointed. Above evenly brown with a row of three or four tiny white spots near tip of forewing, other spots very reduced if present. Below hindwing mottled brown with purplish basal and postmedian bands, *pale vermiculations,* and a pale gray fold near the trailing edge. 🌿 **Larval foodplant:** *Mimosa pigra.*

OUTIS SKIPPER *Cogia outis*

A small scarce skipper of semiopen country, prairies with acacias. Not well known, and may be declining in numbers. Flies spring to fall (2–3 broods). ► Forewings narrow and pointed. Usually smaller than Acacia (p. 258) or Mimosa Skipper. Hindwing fringe brown. Above brown with glassy white forewing spots very small. Below hindwing banded gray-brown. Note *white ring* at base of antennal clubs. 🌿 **Larval foodplant:** Acacias.

COYOTE CLOUDYWING *Achalarus toxeus*

A sporadic resident of south Texas, sometimes straying north to central Texas, in brushy country and thorn scrub. Recorded spring to fall (1–3 broods). ► Hindwing fringe usually bright *white.* Forewings long and pointed, crossed by *meandering, narrow, golden brown bands.* Below brown with darker brown bands. 🌿 **Larval foodplant:** Texas ebony.

JALAPUS CLOUDYWING *Achalarus jalapus*

Rare stray to south Texas, recorded from July to October. ► Practically identical to Coyote Cloudywing, but hindwing has a slight *extended lobe* at the lower angle. 🌿 **Larval foodplant:** Unknown.

VALERIANA SKIPPER *Codatractus mysie*

An Arizona specialty of red rock canyons near the Mexican border. Rare, sometimes seemingly absent for years at a time. Adults fly mainly early in the morning and perch with wings closed. Flies in late summer (1 brood). ► Easily confused with Northern Cloudywing and Acacia Skipper. Fringes brown and *boldly checkered.* Above brown with glassy white forewing spots, usually including an *hourglass-shaped spot* in the cell. Below mottled brown with broad purplish brown band on hindwing and often with buff submarginal band. Northern Cloudywing (p. 260) usually lacks hourglass spot in forewing cell and often perches with wings partly open. Acacia Skipper (p. 258) has white fringe. 🌿 **Larval foodplant:** *Tephrosia leiocarpa.*

SOUTHWESTERN SKIPPERS

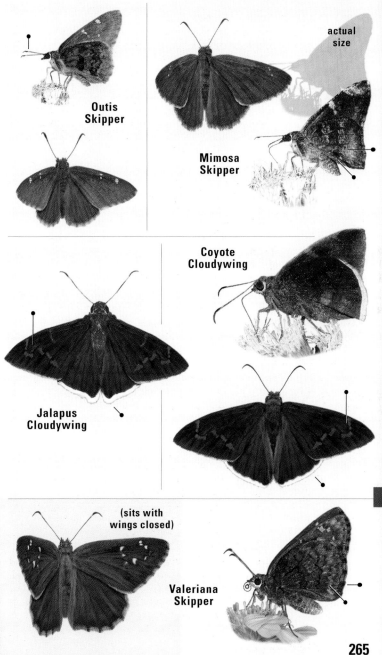

Outis Skipper

Mimosa Skipper

actual size

Coyote Cloudywing

Jalapus Cloudywing

(sits with wings closed)

Valeriana Skipper

SHORT-TAILED SKIPPER   *Zestusa dorus*

A distinctive skipper of southwestern oak woodlands. Males perch on branches on hilltops to await females. May bask with wings open or closed. Flies mainly in spring (1 brood), with an uncommon second brood in south. ▶ Short lobed tail at lower angle of hindwing. Above brown with pale olive hair basally and numerous pale yellow glassy spots, those on the hindwing connected to form a *short band*. Below hindwing mottled brown and gray with distinctive short *postmedian band of pale spots*. 🐛 **Larval foodplant:** Oaks.

HAMMOCK SKIPPER   *Polygonus leo*

Widespread in the tropics, resident in hammock edges in Florida. Strays regularly to Arizona, rarely elsewhere. Adults fly rapidly, often land underneath leaves, may perch with wings open or closed. Flies all year in southern Florida (multiple broods). ▶ Forewings slender and pointed, hindwing curves to *short lobe* at lower angle. Above dark brown with purplish sheen and *three large glassy white forewing spots*. Below hindwing brown with purplish sheen and *black spot near base*. 🐛 **Larval foodplant:** Jamaica dogwood and pongam.

MANGROVE SKIPPER   *Phocides pigmalion*

A large flashy skipper of coastal regions of central and southern Florida only. Locally common in mangrove swamps and coastal hammocks, perching on mangrove leaves and visiting flowers, especially those of morning glory. Flies all year (multiple broods). ▶ Large, colorful, and distinctive. Both above and below, mostly dark violet-blue with *thin turquoise band on hindwing*. 🐛 **Larval foodplant:** Red mangrove.

ZESTOS SKIPPER   *Epargyreus zestos*

Formerly inhabited most of southern Florida, now mainly restricted to Keys. Rare and local in and around tropical hardwood hammocks. A close relative of Silver-spotted Skipper (p. 256) but without the silvery spot. Flies most of year (multiple broods). ▶ *Long pointed forewings* with glassy yellow-orange band and spots. Below brown with purplish sheen and *pale median band* on hindwing. 🐛 **Larval foodplant:** Milk-pea *(Galactia)*.

GUAVA SKIPPER   *Phocides palemon*

South Texas only, and uncommon there, its residency dependent on ornamental plantings of Guava. Flies most of year (multiple broods). ▶ *Highly distinctive*. Above black with turquoise rays and double red spot along forewing leading edge, fringes white, thorax with turquoise stripes. Below deep shiny black with double red spot. 🐛 **Larval foodplant:** Guavas.

TROPICAL SKIPPERS

Short-tailed Skipper

actual size

typical

very fresh condition

Hammock Skipper

Mangrove Skipper

Zestos Skipper

Guava Skipper

Note that any of these in worn condition may lack the hindwing tails.

LONG-TAILED SKIPPER *Urbanus proteus*

Our most common tailed skipper. Resident mainly in the southeast but often strays well northward, especially in late summer, and may breed north of normal range; also a temporary colonist in southern Arizona and California. Larvae can become pests in bean fields in the south. Flies all year in southernmost areas (multiple broods), summer and fall northward and in west (1 brood). ▶ The only tailed skipper found regularly in our area with *green iridescence on body and wing bases above* (but see Tailed Aguna, p. 272). Below similar to Dorantes Longtail but has submarginal dark band on forewing continuous, not broken, and more solid dark postmedian band on hindwing. 🌿 **Larval foodplant**: Many legumes, especially beans.

DORANTES LONGTAIL *Urbanus dorantes*

More limited in the southeast than Long-tailed Skipper, but more regular than that species in Arizona. Usually perches with wings closed or slightly open. Flies all year in Florida and Texas (multiple broods), late summer to fall in the southwest (1 brood). ▶ Similar to Long-tailed Skipper but *lacks green iridescence above*. Below has hindwing pattern more broken up (including dark basal spot), *forewing submarginal band interrupted*. Adults often encountered without tails. 🌿 **Larval foodplant**: Many legumes, including tick trefoils.

BROWN LONGTAIL *Urbanus procne*

A common plain brown tailed skipper of south Texas, often found with the similar Teleus Longtail. Rarely strays to the southwest. Adults may perch with wings closed or wide open. Flies most of year (multiple broods). ▶ Hindwing with long tails. Above evenly brown, sometimes with a short thin white stripe extending down from the leading edge of the forewing. Male has costal fold on forewing. 🌿 **Larval foodplant**: Bermuda, Johnson, and other grasses.

TELEUS LONGTAIL *Urbanus teleus*

South Texas only, common. Often found with the similar Brown Longtail. Flies most of year (multiple broods). ▶ Hindwing with long tails. Above evenly brown, forewing usually crossed by long thin glassy white diagonal band, as well as a short row of white dots near tip. Male lacks costal fold on forewing. 🌿 **Larval foodplant**: *Paspalum* and other grasses.

RESIDENT LONGTAILS

actual size

Long-tailed Skipper

Dorantes Longtail

without tail

Brown Longtail

Teleus Longtail

WHITE-STRIPED LONGTAIL   *Chioides catillus*

Regular in southern Texas, straying north to the center of the state; also a periodic resident of southern Arizona and adjacent New Mexico. Males perch on plants in canyon bottoms, darting out at rival males or other insects, then often returning to the same perch. Adults usually rest with wings closed. Flies all year in south Texas (multiple broods), spring to fall in the southwest (2 broods). ▶ Very long tails and *prominent white stripe on the hindwing below* will readily identify this species. Also note the dark wedge at the tip of the forewing below. 🐛 **Larval foodplant:** Wild beans, milk peas, and other viny legumes.

ZILPA LONGTAIL   *Chioides zilpa*

The zippy Zilpa is a regular stray to south Texas, rarely reaching southeastern Arizona. Attracted to mud as well as flowers. Adults usually perch with wings closed. Recorded spring to late fall in Texas, late summer and fall in Arizona. ▶ Tails very long. Strongly *variegated pattern below*, especially on hindwing, unlike any other species in our area. 🐛 **Larval foodplant:** Legume vines in the genus *Nissolia*.

MOTTLED LONGTAIL   *Typhedanus undulatus*

A rare stray to south Texas, recorded in fall. ▶ Long tails. Below hindwing *mottled* brown with bluish black bands, leaving a *lighter brown area along margin*. Dark spot near tip of forewing below. Above brown with glassy white spots on forewing. 🐛 **Larval foodplant:** Sennas.

EIGHT-SPOTTED LONGTAIL   *Polythrix octomaculata*

Rare stray to south Texas, recorded spring to fall. Lands with wings opened flat. ▶ Tails short (especially on males); two short glassy white bands on forewing. Below brown with darker postmedian band, some females with white median patch. Above brown with two indistinct darker brown bands on hindwing. 🐛 **Larval foodplant:** Legumes.

MEXICAN LONGTAIL   *Polythrix mexicana*

Rare stray to south Texas, recorded summer to fall. Lands with wings opened flat. ▶ Long narrow tails, sometimes expanded at tip. Broad glassy white spotbands across forewings, and two indistinct darker brown bands on hindwing, visible above and below. 🐛 **Larval foodplant:** Legumes.

WHITE-TAILED LONGTAIL   *Urbanus doryssus*

Distinctive rare stray to south Texas, reported in spring and fall. ▶ Tails *short and white*. Evenly dark brown above and below, with white hindwing margins. 🐛 **Larval foodplant:** Legumes.

SCARCER LONGTAILS

actual size

White-striped Longtail

Zilpa Longtail

Mottled Longtail

Eight-spotted Longtail

Mexican Longtail

White-tailed Longtail

271

RARE TROPICAL SKIPPERS

These are all large skippers with white patches or stripes on the hindwing below. They sometimes stray into our tropical border regions, where they are prize finds for butterfly watchers.

GOLD-SPOTTED AGUNA *Aguna asander*

An occasional stray to south Texas, rarely to Arizona. Lands with wings open or closed. Recorded spring to fall in Texas. ▶ Large and brown with a slight tail on the lower angle of the hindwing and large *pale amber spots* across the forewing. Below hindwing purplish brown, with a white band that can be highly variable from narrow, straight, and well developed to faint and diffuse. ❦ **Larval foodplant:** Orchid trees *(Bauhinia)*.

TAILED AGUNA *Aguna metophis*

A rare stray to south Texas, recorded in summer and fall. ▶ Tails *short.* Below brown with white median band *diffused outwardly.* Above brown with glassy pale spots on forewings, *blue-green iridescence at wing bases.* Compare to much more common Long-tailed Skipper (p. 268), also flashers (p. 278). ❦ **Larval foodplant:** Orchid trees.

MERCURIAL SKIPPER *Proteides mercurius*

Very widespread in the tropics; a rare stray north to Florida, Louisiana, Texas, and Arizona. Recorded spring to fall in southern Texas. ▶ Forewings very long and narrow, *head and thorax gold.* Below reddish brown with white frosting. Above dark brown, gold basally with small glassy white spots on forewing. ❦ **Larval foodplant:** Legumes.

WHITE-CRESCENT LONGTAIL *Codatractus alcaeus*

Occasionally reported from southern and western Texas in summer or fall. Usually perches with wings closed. ▶ Tails long. Below hindwing strongly mottled brown with *white patch along submargin.* Above brown with grayish hair basally and large glassy amber spots on forewing. Similar to Zilpa Longtail (previous page), but that species lacks white along submargin on the hindwing below and has a dark brown triangle near the forewing tip below. ❦ **Larval foodplant:** Legumes.

BROKEN SILVERDROP *Epargyreus exadeus*

Rare stray to south Texas. Part of a complex of similar-looking tropical skippers that are most surely identified by lab dissection. ▶ Below hindwing brown with central silver spot and faint silver lines. Above dark brown with pale gold hair basally and glassy white forewing spots. Similar to the very common Silver-spotted Skipper (p. 256), but that species has a larger silver patch below and larger pale gold bands and spots on the forewing. ❦ **Larval foodplant:** Legumes.

RARE TROPICAL SKIPPERS

Gold-spotted
Aguna

actual
size

variations

Tailed
Aguna

Mercurial
Skipper

White-crescent
Longtail

Broken
Silverdrop

ARIZONA POWDERED-SKIPPER   *Systasea zampa*

A small skipper of southwestern deserts, usually perching with wings opened flat. Might be passed off as a moth; appears drab at a distance, but close study of a fresh individual reveals a beautiful pattern. Males perch and patrol at gully junctions or circular alcoves along the base of steep canyon walls. Flies most of year (multiple broods). ▶ *Scalloped hindwing edges* and pale brown tones distinguish this from all but next species. Above variegated tan, orange-brown, and olive; forewing has pale median band with *jagged inner edge*. Below pale tan. ❦ **Larval foodplant:** Various mallows.

TEXAS POWDERED-SKIPPER   *Systasea pulverulenta*

A close relative of the Arizona Powdered-Skipper. Partly separated by range, but the two occur together in west Texas and locally near the Mexican border in Arizona. Adults normally perch with wings open. Flies most of year (multiple broods). ▶ Very much like Arizona Powdered-Skipper, but pale median band on forewing has *inner edge smoothly curved,* not jutting inward. ❦ **Larval foodplant:** Various mallows.

SICKLE-WINGED SKIPPER   *Achylodes thraso*

A distinctive south Texan, fairly common at woodland edges, gardens. Sometimes strays north. Avidly visits flowers, usually perches with wings opened flat. Flies all year (multiple broods). ▶ Forewing tips *hooked*. Above brown with purplish sheen and lighter spots. Female is browner above. Easily identified when in fresh condition, but worn individuals can be more confusing. ❦ **Larval foodplant:** Lime prickly-ash (*Zanthoxylum*).

VARIEGATED SKIPPER   *Gorgythion begga*

Rare stray to extreme southern Texas at various seasons. Small and easily overlooked. Often sits with wings folded downward. ▶ Above strongly variegated dark brown with faint purplish sheen. Tips of forewings somewhat pointed. Below brown. ❦ **Larval foodplant:** Unknown.

GLAZED PELLICIA   *Pellicia arina*

Periodic stray to south Texas, reported March to December. ▶ Above almost black, vaguely banded, with purple sheen extending outward from base. Below banded purplish brown. Female lighter both above and below. ❦ **Larval foodplant:** Unknown.

PURPLISH-BLACK SKIPPER   *Nisoniades rubescens*

Rare stray to south Texas, recorded in fall. ▶ Above banded brownish black with small white dots near forewing tip. Below banded brown. Female lighter both above and below. ❦ **Larval foodplant:** Morning glories.

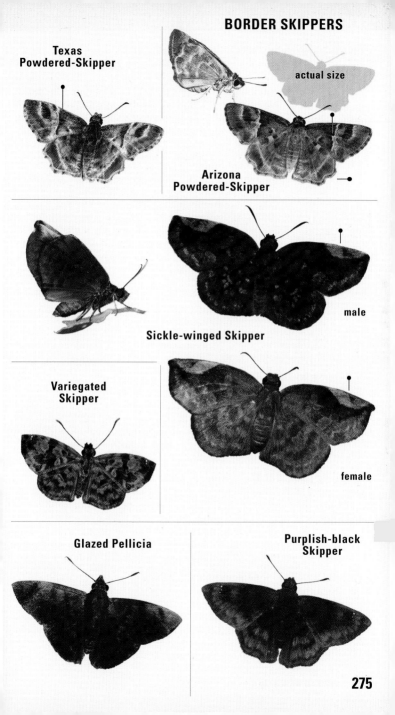

BORDER SKIPPERS

Texas Powdered-Skipper

actual size

Arizona Powdered-Skipper

Sickle-winged Skipper

male

Variegated Skipper

female

Glazed Pellicia

Purplish-black Skipper

275

BROWN-BANDED SKIPPER   *Timochares ruptifasciatus*

A resident of south Texas, straying north to central Texas; irregular stray into the southwest. Adults usually perch with wings open. Flies spring to late fall (multiple broods). ▶ Above orange-brown with broken bands of darker spots on forewing and three dark bands on hindwing. Pattern below similar but paler. ❧ **Larval foodplant**: Barbados cherry.

POTRILLO SKIPPER   *Cabares potrillo*

Resident of south Texas, straying north to central Texas; very rare stray to Arizona. Often lands on shrubs with wings partly opened. Flies all year in south Texas (multiple broods). ▶ Hindwing slightly pointed at outer angle. Above brown with glassy white spotband on forewing containing a *saddle-shaped spot* in cell. Below banded olive-brown. ❧ **Larval foodplant**: Priva.

HERMIT SKIPPER   *Grais stigmatica*

A large brown skipper that strays to south Texas, reported spring to fall; one recent Arizona record. Adults perch with wings fully open, often on the undersides of leaves. ▶ Large, with long forewings. Above brown with slightly darker spots forming bands. Larger and less heavily and evenly banded than Brown-banded Skipper, and with *dark patch in center of forewing*. ❧ **Larval foodplant**: Jopoy.

FALCATE SKIPPER   *Spathilepia clonius*

Periodically found in extreme south Texas, probably resident some years. Rests with wings partly open. Males perch in clearings to await females. Recorded spring and fall (possibly 2 broods). ▶ Forewing tips *extended and squared off*, wing edges slightly scalloped. Above dark brown with *broad glassy white band* on forewing. Below hindwing mottled brown with dark brown triangular mark along leading edge. ❧ **Larval foodplant**: Legumes.

FRITZGAERTNER'S FLAT   *Celaenorrhinus fritzgaertneri*

Rare stray to extreme southern Texas (spring to fall) and Arizona (summer). Active at dawn and dusk, resting during the day under rock overhangs, highway culverts, other dark recesses. Sits with wings opened flat. ▶ Above gray-brown, forewing with glassy white spots and a small dark spot near base; hindwing has pale checkered pattern, and wing fringes checkered gray and white. ❧ **Larval foodplant**: Acanthus family plants.

STALLINGS'S FLAT   *Celaenorrhinus stallingsi*

Stray to south Texas only. Flies mainly in early morning or evening, resting under leaves during the rest of the day. Adults sit with wings opened flat. Recorded spring to fall. ▶ Similar to Fritzgaertner's Flat but smaller, and *lacks* the dark spot near the base of the forewing; wing fringes are usually *plainer*. ❧ **Larval foodplant**: Unknown.

BORDER SKIPPERS

Potrillo
Skipper

Brown-banded
Skipper

actual size

Hermit
Skipper

Falcate
Skipper

Stallings's Flat

Fritzgaertner's Flat

277

FLASHERS

are large, brightly marked skippers of tropical forest regions. In our area they have been found mainly in extreme southern Texas, with one regular species and others occurring as strays.

TWO-BARRED FLASHER   *Astraptes fulgerator*

Regular at times in south Texas; rare stray to southeastern Arizona. Adults usually perch with wings opened flat and will often seek shelter underneath leaves. Flies most of year in Texas (2 or more broods). ▶ Above black with *turquoise-blue* on head, body, and base of wings. Forewing with glassy white diagonal band and minute white dots near tip. Below hindwing brown with leading edge white at base. *Underside of head and thorax are yellow.* Compare to Long-tailed Skipper (p. 268) and Tailed Aguna (p. 272), which sometimes lack tails. ✤ **Larval foodplant:** Coyotillo.

FROSTED FLASHER   *Astraptes alardus*

An irregular stray to wooded areas of south Texas, similar in behavior to Two-barred Flasher. Recorded June to October. ▶ Resembles Two-barred Flasher (with turquoise-blue on head, body, and base of wings above) but larger, and *lacks* pale bands or spots on forewing. Hindwing below brown with *broad white frosted margin.* ✤ **Larval foodplant:** Coral bean.

GILBERT'S FLASHER   *Astraptes gilberti*

Rare stray to south Texas, recorded in October. ▶ Similar to two preceding species, but color above on body and base of wings may be darker blue. Lacks forewing bars shown by Two-barred Flasher and white hindwing margin below of Frosted Flasher; hindwing below is white only at *base of leading edge.* ✤ **Larval foodplant:** Orchid tree *(Bauhinia).*

SMALL-SPOTTED FLASHER   *Astraptes egregius*

Very rare stray to extreme south Texas (once in October). In Mexico males perch on vegetation along forest openings in the afternoon to await females. ▶ Above black with blue-green on head, body, and base of wings. Forewing with small white median spots and tiny white dots near tip. Below banded dark brown with narrow pale yellowish margin on hindwing. ✤ **Larval foodplant:** Unknown.

YELLOW-TIPPED FLASHER   *Astraptes anaphus*

Irregular stray to south Texas. Adults usually perch with wings open. Records are from both spring and fall. ▶ Above mostly brown with vague bands. Hindwing is lobed at lower angle and *tipped bright yellow.* Below hindwing brown with bands more distinct and broad yellow along lower margin. ✤ **Larval foodplant:** Legumes.

FLASHERS

Two-barred Flasher

actual size

Frosted Flasher

Gilbert's Flasher

Small-spotted Flasher

Yellow-tipped Flasher

279

make up a challenging complex. Most are very similar; the problem is compounded by regional variations, differences between sexes, and individuals in worn condition. Adults usually land with wings open but may rest with them closed or folded downward.

JUVENAL'S DUSKYWING   *Erynnis juvenalis*

Common and widespread in eastern oak woodland, local in mountains of southwest. Flies mostly in spring in east (1 brood), spring and summer in southwest (2 broods). ▶ Larger than most eastern duskywings, with more obvious glassy white spots on forewing, usually including *one at end of cell*. Female has forewing grayer, more boldly marked than male. Hindwing below usually has *two pale spots near upper margin*. Southwestern populations have *white fringes* and lack the two pale spots below. ✤ **Larval foodplant:** Oaks.

HORACE'S DUSKYWING   *Erynnis horatius*

Large duskywing of eastern oak woodland. Flies spring to fall (2–3 broods). ▶ Large, fringes brown. Male above dark brown with little contrast and faint white spots on forewing, *usually one at end of cell*. Female forewing above grayer with more contrast and larger glassy spots. Hindwing below *lacks* the two pale spots that Juvenal's *usually* has; male Horace's is often plainer and browner above; eastern Juvenal's fly mainly in spring. Compare Zarucco Duskywing (below), Wild Indigo Duskywing (p. 286). ✤ **Larval foodplant:** Oaks.

ZARUCCO DUSKYWING   *Erynnis zarucco*

Common in southeast in scrub, fields, coastal sandy areas. Flies spring to fall, or all year in south Florida (multiple broods). ▶ Fringes brown (rarely white in south Florida). Male similar to male Horace's, with forewing above dark brown, but has *pale brown patch* at end of cell, whitish cell spot *absent or faint*. Female very similar to female Wild Indigo Duskywing (p. 286); may be more uniformly dark below, but often not identifiable. ✤ **Larval foodplant:** Locusts and other legumes.

FUNEREAL DUSKYWING   *Erynnis funeralis*

Replaces Zarucco Duskywing to the west. Often common in open habitats, from deserts to gardens. Flies spring to fall (multiple broods). ▶ Forewing long and narrow, rather pointed. Hindwing squarish with *prominent white fringes*. Above forewing mostly dark brown with *pale brown patch* at end of cell, cell spot *absent or faint*. Compare to other white-fringed duskywings (next page). ✤ **Larval foodplant:** Legumes.

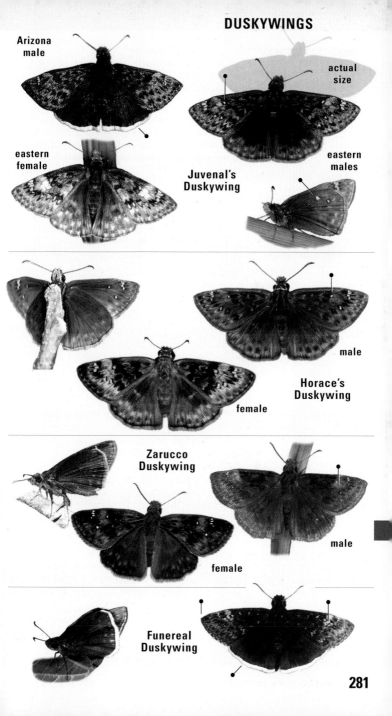

DUSKYWINGS

Arizona male

actual size

eastern female

Juvenal's Duskywing

eastern males

Horace's Duskywing

male

female

Zarucco Duskywing

female

male

Funereal Duskywing

PROPERTIUS DUSKYWING   *Erynnis propertius*

Common in oak woodlands of the far west. Flies in spring to early summer (1 brood). ► Large, with *brown* fringes, *much gray on forewing*. Hindwing below usually has *two pale spots* near leading edge. Within its range, most duskywings are smaller or have white fringes. Pacuvius Duskywing on West Coast similar but smaller, not so gray above, lacks pale spots near leading edge of hindwing below. 🐛 **Larval foodplant:** Oaks.

MERIDIAN DUSKYWING   *Erynnis meridianus*

Essentially replaces Propertius Duskywing in southwestern oak woodlands. Uncommon. Males hilltop. Flies spring and summer (2 broods). ► Fringes brown. Male above brown with indistinct black lines. Female forewing gray-brown with bold black markings. Hindwing below lacks two pale spots near upper margin. Rocky Mountain Duskywing (next page) is grayer and often flies at higher elevations. 🐛 **Larval foodplant:** Oaks.

PACUVIUS DUSKYWING   *Erynnis pacuvius*

Medium-sized duskywing of western mountains. Variable: dark-fringed along Pacific Coast, white-fringed from Colorado to Mexico. Males hilltop. Flies summer in north (1 brood), spring and late summer in south (2 broods). ► Above forewing patterned brown, black, or gray, with *orange-brown patches fairly prominent, one at end of cell*. Westernmost populations show less contrast above. 🐛 **Larval foodplant:** Buckbrushes.

MOURNFUL DUSKYWING   *Erynnis tristis*

Fairly common in southwestern oak woodlands, scarce in California. Males hilltop. Flies spring to fall (3 broods). ► Large with white hindwing fringe. In southwest, indentified by *white marginal patches* on hindwing below. In California these marks are faint; separated from Funereal Duskywing there (previous page) by pattern of forewing above, usually *lacking* obvious pale patch beyond end of cell. 🐛 **Larval foodplant:** Oaks.

SCUDDER'S DUSKYWING   *Erynnis scudderi*

Rare and restricted in southwest. Males occur on hilltops, usually above 6,000 feet in mountains. Flies spring and summer (2 broods). ► Small, white-fringed. Very similar to southwestern form of Juvenal's Duskywing (previous page); averages smaller, but probably not safely identified in the field, requiring lab dissection. 🐛 **Larval foodplant:** Unknown, presumed to be oaks.

WESTERN DUSKYWINGS

Propertius Duskywing

females

actual size

male

Meridian Duskywing

male

female

Pacuvius Duskywing

southwest

Pacific coast

Mournful Duskywing

California

southwest

Scudder's Duskywing

DREAMY DUSKYWING   *Erynnis icelus*

A small duskywing of boreal forests. Flies late spring and early summer (1 brood). ▶ This and next are the only two duskywings *without* glassy white forewing spots. Forewings short and rounded. Above forewing gray with *two black chainlike bands enclosing gray scales.* Hindwing above brown with two rows of pale spots.
🌿 **Larval foodplant:** Willow, aspen, poplar, others.

SLEEPY DUSKYWING   *Erynnis brizo*

An early season duskywing of oak woods. Males hilltop. Flies early to late spring (1 brood). ▶ Usually larger than Dreamy with longer, more pointed forewing. Above forewing gray with *broad gray chainlike bands enclosing gray scales; no white spots.* Hindwing above dark brown with pale spots, often fainter than those of Dreamy Duskywing. 🌿 **Larval foodplant:** Oaks.

AFRANIUS DUSKYWING   *Erynnis afranius*

A small duskywing, common in western mountains. Flies spring and summer (2 broods). ▶ Fringes brown (often white edged). Difficult to separate from Persius Duskywing where they overlap in late spring and early summer. Male Afranius usually has a stronger pattern above, often including a *brown patch past the end of the forewing cell.* Female above similar to male. 🌿 **Larval foodplant:** Lupines, lotuses, other legumes.

PERSIUS DUSKYWING   *Erynnis persius*

Rare and local in upper midwest, more widespread in west. Males hilltop. Flies late spring to early summer (1 brood). ▶ Very similar to Afranius Duskywing. Male has forewing pattern above largely obscured with gray hairs, creating a *duskier look.* Female above lighter than male with stronger pattern, and may be impossible to separate from Afranius female in field. In far west, compare Pacuvius Duskywing (previous page). 🌿 **Larval foodplant:** Golden banner, lupines, and other legumes.

ROCKY MOUNTAIN DUSKYWING   *Erynnis telemachus*

Southern Rocky Mountain region, mainly associated with Gambel oak thickets and woodlands. Flies late spring and early summer (1 brood). ▶ Male above forewing strongly gray with black lines and small glassy spots. Female similar with stronger pattern. Hindwing below usually shows *two pale spots near leading margin.* Compare Meridian Duskywing (previous page).
🌿 **Larval foodplant:** Oaks, especially Gambel oak.

BROWN-FRINGED DUSKYWINGS

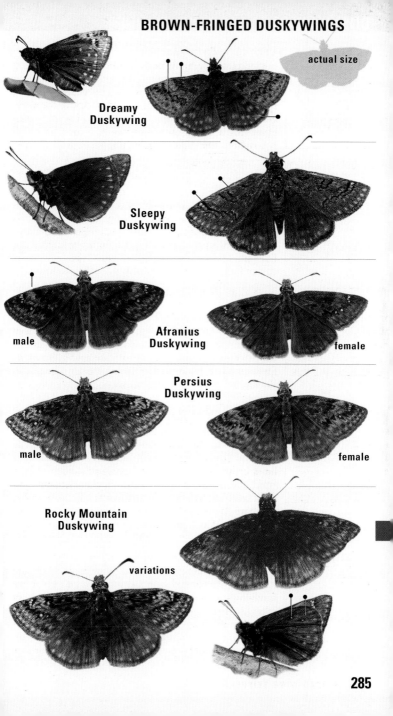

actual size

Dreamy Duskywing

Sleepy Duskywing

male **Afranius Duskywing** female

Persius Duskywing

male female

Rocky Mountain Duskywing

variations

WILD INDIGO DUSKYWING   *Erynnis baptisiae*

Formerly scarce, now expanding its range because it has adapted to the introduced crown vetch as a larval foodplant. Flies spring to fall (2–3 broods). ▶ Brown-fringed, medium-sized, variable. Forewing above *darkened at base*, with brown patch beyond cell and small glassy white spots. Hindwing above brown with *pale cell-end bar and pale spots*. Female above with sharper pattern than male. Hindwing below has *pale marginal spots*. Compare Horace's and Zarucco Duskywings (p. 280). 🌱 **Larval foodplant:** Crown vetch and wild indigo.

COLUMBINE DUSKYWING   *Erynnis lucilius*

A small northeastern duskywing. Local in ravines, gorges, and on shale or limestone slopes where wild columbines grow. Flies spring to fall (2–3 broods). ▶ Almost identical to Wild Indigo Duskywing. Averages darker and smaller, but probably not safely identified in the field, except perhaps by association with the larval foodplant. 🌱 **Larval foodplant:** Wild columbine.

MOTTLED DUSKYWING   *Erynnis martialis*

Small distinctive duskywing of open woodlands, usually uncommon to rare. Has disappeared from some of former range in northeast. Males are avid hilltoppers. Flies spring to fall in east (2 broods), early summer in Rockies (1 brood). ▶ Told from other duskywings by *strongly mottled pattern* on both wings above. Has purplish sheen when in fresh condition. 🌱 **Larval foodplant:** New Jersey tea, also Fendler's buckbrush in Colorado.

FLORIDA DUSKYWING   *Ephyriades brunneus*

Extreme south Florida only, usually uncommon. A large brown skipper of open pinelands. Flies all year (multiple broods). ▶ Similar to typical duskywings, but both sexes fairly *uniform* brown above with *semicircle of small white spots* near forewing tip. Female paler with purple sheen and larger forewing spots. 🌱 **Larval foodplant:** Locustberry.

FALSE DUSKYWING   *Gesta gesta*

A tropical species resident in southern Texas. Adults often rest open-winged with the forewings covering the hindwings, or with wings folded downward. Flies spring to fall (multiple broods). ▶ Above banded brown and black with no white spots. Forewing with *bluish gray submarginal band* and *lighter brown patch curving outward just beyond end of cell.* 🌱 **Larval foodplant:** *Indigofera* species.

DUSKYWINGS

Wild Indigo Duskywing

actual size

male

female

Columbine Duskywing

Mottled Duskywing

Florida Duskywing

female

male

False Duskywing

CHECKERED-SKIPPERS

Small skippers with black and white checkered upper surfaces. Most can be difficult to identify to species. Field marks on undersides of wings are often not easily seen, since adults usually rest with wings open.

COMMON CHECKERED-SKIPPER   *Pyrgus communis*

The most common and widespread skipper in North America. Found in nearly all habitats from high to low elevations, and adapts well to disturbed areas. Flies all year in southern regions (multiple broods), spring to fall northward (2 broods). ▶ Above checkered black and white, female with more black, male often with sparse blue hair basally. Below hindwing white with bands and spots of tan or olive. Compare to others on this and next page. 🌱 **Larval foodplant:** Mallows.

WHITE CHECKERED-SKIPPER   *Pyrgus albescens*

Recently shown to be a distinct species from Common Checkered-Skipper. Mostly in hot arid habitats in the southwest, and recently has invaded the southeast, but the two species are found together over a broad front and cannot be identified in the field where they overlap. Flies most of year (multiple broods). ▶ Essentially identical to Common Checkered-Skipper, separated only by dissection in the lab. 🌱 **Larval foodplant:** Mallows.

TROPICAL CHECKERED-SKIPPER   *Pyrgus oileus*

Resident only along Gulf Coast from Florida to south Texas; a periodic stray to southwest. Recorded spring to fall in southwest (2 broods), most of year elsewhere (multiple broods). ▶ Very much like Common and White Checkered-Skippers. On the forewing fringe near tip, *dark checks run together* (they are evenly spaced on other species). White spot at end of forewing cell, and white marginal spots on hindwing above, are *usually larger* on Tropical. Below hindwing has *three evenly spaced dark elongated spots* along leading edge, the center one absent on both Common and White Checkered-Skippers. 🌱 **Larval foodplant:** Mallows.

DESERT CHECKERED-SKIPPER   *Pyrgus philetas*

Strictly southwestern, uncommon in hot desert regions. Often congregates at mud in small numbers. Flies most of year (multiple broods). ▶ Similar to other checkered-skippers but *much plainer below,* whitish or tan, with *two small black dots* near center of hindwing leading edge. Above much like Tropical Checkered-Skipper but usually has smaller white marginal spots on hindwing and has dark checks in forewing fringe *evenly spaced.* 🌱 **Larval foodplant:** Mallows.

CHECKERED-SKIPPERS

actual size

variations

male

variations

female

Common Checkered-Skipper
White Checkered-Skipper
(essentially identical)

male

female

**Tropical
Checkered-Skipper**

**Desert
Checkered-Skipper**

female

male

289

GRIZZLED SKIPPER   *Pyrgus centaureae*

Mainly in far north, also scattered at high elevations in Rockies. Isolated population in Appalachians *(P. c. wyandot)*, possibly a distinct species, is rare and declining. Flies in spring in east, late spring and summer in west (1 brood), biennial in some areas. ▶ Large like Common Checkered-Skipper but with white checks reduced. On forewing above, white basal spotband *lacks a spot* just below forewing cell, unlike similar species. Forewing lacks the white spots along margin usually present on Common Checkered-Skipper. Below banded olive-gray. 🌿 **Larval foodplant:** Cinquefoils.

TWO-BANDED CHECKERED-SKIPPER   *Pyrgus ruralis*

A small montane species, found in moist clearings and meadows up to above treeline; also down to sea level on west coast. Isolated population in southern California is endangered. Flies late spring to early summer (1 brood). ▶ Smaller than Common Checkered-Skipper, with two white spotbands on forewing forming a loose X. Hindwing above usually with white basal spot. Difficult to separate from next species where ranges meet, but banded *reddish brown* below, not gray-brown. 🌿 **Larval foodplant:** Cinquefoils and horkelias.

MOUNTAIN CHECKERED-SKIPPER   *Pyrgus xanthus*

Replaces Two-banded Checkered-Skipper to the southeast, with only a slight overlap in range. Males patrol stream bottoms, shallow depressions, and gullies to find females. Flies late spring to early summer (1 brood). ▶ Very similar to previous species, but banded *gray-brown* below, not reddish brown. Also similar to next species, but hindwing above usually has a *distinct white basal spot.* 🌿 **Larval foodplant:** Cinquefoils.

SMALL CHECKERED-SKIPPER   *Pyrgus scriptura*

A small versatile skipper of varied western habitats, including prairies, dry mountain slopes, alkali flats, weedy fields. Flies spring to fall (2–3 broods). ▶ Above with white checks often reduced, but varying in size and number. Similar to Two-banded and Mountain Checkered-Skippers, but hindwing above usually *lacks* white basal spot, except on some spring individuals. Hindwing fringe usually *incompletely checkered,* with dark checks only weakly touching outer edge or failing to reach it. Often a gray area at *base* of forewing leading edge. Below varies from vaguely banded olive-brown to plain white. 🌿 **Larval foodplant:** Mallows.

CHECKERED-SKIPPERS

actual size

Grizzled Skipper

Appalachians

Two-banded Checkered-Skipper

Mountain Checkered-Skipper

Small Checkered-Skipper

WHITE-SKIPPERS

These are fast fliers, usually perching with their wings open flat.

NORTHERN WHITE-SKIPPER *Heliopetes ericetorum*

The only white-skipper in most of the west, in dry canyons and brushy country. Flies late spring to early summer and late summer to fall (2 broods). ► Above male mostly white with black marginal chevrons. Female has more submarginal black and more gray at wing bases; compare to next species, also to checkered-skippers (preceding pages). Below hindwing vaguely banded brown and white. 🐛 **Larval foodplant:** Mallows.

ERICHSON'S WHITE-SKIPPER *Heliopyrgus domicella*

An uncommon species of southwestern deserts and southern Texas, rarely seen in numbers. Flies early spring to late fall (3 broods). ► Above brownish black with a broad white median band; dark markings heavier, more sharply defined than on female Northern White-Skipper. Below hindwing white with light olive green along margin and near base. Forewing below has darker patch on leading edge near base, absent on other white-skippers. 🐛 **Larval foodplant:** Mallows.

LAVIANA WHITE-SKIPPER *Heliopetes laviana*

Common resident of south Texas, straying northward. Regular stray, probably breeding, in Arizona. Flies most of year in south Texas (multiple broods), spring and fall in Arizona (2 broods?). ► Above mostly white, with black along margins often reduced or absent on hindwing. Female with black more extensive. On hindwing below, brown marginal patch has *relatively straight inner edge,* and dark median band slants in toward body and wing base. 🐛 **Larval foodplant:** Mallows.

TURK'S-CAP WHITE-SKIPPER *Heliopetes macaira*

Mainly south Texas, rarely strays north. Prefers brushy openings near tropical woodlands. Flies most of year (multiple broods). ► Above mostly white, with black more extensive on female and often absent on hindwing. Similar to Laviana White-Skipper, but black near tip of forewing is *interrupted by a white dash.* On hindwing below, inner edge of brown marginal patch *parallels edge of wing.* Tip of forewing below shows less contrast. 🐛 **Larval foodplant:** Turk's-cap and other mallows.

VEINED WHITE-SKIPPER *Heliopetes arsalte*

Rare stray to south Texas, recorded in October. ► Above mostly white with black at forewing tip and along margin edge, *extending slightly inward* along veins. Below hindwing white with black veins and *orange* along base of leading edge. 🐛 **Larval foodplant:** Mallows.

WHITE-SKIPPERS

actual size

male

female

Northern White-Skipper

Erichson's White-Skipper

male

female

Laviana White-Skipper

female

male

Turk's-cap White-Skipper

Veined White-Skipper

SOUTHWESTERN SKIPPERS

WHITE-PATCHED SKIPPER   *Chiomara asychis*

A small tropical skipper resident in south Texas, straying northward; regular but rare in southwest. Adults mainly sit with wings open, sometimes folded downward. Males hilltop, or perch on twigs along clearings, flying out at any passing butterfly. Flies most of year in Texas (multiple broods), recorded spring to fall in southwest (2 broods). ▶ Above variable. Forewing mottled gray, brown, black, and white; hindwing with prominent white patch. Female has less extensive white. Overall lacks checkered "look" of checkered-skippers (pp. 288–291). Below mostly white with variable brown spotting along margin. 🐛 **Larval foodplant:** Barbados cherry in Texas; Janusia suspected in Arizona.

HOARY SKIPPER   *Carrhenes canescens*

Rare stray to south Texas, recorded spring and fall. Usually perches with wings open. ▶ Above brown, tan, or grayish with circular pattern of transparent spots on forewing, often with pair of small glassy spots near center of hindwing and transparent band near base. Below tan with thin brown bands. 🐛 **Larval foodplant:** Mallows.

GLASSY-WINGED SKIPPER   *Xenophanes tryxus*

Periodic resident in south Texas, flying in spring and fall. ▶ Distinctive. Above gray-brown with large irregular *transparent median patches* on both wings. Below with expanded transparent patches on white extending to brown margins. 🐛 **Larval foodplant:** Mallows.

COMMON STREAKY-SKIPPER   *Celotes nessus*

A distinctive little skipper of Texas and the southwest. Easily overlooked owing to its small size and weak, low flight, but shows a striking pattern on close inspection. Males patrol gullies and canyon bottoms during the heat of the day to find females. Flies spring to fall (2–3 broods). ▶ Above brown with dazzling array of lines, chevrons, and spots creating an overall *pleated* or *crinkled* appearance; pattern below similar. 🐛 **Larval foodplant:** Mallows, also Ayenia in Arizona.

SCARCE STREAKY-SKIPPER   *Celotes limpia*   *(not illustrated)*

A cryptic species of west Texas and northeastern Mexico, living in dry canyons and washes. Not identifiable in the field, so status is poorly known. Flies spring to fall (multiple broods). ▶ Essentially identical to Common Streaky-Skipper, which overlaps its range; not identified with certainty without lab dissection. 🐛 **Larval foodplant:** Mallows.

SOUTHWESTERN SKIPPERS

actual size

variations

White-patched Skipper

Hoary Skipper

Glassy-winged Skipper

Common Streaky-Skipper

295

SCALLOPWINGS

Small black skippers with scalloped hindwings, usually perching with wings open flat. Flight is relatively slow and close to the ground.

HAYHURST'S SCALLOPWING   *Staphylus hayhurstii*

Widespread but usually rather uncommon, in woodland clearings, fields, roadsides, gardens. Flies spring to fall (2 broods, perhaps 3 in southern Florida). ▶ The only small black skipper in the east with *scalloped margins* on the hindwings. Fringes usually checkered dark brown and tan. Above male blackish, female brown with more contrast and with pale flecked appearance, both with darker bands and small white dots on forewing. Common Sootywing (next page) is similar but has rounded hindwing and usually more white dots on forewing. In central Texas, see Mazans Scallopwing. 🌿 **Larval foodplant:** Lambsquarters and others.

MAZANS SCALLOPWING   *Staphylus mazans*

Replaces Hayhurst's Scallopwing from central Texas southward to Mexico, haunts open weedy areas adjacent to woodlands. Flies most of year (3 broods). ▶ Very similar to Hayhurst's Scallopwing, with scalloped margin of hindwings and small white dots on forewings; above male blackish, female dark brown with pale flecks. This species usually *lacks* the checkering on the fringes shown by Hayhurst's (but fringes can be hard to see on worn individuals). 🌿 **Larval foodplant:** Lambsquarters and pigweeds.

GOLDEN-HEADED SCALLOPWING   *Staphylus ceos*

Mainly southern Arizona to south Texas, straying northward. Common in a variety of habitats, from deserts to mountain clearings. Attracted to damp soil as well as flowers, perching with wings opened flat or only partially open. Flies early spring to late fall (2 broods). ▶ Black above with one or two tiny white spots near forewing tip, hindwing margin vaguely scalloped. Usually easily recognized by *gold scales on head and palpi*. Females and worn individuals may look dark-headed; compare to Common Sootywing (next page). 🌿 **Larval foodplant:** Pigweeds.

MOTTLED BOLLA   *Bolla clytius*

Rare stray to south Texas and southeastern Arizona. Recorded summer and fall in Texas, August to October in Arizona. ▶ Easily confused with scallopwings, but averages a bit larger. Hindwing less scalloped, slightly squared. Mostly brown above with broad, diffusely darker band through middle of forewing. 🌿 **Larval foodplant:** Unknown.

SCALLOPWINGS

actual size

underside

male

female

Hayhurst's Scallopwing

Mazans Scallopwing

male

female

Golden-headed Scallopwing

worn

Mottled Bolla

male

female

SOOTYWINGS

usually perch with wings open. Flight is slow and close to the ground.

COMMON SOOTYWING   *Pholisora catullus*

Most widespread of small black skippers. Found in open habitats, especially disturbed areas such as weedy vacant lots. Flies spring to fall (2–3 broods). ► Above uniform black or blackish brown with a curved row (or two) of small white spots on forewing. Number of spots varies. Usually has several *small white spots on head*. Below hindwing veins not lined in black. 🌱 **Larval foodplant:** Pigweeds and careless-weeds *(Amaranthus).*

MEXICAN SOOTYWING   *Pholisora mejicana*

Rare, with limited range, occurring in canyons, washes, fields. Flies late spring to summer (2 broods). ► Above identical to Common Sootywing. Below hindwing with bluish sheen (which Common Sootywing usually lacks) and black-lined veins. Difficult to identify in the field, since sootywings usually perch with wings opened flat. 🌱 **Larval foodplant:** Careless-weeds.

MOJAVE SOOTYWING   *Hesperopsis libya*

A small black skipper of alkali salt flats and other hot arid habitats. Males patrol around saltbushes to locate females. Flies spring to fall (1–2 broods). ► Variable. Above black or black-brown; white forewing spots may be conspicuous, forming bands, or nearly absent. Below hindwing pale to dark, usually with roundish white spots, fewer in north. Fringes not strongly checkered. 🌱 **Larval foodplant:** Saltbushes *(Atriplex).*

SALTBUSH SOOTYWING   *Hesperopsis alpheus*

Occupies similar habitats to Mojave Sootywing and their ranges overlap broadly, although the two are rarely found together at the same time. Flies spring and late summer (1–2 broods). ► Similar to Mojave Sootywing above but usually has ground color much more mottled; fringes strongly checkered. Below hindwing blackish brown with thin white bar in center and other reduced white dashes. 🌱 **Larval foodplant:** Saltbushes.

"MACNEILL'S" SALTBUSH SOOTYWING   *H. a. gracielae*

Lower Colorado River region only. Sometimes considered a distinct species from other Saltbush Sootywings. Flies spring to fall (2 broods). ► Smaller than other Saltbush Sootywings, *fringes not strongly checkered.* Above very dark, with markings extremely vague. Below blackish brown with thin white bar on hindwing and other reduced white markings. 🌱 **Larval foodplant:** Primarily quail bush *(Atiplex lentiformis).*

SOOTYWINGS

Mexican Sootywing

variations

actual size

Common Sootywing

male

Mojave Sootywing

female

Saltbush Sootywing

"MacNeill's" Saltbush Sootywing

299

make up a separate subfamily (**Heteropterinae**) of small species. Their flight is weak and close to the ground, and when perched they open their wings in unison, unlike the true grass skippers (beginning on p. 302). Their antennal tips lack the terminal extension of other skippers.

ARCTIC SKIPPER   *Carterocephalus palaemon*

A distinctive boreal species, common in parts of the far north, mostly rare south of Canada. Found mainly in moist clearings in coniferous or mixed woodlands. Flies mostly in late spring and early summer (1 brood). ▶ Above dark brown with orange checkered pattern. Below yellow-orange or tan with black-outlined pale yellow or cream spots. Nothing in its range is really similar. 🌿 **Larval foodplant:** Grasses.

RUSSET SKIPPERLING   *Piruna pirus*

Local but sometimes common in the central and southern Rockies. Best observed visiting flowers or mud along creeks or in moist grassy gullies. Flies in late spring and early summer (1 brood). ▶ Small and mostly unmarked. Above dark brown with small white spots limited to forewing. Below hindwing *unmarked rich reddish brown*. 🌿 **Larval foodplant:** Grasses.

FOUR-SPOTTED SKIPPERLING   *Piruna polingi*

A species of high mountain streamsides and wet meadows in Arizona and New Mexico, also recently reported from Davis Mountains, Texas. Flies in summer (1 brood). ▶ Above dark brown with white spots on both wings, including a conspicuous white spot in center of hindwing. Below hindwing *reddish brown* with four large *squarish white spots*. 🌿 **Larval foodplant:** Grasses.

MANY-SPOTTED SKIPPERLING   *Piruna cingo*

A southeastern Arizona specialty, usually rare and local in shaded grassy swales along creeks or canyons in mid-elevation oak woodland. Adults visit mud but rarely gather in any numbers. Flies in late summer (1 brood). ▶ Above dark brown with *small white spots* on *both wings*. Below hindwing golden brown with many *small bold white spots*. 🌿 **Larval foodplant:** Side-oats grama.

CHISOS SKIPPERLING   *Piruna haferniki*

Rare and local in pine-oak woodland of Chisos Mountains, Big Bend National Park, Texas. Flights of adults may be closely tied to rains, which are sporadic and unpredictable. Flies spring to fall (2 broods). ▶ Above dark brown with small white spots limited to forewing. Below hindwing unmarked blackish brown with *base and outer angle gray*. Compare to roadside-skippers (pp. 342–350). 🌿 **Larval foodplant:** Unknown.

SKIPPERLINGS

actual size

Arctic Skipper

Russet Skipperling

Four-spotted Skipperling

Many-spotted Skipperling

Chisos Skipperling

(subfamily Hesperiinae) are mostly small and usually orange or brown. Adults rest with wings closed or bask with hindwings opened farther than forewings (the "jet-plane position"), a posture unique to grass skippers. Their flight is fast and agile. Males of most have a black stigma of specialized scales on the forewing. Larvae eat grasses and related plants.

FIERY SKIPPER *Hylephila phyleus*

Often noticed by the public as "that little orange moth" of lawns and gardens. Common in southern regions; strays north, especially in the east, finding its way to the Great Lakes and New England. Favors open habitats with Bermuda grass. Flies most of year in hot regions, spring to fall northward (multiple broods). ▶ Antennae short. Above male yellow-orange with black stigma; wings with *black "toothed" margins.* Below hindwing yellow-orange with *small brown spots* of varying intensity. Female similar but more orange-brown above and below. Whirlabout (more limited to far south) has larger dark spots below, different hindwing pattern above. 🌿 **Larval foodplant:** Primarily Bermuda grass.

SACHEM *Atalopedes campestris*

Another orange skipper widespread and common in the south, straying north to Canada. Prefers rural habitats but also found near lawns and gardens. Flies most of year in south, late spring to fall northward (multiple broods). ▶ Often mistaken for skippers in the genus *Hesperia* (beginning p. 312). Above male golden-orange with *large square black stigma.* Female mostly brown with large glassy spot at end of forewing cell. Hindwing below variable, male pale yellow, female brown, both with paler postmedian band or chevron; look for *dark square patch near trailing edge.* 🌿 **Larval foodplant:** Crab, Bermuda, and other grasses.

WHIRLABOUT *Polites vibex*

Mainly southeastern, common in Florida and south Texas. Adults habitually land and take off with a circular (or "whirling") flight. Flies most of year in southernmost areas (multiple broods), spring to fall northward (2 broods). ▶ Male above has black stigma connected to black patch extended toward tip of forewing (absent on Sachem); black margin on hindwing *smooth* (jagged on Fiery Skipper). Below male has hindwing yellow to orange with two broken rows of *large brown spots.* Female above mostly dark brown with small creamy spots on forewing, below hindwing olive-gray or brown with shadow of male's spots. 🌿 **Larval foodplant:** Weedy grasses.

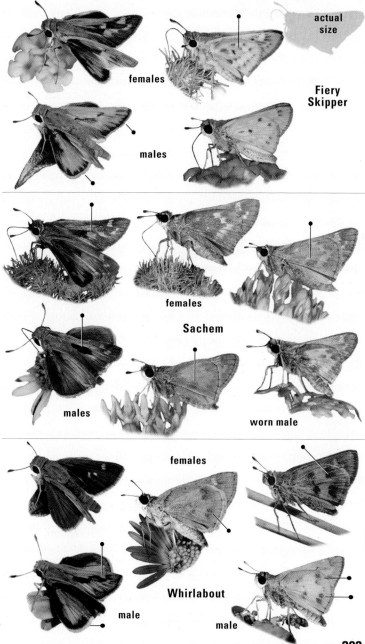

actual size

females

Fiery Skipper

males

females

Sachem

males

worn male

females

Whirlabout

male

male

303

TINY ORANGE SKIPPERS

EUROPEAN SKIPPER *Thymelicus lineola*

Accidentally introduced into Ontario, Canada, in 1910, and still spreading. Often abundant in various habitats with Timothy grass. Flight is weak and low. Flies early summer (1 brood). ▶ Fringes *orange*. Below plain pale orange, above with black borders and veins blackened inward from margins. Male has thin black stigma. Delaware Skipper (p. 336) larger with longer antennae. ✿ **Larval foodplant:** Timothy and other grasses.

LEAST SKIPPER *Ancyloxypha numitor*

Tiny eastern species, common at wet grassy habitats. Adults meander through grass with weak fluttering flight. Flies most of year in south (multiple broods), spring to fall northward (2–3 broods). ▶ Forewing rounded. Below plain orange. Above black and orange, more black than on similar species in same range (female often all black above). ✿ **Larval foodplant:** Grasses.

TROPICAL LEAST SKIPPER *Ancyloxypha arene*

Tiny local skipper of streamsides in arid southwest. Adults weakly fly among grasses near water. Flies spring to fall (multiple broods), more common late in season. ▶ Forewing rounded. Below hindwing pale orange with *paler ray (barely visible)* extending from base to margin. Above bright orange with dull black border on forewing. ✿ **Larval foodplant:** Grasses of wet habitats.

ORANGE SKIPPERLING *Copaeodes aurantiaca*

A common plain skipper of arid canyons in southwest; also adapts to urban gardens. Adults are rapid fliers, hard for the eye to follow. Males perch in gullies to await females. Flies all year, mainly spring to fall (multiple broods). ▶ Forewing less rounded than Tropical Least Skipper. Below *unmarked yellow-orange.* Above male mostly bright orange with thin black stigma. Female above bright orange, often with black below forewing cell and along margin. ✿ **Larval foodplant:** Bermuda and other grasses.

SOUTHERN SKIPPERLING *Copaeodes minima*

Mainly Gulf Coast from Texas to Florida; rare stray to Arizona. Our smallest skipper. Flies all year some areas, spring to fall elsewhere (multiple broods). ▶ Below hindwing orange with narrow white ray from base to margin. Above male mostly unmarked bright orange with thin black stigma. Female above bright orange with black below forewing cell, on veins and along margin. ✿ **Larval foodplant:** Bermuda and other grasses.

TINY GRASS SKIPPERS

actual size

European Skipper

Least Skipper

Tropical Least Skipper

Orange Skipperling

Southern Skipperling

305

GARITA SKIPPERLING   *Oarisma garita*

A small dusky skipper, sometimes common in prairies and western mountain grasslands, with an isolated population in Ontario, Canada. Flight is weak and close to ground. Flies in summer (1 brood). ▶ Above unmarked dark brown with variable orange dusting. Below hindwing pale orange with *whitish fringe* and usually *whitish veins*. ✢ **Larval foodplant:** Grasses.

EDWARDS'S SKIPPERLING   *Oarisma edwardsii*

Uncommon in midelevation grassy habitats of southern Rockies and southwest. Usually found at lower elevations than Garita Skipperling. Flies in summer (1 brood). ▶ Above unmarked orange-brown, not as dark as Garita Skipperling. Below hindwing pale orange, veins not outlined with white. Fringes below may be dark. Orange Skipperling (previous page) is smaller, with faster flight. ✢ **Larval foodplant:** Unknown.

POWESHIEK SKIPPERLING   *Oarisma poweshiek*

A specialty of the northern Great Plains, thriving in undisturbed native tall-grass prairie. Still locally common, but endangered by loss of habitat. Flies in midsummer (1 brood). ▶ Above dark brown with orange near leading edge of forewing. Below hindwing dark brown with some white overscaling and with distinctive *white-outlined veins*. Garita Skipperling less contrasty below and above. ✢ **Larval foodplant:** Spikerush.

ALKALI SKIPPER   *Pseudocopaeodes eunus*

Rare in alkaline saltgrass flats near water in deserts, where its pale color blends with the habitat. Flight is fast. Flies spring to fall at low elevations (2 broods), summer higher (1 brood). ▶ Above mostly orange with thin black borders, veins slightly blackened inward from margins. Male has thin black stigma. Below hindwing pale orange or yellow with *paler ray* extending from base to margin. ✢ **Larval foodplant:** Saltgrass.

SUNRISE SKIPPER   *Adopaeoides prittwitzi*

Rare in midelevation (4,000–6,000 feet) cienegas along Mexican border. Also reported from west Texas. Flies late spring to fall (2–3 broods), more numerous by late summer. ▶ Below hindwing pale orange with *yellow ray* extending from base to margin. Above note veins slightly *blackened inward from margins*. Female has blacker veins, thin cell end bar on forewing, often an overlay of black scales. ✢ **Larval foodplant:** Knotgrass.

VERY SMALL SKIPPERS

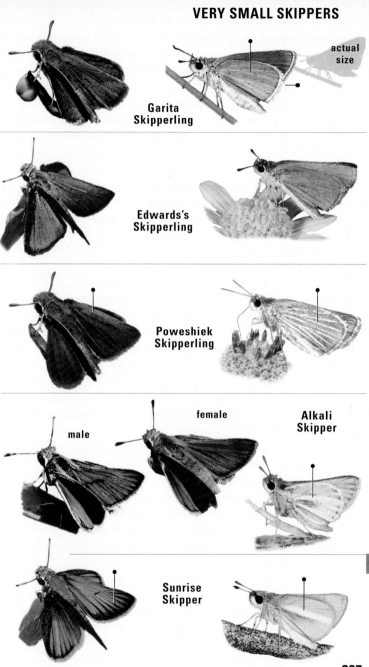

actual size

Garita Skipperling

Edwards's Skipperling

Poweshiek Skipperling

male

female

Alkali Skipper

Sunrise Skipper

DARK SOUTHERN SKIPPERS

CLOUDED SKIPPER *Lerema accius*

Common in southeast, especially Florida and Texas, straying northward; periodic resident in southwest. Often basks in early morning on low plants at forest edge. Flies most of year in southern areas (multiple broods), spring to fall northward (1–2 broods). ▶ Below hindwing dark brown with *pale areas* (often purple frosted when fresh) along margin and near middle, setting off a *dark broad band* extending down from leading margin. Above dark brown with small white forewing spots better developed on female; male has large stigma.
🌿 **Larval foodplant**: Primarily weedy grasses.

FAWN-SPOTTED SKIPPER *Cymaenes odilia*

South Texas only, generally uncommon. Flies spring to late fall (multiple broods). ▶ Very similar to Clouded Skipper (which is more common in south Texas) but averages smaller, especially body size, and has *more distinct* pale bands on hindwing below. Above dark brown with small white forewing spots; male lacks stigma. Below hindwing dark brown, paler basally, with well-defined pale postmedian band not reaching the leading edge. 🌿 **Larval foodplant**: Grasses.

THREE-SPOTTED SKIPPER *Cymaenes tripunctus*

South Florida only, locally common in woodland edges and clearings. Flies all year (multiple broods). ▶ Above dark brown with small white forewing spots, the base of the forewing leading edge often tawny. Below hindwing yellow-brown with faint row of postmedian spots. Eufala Skipper (p. 352), common in Florida, is very similar, but generally paler gray-brown below with fainter spots, and antennae shorter. 🌿 **Larval foodplant**: Primarily weedy and ornamental grasses.

MALICIOUS SKIPPER *Synapte malitiosa*

South Texas only. Prefers edges of well-shaded understories. Reported spring to fall. ▶ Above brown with diffuse pale yellow forewing patch crossed by broad dark brown streak. Below hindwing pale yellowish brown crossed by *tiny dark striations*. 🌿 **Larval foodplant**: Grasses.

VIOLET-PATCHED SKIPPER *Monca tyrtaeus*

South Texas only. Flies most of year (2–3 broods). ▶ Smaller than Clouded Skipper, forewings more rounded than those of Fawn-spotted Skipper. Above dark brown with small white forewing spots. Below hindwing with *well-defined bright violet basal and postmedian bands*. Similar to Fawn-spotted Skipper above but has much brighter hindwing markings below. Forewing below with violet marginal patch. 🌿 **Larval foodplant**: Grasses.

DARK SOUTHERN SKIPPERS

actual size

female

male

Clouded
Skipper

Fawn-spotted
Skipper

Three-spotted
Skipper

Malicious
Skipper

Violet-patched
Skipper

309

SWARTHY SKIPPER   *Nastra lherminier*

A small drab skipper, fairly common in the east, sometimes straying north of mapped range. Favors grassy areas such as roadsides and meadows. Flies spring to fall (2 broods). ▶ Above dark brown, rarely with a trace of forewing spots. Below hindwing yellow-brown with veins slightly paler. In most of its range, few other skippers are so dull. 🌱 **Larval foodplant:** Little bluestem grass.

NEAMATHLA SKIPPER   *Nastra neamathla*

Localized in the south, mainly Florida and eastern Texas, in open grassy areas. Flies early spring to fall (2–3 broods). ▶ Similar to the more common Swarthy Skipper, which overlaps its range, but hindwing below is browner and mostly *lacks* the paler veins. Above dark brown, with or without traces of forewing spots. 🌱 **Larval foodplant:** Probably bluestem grasses.

JULIA'S SKIPPER   *Nastra julia*

Common in south Texas; rare in southwest. May intergrade with Swarthy Skipper in Houston area. Flight is fast. Flies all year in Texas (multiple broods). ▶ Resembles two preceding species but hindwing below may be *warmer* yellowish brown, *without* paler veins. Above usually has yellowish forewing spots below cell and near tip. Eufala Skipper (p. 352) has forewings longer with white spots. 🌱 **Larval foodplant:** Grasses.

DOUBLE-DOTTED SKIPPER   *Decinea percosius*

Extreme south Texas only, rare. Reported spring to fall. ▶ Above dark brown with glassy white forewing spots, notably *two prominent ones near center*. Below hindwing pale yellow-brown with two small glassy spots near center. 🌱 **Larval foodplant:** Unknown for U.S.

HIDDEN-RAY SKIPPER   *Conga chydaea*

Rare stray to south Texas, July to October. ▶ Above blackish brown with variable white forewing dots. Below dark brown with white streak above trailing edge of forewing (rarely visible). 🌱 **Larval foodplant:** Unknown.

PALE-RAYED SKIPPER   *Vidius perigenes*

Rare in scrubby areas of south Texas, spring to fall (2 broods?). ▶ Above unmarked dark brown. Below hindwing yellow-brown, veins slightly paler, with *white streak* from base to margin. 🌱 **Larval foodplant:** Unknown.

REDUNDANT SKIPPER   *Corticea corticea*

A small dark skipper that strays to south Texas, reported in fall. ▶ Above forewing blackish brown with diffuse pale yellow band. Similar to Malicious Skipper (previous page) but smaller with more rounded forewings. Below hindwing *unmarked* orange-brown. 🌱 **Larval foodplant:** Unknown.

DULL SKIPPERS

Neamathla Skipper

Swarthy Skipper

actual size

Julia's Skipper

Double-dotted Skipper

Hidden-ray Skipper

Pale-rayed Skipper

Redundant Skipper

311

HESPERIA SKIPPERS

(genus *Hesperia*) make up a group of similar species, often with a prominent band or chevron of white spots on the hindwing below. Many of them overlap in range. Identification is challenging, often relying on minor differences in the spot configuration of the hindwing chevron, but differences in flight season also help. All are fast in flight. Males have narrow black stigmas on their forewings.

COMMON BRANDED SKIPPER   *Hesperia comma*

Most widespread and variable Hesperia. Some populations included here may be full species, especially those of the west and the Canadian prairies. Males are avid hilltoppers. Flies anywhere from late spring to early fall, mostly late summer (1 brood). ► Below hindwing varies from green or yellow to brown. Chevron of white or yellow spots is usually *sharply curved* and encloses basal spots that *often form the shape of a* C. Spots below reduced or (rarely) entirely absent in some western populations. Above orange with brown borders of variable width blending into orange, with or without lighter spots. 🌿 **Larval foodplant:** Grasses.

JUBA SKIPPER   *Hesperia juba*

Common and widespread in west. Males patrol gullies and slopes in search of females. Flies in late spring and early fall (2 broods). ► Larger than most western Hesperia. Below hindwing olive or green with *large squarish white spots,* often extending along veins, bottom spot of chevron often displaced inward. Above orange with jagged brown borders, more *sharply defined* than on most Hesperia. 🌿 **Larval foodplant:** Grasses.

COLUMBIAN SKIPPER   *Hesperia columbia*

Mainly limited to chaparral of coastal mountains of California. Uncommon and local. Males hilltop. Flies late spring and early fall (2 broods). ► Below hindwing usually rather bright brownish yellow with *abbreviated pattern:* the upper of two basal white spots and the upper white spots of chevron are partial or absent. Above orange with brown borders. 🌿 **Larval foodplant:** Grasses.

DOTTED SKIPPER   *Hesperia attalus*

Brownish skipper of sandy barrens in the east, short-grass prairie in the plains. Local and uncommon. Flies spring to fall (mainly 2 broods). ► Below hindwing brown, usually with *tiny pale spots* in postmedian area and near base (may be lacking on southern plains). See Ottoe Skipper, p. 318. Above mostly brown with yellow spots, including two near forewing margin and row on hindwing. 🌿 **Larval foodplant:** Grasses.

HESPERIA SKIPPERS

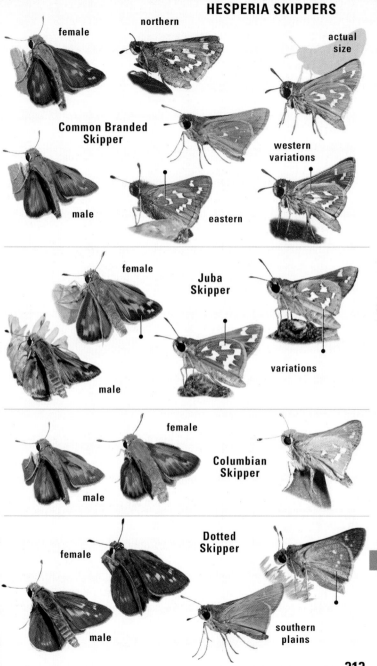

female

northern

actual size

Common Branded Skipper

western variations

male

eastern

Juba Skipper

female

male

variations

female

Columbian Skipper

male

Dotted Skipper

female

male

southern plains

313

NEVADA SKIPPER — *Hesperia nevada*

A species of high mountain grasslands and northern prairies. Common but local in west, uncommon in Canada. Males hilltop. Flies in early to midsummer (1 brood). ► Below olive or green with sharp white chevron, the lower spot *displaced inward,* often almost disconnected. Above orange with brown borders poorly defined. 🌿 **Larval foodplant:** Grasses.

GREEN SKIPPER — *Hesperia viridis*

Central Rockies south to Arizona (rare), New Mexico, and west Texas. Males perch in gullies to await females. Flies in summer in north and Arizona (1 brood), late spring to early summer and again early fall southward (2 broods). ► Below hindwing yellow or olive. The lower three spots of the white chevron *arc outward slightly.* Some Pahaska Skippers match this pattern and cannot be reliably separated. Above orange with brown borders poorly defined. 🌿 **Larval foodplant:** Grasses.

PAHASKA SKIPPER — *Hesperia pahaska*

Very similar to Green Skipper but more widespread and often in more arid habitats. Males avidly hilltop. Flies in early summer in north (1 brood), spring to fall near Mexican border (2–3 broods). ► Below hindwing yellow, olive, or green. Spots in white chevron connected or not; lower three spots are *fairly straight* or arc outward slightly. Above orange with brown borders poorly defined. 🌿 **Larval foodplant:** Grasses.

APACHE SKIPPER — *Hesperia woodgatei*

A fall-flying Hesperia of southwestern mountains. Uncommon and local, mostly in pine-oak forests. Flies in September and October (1 brood). ► Antennae with white below tips. Below hindwing greenish brown, chevron white, loosely connected or broken into spots. Above rich orange with brown borders poorly defined. Note *season and habitat.* 🌿 **Larval foodplant:** Grasses.

MORRISON'S SKIPPER — *Stinga morrisoni*

Often mistaken for a Hesperia; flies with Pahaska Skipper and others in late spring. Adults visit both flowers and mud. Males hilltop. Flies late spring to early summer in most of range (1 brood), spring and late summer in west Texas (2 broods). ► Below hindwing with *white streak out from base* but not meeting chevron. Above orange, forewing with brown jagged border. Male has stigma and female has dark brown stigma-like mark on forewing above. 🌿 **Larval foodplant:** Grasses.

WESTERN HESPERIA

Nevada Skipper

female

male

variations

actual size

female

Green Skipper

male

female

male

Pahaska Skipper

Apache Skipper

female

male

Morrison's Skipper

COBWEB SKIPPER *Hesperia metea*

A dark early-season skipper of the east, widespread but local in clearings and grassy areas. Flies spring to early summer (1 brood). ▶ Variable. Below hindwing with sharply curved white chevron and white sometimes extending along veins creating *cobweb look*. Above mostly dark brown with limited pale orange. Leading edge of forewing *whitish*. In Texas and Arkansas, may be nearly or entirely unmarked both above and below. 🌱 **Larval foodplant**: Big bluestem and little bluestem.

LEONARD'S SKIPPER *Hesperia leonardus*

A late-season species with two very different-looking subspecies. The plainer western population was formerly treated as a separate species **(Pawnee Skipper)**, but intermediates occur in the upper midwest. Favors prairies and large open fields. Flies late summer to early fall (1 brood). ▶ Large. **East:** Below hindwing *reddish brown* with *bright white or cream spotband*. Above mostly blackish brown with limited orange bands. **West (Pawnee Skipper):** Below hindwing yellow-orange with postmedian spots *reduced or absent*. Above male orange with broad dark brown borders. Female above mostly brown with glassy forewing spots and pale orange hindwing spots. Ottoe Skipper (p. 318) is similar to western subspecies but flies in midsummer, not late summer. 🌱 **Larval foodplant**: Grasses.

LINDSEY'S SKIPPER *Hesperia lindseyi*

West Coast only, a bright orange skipper of foothill chaparral and oak woodland habitats. Flies late spring to early summer (1 brood). ▶ Below hindwing yellow or greenish brown with chevron of muted cream or pale white spots, the outer edges of these spots usually looking *jagged*. Above yellow-orange with indistinct brown margins, especially reduced on some females. 🌱 **Larval foodplant**: Grasses.

SIERRA SKIPPER *Hesperia miriamae*

A physically challenging skipper, rarely observed, living only above timberline along the crest of California's Sierra Nevada and adjacent White Mountains. Among the fastest flying of all skippers. Males hilltop at 11,000 feet and above. Flies mid- to late summer (1 brood). ▶ Below hindwing *dusky bluish brown* with pale white chevron. Above orange with broad brown border on forewing, more well defined on female. Habitat is best field mark. 🌱 **Larval foodplant**: Grasses.

HESPERIA SKIPPERS

male female **Cobweb Skipper** actual size

eastern male eastern female **Leonard's Skipper**

"Pawnee" male female "Pawnee"

Lindsey's Skipper male female

Sierra Skipper male

INDIAN SKIPPER *Hesperia sassacus*

This early-season skipper inhabits brushy fields, pastures, woodland clearings. Flies late spring to early summer (1 brood). ▶ Below hindwing orange with *rather indistinct* paler chevron; one spot on band *juts out toward margin.* Above male orange with well-defined, slightly jagged black borders; female blackish brown and orange, borders well defined, hindwing veins through orange patch not blackened. Long Dash (p. 322) similar but has thicker, more curved stigma on male; female has blackened veins on hindwing above; hindwing band below usually wider and lacks outward displaced spot. 🌿 **Larval foodplant:** Grasses.

OTTOE SKIPPER *Hesperia ottoe*

A large Hesperia of tall-grass prairie. Uncommon and local, limited to a dwindling habitat. Flies mid- to late summer (1 brood). ▶ Below hindwing *unmarked pale yellow,* sometimes with trace of postmedian spotband. Above male orange with broad dark borders. Female above orange with broad borders and large glassy spot near forewing cell. Male Leonard's Skipper (previous page) nearly identical to male Ottoe but flies later in year. 🌿 **Larval foodplant:** Bluestems and other grasses.

DAKOTA SKIPPER *Hesperia dacotae*

A small orange skipper of undisturbed alkaline tall-grass prairies. Rare and local, limited to a dwindling habitat. Flies early to midsummer (1 brood). ▶ Small, forewings more rounded than those of other Hesperia. Below male hindwing unmarked yellow-orange, rarely with faint trace of spotband. Female hindwing below grayish brown, usually with white basal spot, and with or without white spotband; compare to Dotted Skipper (p. 312). Above male orange with light black border. Female above orange and black with large glassy spot near forewing cell. 🌿 **Larval foodplant:** Grasses.

MESKE'S SKIPPER *Hesperia meskei*

An elusive skipper of the southeast, with isolated populations in Arkansas and eastern Texas. Rare and local within range; may have disappeared from Florida Keys. Flies late spring and fall most areas (2 broods), all year southern Florida (3 broods). ▶ Below hindwing golden orange, with or without faint spotband. Above mostly dark brown with orange bands. Arogos Skipper and others on p. 336 are similar below but quite different above. 🌿 **Larval foodplant:** Grasses.

HESPERIA SKIPPERS

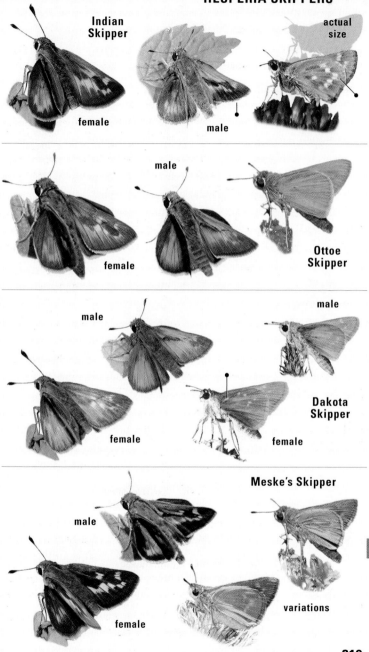

Indian Skipper
female
male
actual size

Ottoe Skipper
male
female

Dakota Skipper
male
male
female
female

Meske's Skipper
male
female
variations

319

Although they wear bold patches and lines on the hindwings below, their patterns actually provide perfect camouflage in the wild. When they land on the ground among short dry grass, these skippers virtually disappear.

UNCAS SKIPPER *Hesperia uncas*

Widespread and local in short-grass and alkaline grasslands. Sometimes common, clustering on southwestern roadside thistles by the dozens, their triangular silhouettes visible from inside a passing vehicle. Males hilltop, perching just below summits. Flies early and late summer (2 broods) in some areas, midsummer (1 brood) in others. ▶ Variable. Below hindwing olive-yellow with darker spots and *white chevron and veins* (subspecies *macswaini*, California-Nevada border, lacks white veins). Above variable, usually with lighter spots near forewing tip. At east edge of range, see Cobweb Skipper (p. 316). ☙ **Larval foodplant:** Primarily blue grama.

SANDHILL SKIPPER *Polites sabuleti*

Widespread in many habitats, from coastal dunes to rocky slopes above treeline. Flies spring to fall depending on locality and altitude (1–3 broods). ▶ Extremely variable, even varying sharply over short distances. Resembles Uncas Skipper in some areas but is much smaller with shorter forewings. On hindwing below, *cobweb pattern* is usually visible. Above male usually orange or pale orange with jagged black margins, especially on hindwing, and a black stigma often bordered by dark patch. Female above tends to be darker. ☙ **Larval foodplant:** Saltgrass, Bermuda grass, and others.

RHESUS SKIPPER *Polites rhesus*

An early-season skipper of dry short-grass prairies, often on volcanic soils. Males perch on gully edges or on high points in flat areas to await females. Flies late spring to early summer (1 brood). ▶ Fringes white. *Bold pattern on hindwing below,* pale yellow with black patches next to white veins and white spotband. Above blackish brown with white markings, more extensive on female. ☙ **Larval foodplant:** Primarily blue grama.

CARUS SKIPPER *Polites carus*

Uncommon in southwest. Males perch on grassy flats at gully edges or below hilltops to await females. Flies late spring to late summer (2–3 broods). ▶ Fringes white to gray. Below hindwing gray-brown with dark patches next to creamy veins and spotband. Duller, less contrasty than Rhesus Skipper. Above dark gray-brown with pale yellow spots. ☙ **Larval foodplant:** Unknown.

WESTERN SKIPPERS

male

actual size

variations

Uncas
Skipper

female

macswaini

Sandhill
Skipper

variations

variations

male

female

Rhesus
Skipper

Carus
Skipper

DRACO SKIPPER   *Polites draco*

A common species mainly of dry high mountain grass-lands and meadows. Flies early to midsummer (1 brood). ▶ Below hindwing orange-yellow, brown, or green. Cream or white chevron has *very large jagged spot* in center (*Hesperia* skippers on preceding pages lack this jagged spot). Sandhill Skipper (previous page) is smaller, prefers wet meadows at lower elevations where ranges overlap. 🌿 **Larval foodplant:** Grasses.

SONORAN SKIPPER   *Polites sonora*

Common near wet meadows in mountain west (but not in Sonora!), with some colonies at sea level in northwest. Flies in summer (1 brood). ▶ Below hind-wing yellow-orange to gray-brown with narrow yellow or cream spotband enclosing *long basal spot*. Long Dash similar below but usually has short basal spot and wider spotband. Above orange with variable black bor-ders. 🌿 **Larval foodplant:** Grasses.

LONG DASH   *Polites mystic*

Widespread in north, more local southward in moun-tains; common in grassy habitats. Flies in summer (mainly 1 brood). ▶ Below hindwing orange-brown with contrasting broad yellow spotband and *short basal spot*. Many individuals from midwestern prairies are al-most entirely orange-brown below with little contrast (compare to Indian Skipper, p. 318). Above orange and black, orange patch on hindwing highlighted by black veins. 🌿 **Larval foodplant:** Grasses.

PECK'S SKIPPER   *Polites peckius*

Small classy skipper of moist grassy meadows and marsh edges. Adapts to lawns, roadsides, power-line cuts, other disturbed areas. Common in most of range. Flies spring to fall in much of eastern U.S. (2 broods), summer in north and west (1 brood). ▶ Below hind-wing brown to tan with two connected yellow patches; a *central spot juts outward* on outer patch. Above orange and black. 🌿 **Larval foodplant:** Grasses.

MARDON SKIPPER   *Polites mardon*

Rare and local. Isolated populations in northwest, in grassy lowlands or subalpine meadows, rocky serpen-tine meadows in northwestern California. Flies in early summer (1 brood). ▶ Wings short, stubby, rather rounded. Below hindwing yellow to olive-brown with *thick yellowish spotband*. Above dusky orange and black. 🌿 **Larval foodplant:** Grasses.

POLITES SKIPPERS

Draco Skipper
male
female
variations
actual size

Sonoran Skipper
male
female

Long Dash
male
female
variations

Peck's Skipper
female
male
variations

Mardon Skipper
male
female

323

TAWNY-EDGED SKIPPER   *Polites themistocles*

Very common and widespread in east, more local in west. Flies mostly early and late summer in southeast, spring to fall in deep south (2–3 broods), mostly early summer in north and west (1 brood). ▶ Small, rather dull. Hindwing below olive to brown, sometimes with faint pale crossband, but *contrasts sharply with tawny orange leading edge of forewing below.* Crossline Skipper very similar but usually a bit larger, and hindwing below is usually more yellowish brown and more often has a pale spotband. Above male Tawny-edged has thicker black stigma setting off orange leading edge; female brown with pale spots, usually some orange near forewing leading edge. ❦ **Larval foodplant:** Grasses.

CROSSLINE SKIPPER   *Polites origenes*

Mainly eastern, locally common in open areas. Flies midsummer in west and north (1 brood), spring to fall elsewhere (2 broods). ▶ Variable; can be very similar to Tawny-edged Skipper and hard to distinguish, but more often has *pale spotband* on hindwing below, and usually shows *less contrast* between hindwing and leading edge of forewing below. Above male stigma is narrower and more tapered toward base. Females above very similar, not always safely identified. ❦ **Larval foodplant:** Grasses.

BARACOA SKIPPER   *Polites baracoa*

Common around lawns and weedy disturbed areas in south Florida, more local in scrubby woodlands in central Florida. Flies spring to fall, or all year in south (multiple broods). ▶ Similar to Crossline and Tawny-edged Skippers but usually *smaller.* Hindwing below dark, contrasting with orange on forewing, and usually with a *short, thick pale band.* Above male golden orange and brown, with short black stigma almost meeting additional black streak on forewing. Female above mostly brown with pale spots. ❦ **Larval foodplant:** Grasses.

BLACK DASH   *Euphyes conspicua*

Local in marshes and wet meadows from upper midwest to Atlantic Coast. Look for adults on flowers of swamp milkweed. Flies in summer (1 brood). ▶ Large. Below hindwing *rusty yellow-brown* with *thick pale yellow patch.* Above male dark with variable orange patches and thick black stigma; female with or without orange patch or band on hindwing. See broken-dashes (next page). ❦ **Larval foodplant:** Sedges.

SKIPPERS

female

variations

actual
size

male

**Tawny-edged
Skipper**

**Crossline
Skipper**

female

male

variations

Baracoa Skipper

male

female

Black Dash

male

female

SOUTHERN BROKEN-DASH   *Wallengrenia otho*

A versatile skipper of a wide variety of habitats, often common. Flies spring to fall in most of range (2 broods), all year in south Texas and Florida (3 broods). ► Below red-orange (sometimes yellow-orange) with short pale spotband on hindwing often shaped like a 3. Many can be identified at a glance by *typical red-orange color*. Forewing below has contrasting *gray fringe*. Above male has an orange dash next to broken black stigma on forewing. Female above mostly brown with pale orange spots, including near center of forewing. 🦋 **Larval foodplant:** Grasses.

NORTHERN BROKEN-DASH   *Wallengrenia egeremet*

Widespread in east. Formerly considered same species as Southern Broken-Dash, but their ranges overlap in the southeast. Flies in summer in north (1 brood), spring to fall southward (2 broods). ► Similar to Southern Broken-Dash (including shape of spotband on hindwing below) but below *duller yellow-brown,* often with a purple sheen. Above male with yellow dash (often faint) next to broken black stigma on forewing. Female above mostly brown, often with two pale yellow spots near center of forewing. 🦋 **Larval foodplant:** Grasses.

LITTLE GLASSYWING   *Pompeius verna*

Local, sometimes common in damp brushy meadows. Flies in summer in north (1 brood), spring to fall southward (2 broods). ► Below hindwing brown, often with purple sheen, and tiny pale spots forming a band. Best separated from similar species by the prominent (and often squarish) *glassy white spot* near center of forewing and other glassy white spots. Also note white at base of antennal clubs. Male has black stigma. 🦋 **Larval foodplant:** Purple top grass.

DUN SKIPPER   *Euphyes vestris*

Our most widespread "plain" brown skipper, in a wide array of habitats but usually near wet areas. Flies mainly in summer in north (1 brood), spring and summer in south (2 broods). ► Below hindwing usually unmarked brown, rarely with hint of spotband. Above male unmarked dark brown with black stigma. Female above dark brown with up to two pale white spots near center of forewing; compare to the two preceding species. Adults in some regions have gold on head, suggesting Orange-headed Roadside-Skipper (p. 350). 🦋 **Larval foodplant:** Sedges.

SKIPPERS

male

actual size

female

Southern Broken-Dash

Northern Broken-Dash

female

male

male

female

Little Glassywing

male

female

Dun Skipper

327

WOODLAND SKIPPER   *Ochlodes sylvanoides*

Widespread in west, often the most common orange skipper of many habitats late in the season. Flies mainly midsummer to fall (1 brood). ▶ Below variable, hindwing yellow-brown to purplish, usually with spotband of yellow or cream squarish spots. Above with jagged dark borders; male has prominent black stigma, female has dark patch in place of stigma with second dark patch outward toward tip. ❦ **Larval foodplant:** Grasses.

RURAL SKIPPER   *Ochlodes agricola*

Common in lowlands and foothills of far west. Usually flies earlier than Woodland Skipper, late spring to early summer (1 brood). ▶ Male hindwing below orange, may have yellow spotband. Female below orange-brown to purplish, yellow spotband prominent or faint. Look for dark area in center of hindwing below. Smaller, usually less strongly marked than Woodland Skipper. Coastal populations tend to be darker. ❦ **Larval foodplant:** Melic and other grasses.

YUMA SKIPPER   *Ochlodes yuma*

Widespread but very local, around scattered colonies of giant reed. Flies late spring to early fall (1–2 broods). ▶ Large and plain. Below hindwing unmarked yellow (male) or yellow-tan (female), sometimes with trace of pale spotband. Above mostly orange with diffuse dark margins, male with stigma, female with lighter markings. Population in northern New Mexico much darker above and below. ❦ **Larval foodplant:** Giant reed.

SNOW'S SKIPPER   *Paratrytone snowi*

Uncommon and limited in range, found in clearings in mountain pine woodlands. Very fast in flight. Flies in mid- to late summer (1 brood). ▶ Below hindwing *reddish brown,* usually with narrow pale yellow spotband and lone spot toward base; *hindwing fringe is whitish.* Above mostly brown; note the hourglass-shaped spot near end of forewing cell. ❦ **Larval foodplant:** Grasses.

UMBER SKIPPER   *Poanes melane*

Common garden visitor along California coast, rare in southwest. Flies spring to fall (2 broods). ▶ Below hindwing purplish brown, with yellow postmedian spotband either faint (California) or bold (southwest). Above reddish brown with dark area in center of forewing, yellow-orange row of spots on forewing, and orange flush on hindwing. Yellow spots are bolder and better defined in southwest. ❦ **Larval foodplant:** Grasses.

WESTERN SKIPPERS

female

Woodland Skipper

actual size

male

variations

interior

coastal

Rural Skipper

variations

Yuma Skipper

female

male

female

Snow's Skipper

male

southwest

Umber Skipper

California

329

Most have yellow patches on the hindwing below; males lack stigmas.

HOBOMOK SKIPPER   *Poanes hobomok*

Common in clearings and edges of woodlands in north and east, with isolated population in southern Rockies. Female has two color forms. Flies late spring to midsummer (1 brood). ▶ Below hindwing purplish brown with broad yellow postmedian patch. Above orange with broad dark brown borders on both wings and cell-end bar on forewing, hindwing patch highlighted by brown veins. Brown female (form "pocahontas") is mostly dark above, with white spot in forewing cell, and hindwing mostly purplish brown below; compare to Zabulon Skipper. ❧ **Larval foodplant**: Grasses.

ZABULON SKIPPER   *Poanes zabulon*

Primarily eastern. Males perch on tall shrubs and other vantage points along streams and trails to await females. Flies late spring to fall (2 broods). ▶ Male hindwing below mostly yellow, brown at base and along margin; brown basal area *encloses a yellow spot,* lacking on Hobomok Skipper. Above male has thin cell-end bar on forewing, dark brown borders usually narrower than those of male Hobomok; hindwing patch not highlighted by veins. Female resembles "pocahontas" form of female Hobomok, but has *sharp white margin* at upper angle of hindwing below and lacks white cell spot above. ❧ **Larval foodplant**: Grasses.

TAXILES SKIPPER   *Poanes taxiles*

Primarily in mountain woodlands, often very common. A western replacement for the Zabulon Skipper. Flies in summer (1 brood). ▶ Male hindwing below mostly yellow with brown spots at base and narrowly along margin. Female below purplish or reddish brown with some orange suffusion and with *very narrow white leading edge* on hindwing. Above male mostly yellow-orange with narrow brown borders, female somewhat darker. ❧ **Larval foodplant**: Grasses.

MULBERRY WING   *Poanes massasoit*

A dark, distinctive skipper of wetland habitats in the upper midwest and east. Local, sometimes common. Adults fly weakly and low in sedgy spots. Flies in summer (1 brood). ▶ Wings rounded. Below reddish brown with *bold yellow patch* in shape of *thick crossbow* (rarely absent). Above velvety blackish brown, with or without spots (yellow on male, white on female). ❧ **Larval foodplant**: Sedges.

WELL-MARKED SKIPPERS

actual size

dark form females

Hobomok Skipper

females

Zabulon Skipper

males

females

males

Taxiles Skipper

male

Mulberry Wing

female

variant

typical

331

BROAD-WINGED SKIPPER *Poanes viator*

Sometimes common in coastal marshes, local in inland sedge meadows. Flies spring to fall (or spring and fall) in southern coastal areas, mainly summer in north and inland. ▶ *Rounded wings.* Variable. Below hindwing with paler ray out from base crossing row of yellowish spots. Mulberry Wing (previous page) smaller with stronger pattern. Above male has orange spots on forewing and hindwing, no stigma; female similar but with white spots on forewing. 🐛 **Larval foodplant:** Common reed, wild rice, sedges, and others.

AARON'S SKIPPER *Poanes aaroni*

A localized inhabitant of fresh and salt-water marshes of the southeast, common in some limited areas. Flies mostly late spring and late summer (2 broods). ▶ Hindwing below orange-tan with pale ray extending from base to margin. Above orange with broad dark brown borders, male with slender black stigma. 🐛 **Larval foodplant:** Maidencane and other grasses.

YEHL SKIPPER *Poanes yehl*

A skipper of moist or swampy southeastern woods, usually uncommon. Ranges north to southern Illinois. Flies late spring to early summer and late summer to fall (2 broods). ▶ Hindwing below orange or yellow on male, brown on female, both with pale postmedian spots. Above orange with black borders, male has stigma, female paler. 🐛 **Larval foodplant:** Unknown.

PALATKA SKIPPER *Euphyes pilatka*

Mainly coastal from Virginia to Florida Keys. Prefers brackish marshes, but other wetlands with sawgrass will suffice. Flies mainly early and late summer (2 broods), most of year in south Florida (3 broods?). ▶ *Large.* Below hindwing unmarked rich warm brown. Above orange with black borders, female with more black basally and with broader borders blending into orange. 🐛 **Larval foodplant:** Sawgrass.

TWO-SPOTTED SKIPPER *Euphyes bimacula*

Rare and highly localized in sedgy meadows, marshes, bogs. Flies in summer in north (1 brood), late spring to early summer and late summer in south (2 broods). ▶ Fringes white. Below hindwing orange-brown with paler veins and *conspicuous white trailing edge.* Above mostly brown, male with variable orange patch around stigma, female usually with two creamy spots near forewing center. 🐛 **Larval foodplant:** Sedges.

WETLAND SKIPPERS

Broad-winged Skipper
male
female
actual size

Aaron's Skipper
male
female

Yehl Skipper
male
female

Palatka Skipper
male
female

Two-spotted Skipper
male
female

333

DION SKIPPER *Euphyes dion*

A large eastern skipper of wet marshes and bogs. Local and uncommon. Some populations have been described as different species (see below). Flies in summer in north (1 brood), late spring to early summer and late summer in south (2 broods). ► Variable. Below hindwing red or orange-brown with two pale rays extending out from base, the upper one not reaching margin. Above male orange with broad dark brown borders, black stigma, and orange ray on hindwing. Female mostly brown with pale orange spots on forewing and orange ray on hindwing. Southern populations tend to be darker above. ❦ **Larval foodplant:** Sedges.

BAY SKIPPER *Euphyes bayensis* **(not illustrated)**

Recently described from brackish marsh in coastal Mississippi, reported elsewhere on Gulf Coast. Flies late spring and fall (2 broods). ► Essentially identical to Dion Skipper except that males have slightly narrower stigma and more extensive orange above. ❦ **Larval foodplant:** Unknown.

DUKES'S SKIPPER *Euphyes dukesi*

Dark skipper of shaded eastern swamps and wet roadside ditches. Local. Adults are slow fliers. Flies in summer in north (1 brood), late spring to early summer and late summer in south (2 broods). ► Wings rounded. Below hindwing orange-brown with pale ray extending from base to margin, center of forewing black. Above mostly dark, male sometimes with orange on leading edge of forewing; female may have pair of white spots near center of forewing. ❦ **Larval foodplant:** Sedges.

PALMETTO SKIPPER *Euphyes arpa*

Mainly in Florida, local in woodland scrub with saw palmetto. Flies late spring to fall (2 broods). ► *Large, uniformly orange. Head and shoulders yellow-orange.* Below hindwing unmarked orange. Above male orange with dark brown borders and long narrow black stigma; female above mostly dark brown with pale yellow spots. ❦ **Larval foodplant:** Saw palmetto.

BERRY'S SKIPPER *Euphyes berryi*

Rare and local in southeast, mainly Florida. Adults cling to pond edges, swamps, and other wet habitats. Flies spring and fall (2 broods). ► Below hindwing orange with light veins. Byssus Skipper (next page) usually has pale postmedian patch on hindwing. Above orange with brown borders, male with stigma, female with forewing cell spot. ❦ **Larval foodplant:** Sedges.

EASTERN SKIPPERS

actual size

male

female

Dion Skipper

male

female

Dukes's Skipper

male

female

Palmetto Skipper

Berry's Skipper

male

female

335

DELAWARE SKIPPER · *Anatrytone logan*

Widespread east of the Rockies in a variety of wet grassy habitats, including disturbed areas. Flies in summer in north (1 brood), late spring to early summer and late summer in south (2 broods). ▶ Below unmarked yellow-orange, including *orange fringes*. Above orange with *black cell-end bar* on forewing and black veining, female with more black. Compare to European Skipper (p. 304). 🐛 **Larval foodplant:** Grasses.

AROGOS SKIPPER · *Atrytone arogos*

Local, scarce at undisturbed prairies on Great Plains, serpentine barrens and sandy pine flats in east. Flies in summer in north (1 brood), late spring to early summer and late summer in south (2 broods). ▶ *Small*, fringes *white*. Below orange-yellow, sometimes with paler veins. Above male yellow with broad dark margins, *no cell-end bar* on forewing. Female similar with broader margins, hindwing mostly brown, forewing often with black streak below cell. 🐛 **Larval foodplant:** Big bluestem (prairies), lopsided Indian grass (Florida).

BYSSUS SKIPPER · *Problema byssus*

Local at wooded wetlands and marsh edges in southeast, tall-grass prairies farther west. Flies in summer on prairies (1 brood), late spring to early summer and late summer to fall in southeast (2 broods). ▶ Variable. Male hindwing below orange to orange-brown, usually with pale patch. Female hindwing below orange or reddish brown, usually with pale band. Above male orange with sharp black margins and cell-end bar on forewing; female similar to male or mostly black with orange reduced. 🐛 **Larval foodplant:** Grama grass and others.

RARE SKIPPER · *Problema bulenta*

Despite the name, can be locally common in brackish coastal marshes, but habitat is limited and many colonies are inaccessible. Flies in summer (1–2 broods). ▶ Similar to Delaware Skipper but larger, with broader black margins above in both sexes; from below, black cell-end bar on forewing often visible. Note range and habitat. 🐛 **Larval foodplant:** Wild rice and other grasses.

COMMON MELLANA · *Quasimellana eulogius*

Regular stray to south Texas. Males perch along woodland trails in late afternoon to await females. Reported most of year. ▶ Below hindwing yellow-orange, pale postmedian band very faint. Above male with black streak from base to margin above trailing edge of forewing, no stigma. Female above mostly brown with paler spots. 🐛 **Larval foodplant:** Unknown.

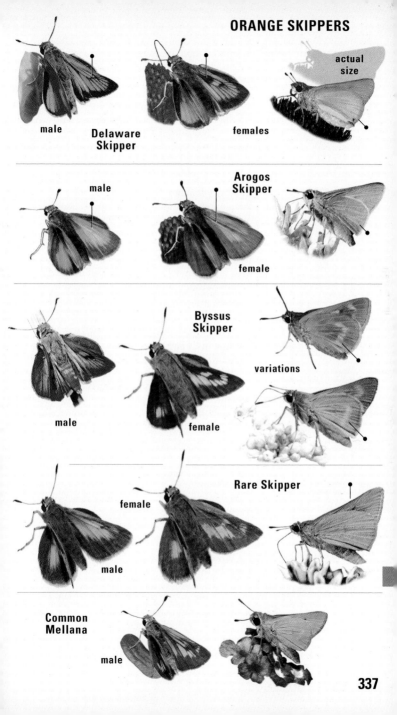

ORANGE SKIPPERS

actual size

male

females

Delaware Skipper

male

Arogos Skipper

female

Byssus Skipper

variations

male

female

Rare Skipper

female

male

Common Mellana

male

337

DUSTED-SKIPPERS

(genus *Atrytonopsis*) are medium-sized to large, fast in flight. Avid flower visitors, some are the only skippers known to visit cholla cactus flowers.

DUSTED SKIPPER   *Atrytonopsis hianna*

Widespread but local in the east, in prairies, overgrown fields, barrens. Flies late spring to early summer (1 brood). ▶ Palps white and eye half-circled with white, giving face a *"bandit mask."* Below hindwing brown, grayer toward margin, usually with white basal spot and occasionally more spots. Above brown with white dots on forewing. ❦ **Larval foodplant:** Bluestem grasses.

LOAMMI SKIPPER   *Atrytonopsis loammi*

Local but sometimes common in dunes, sand flats, overgrown fields in southeast. Sometimes treated as a subspecies of Dusted Skipper. Flies in late spring and again late summer to fall (2 broods). ▶ Similar to Dusted Skipper, including "masked" face, but hindwing below with *sharp white spotband curving outward.* Note that Dusted Skipper sometimes has variable white spotting below. ❦ **Larval foodplant:** Bluestem grasses.

DEVA SKIPPER   *Atrytonopsis deva*

Locally very common at middle elevations in mountains and canyons. Flies late spring to early summer (1 brood). ▶ Distinct *white or tan fringe* on hindwing. Below hindwing smooth gray-brown, grayer toward margin, usually with two darker parallel lines across center. Above forewing brown with glassy white spots. Moon-marked Skipper flies later in season, has hourglass spot in forewing cell. ❦ **Larval foodplant:** Unknown.

VIERECK'S SKIPPER   *Atrytonopsis vierecki*

A species of rugged southwestern canyons in oak-juniper-pinyon woodland. Flies late spring to early summer (1 brood). ▶ Similar to Deva and Moon-marked Skippers but hindwing fringe is *gray,* not white or tan. Unlike Deva Skipper, forewing above has hourglass-shaped spot in cell. Dusted Skipper may overlap range in New Mexico. ❦ **Larval foodplant:** Unknown.

MOON-MARKED SKIPPER   *Atrytonopsis lunus*

Uncommon and local in southwestern oak-juniper woodland at middle elevations. Flies in mid- to late summer (1 brood). ▶ Large with *hindwing fringe usually cream* (shape suggesting a crescent moon). Large pale spots above, including hourglass-shaped spot in forewing cell. Deva Skipper flies earlier in season and lacks the hourglass spot. ❦ **Larval foodplant:** Bullgrass.

DUSTED-SKIPPERS

actual size

Dusted Skipper

Loammi Skipper

Deva Skipper

Viereck's Skipper

Moon-marked Skipper

339

WHITE-BARRED SKIPPER   *Atrytonopsis pittacus*

Fairly common in open oak woodlands at middle elevations. Attracted to mud and to flowers, and males are avid hilltoppers. Flies in spring, with partial second brood in early fall (1–2 broods). ► Fringes are *plain whitish*. Below gray with a narrow postmedian bar of pale glassy spots. Above brown with glassy forewing spots and glassy postmedian straight bar on hindwing.
🌿 **Larval foodplant:** Probably grasses.

PYTHON SKIPPER   *Atrytonopsis python*

Uncommon but widespread in oak woodland of southwest, found cavorting among the same flowers (thistle, locust, or cholla) as Deva Skipper (previous page). Flies late spring to early summer (1 brood). ► Fringes *checkered*. Below hindwing brown with gray overlay and a narrow cream to white postmedian band that curves outward. Above brown with pale yellow glassy spots, including a curved bar on hindwing. In eastern part of range, postmedian band reduced below and spots whiter above. 🌿 **Larval foodplant:** Unknown.

CESTUS SKIPPER   *Atrytonopsis cestus*

Rare and local from central Arizona southward. Inhabits deep canyons with shaded walls where stands of the larval foodplant thrive. Males often mingle with more widespread Sheep Skipper, frequently sharing perching spots on sunny steep canyon walls. Flies late spring and late summer (2 broods). ► Fringes *checkered*. Below hindwing gray-brown with broad glassy postmedian and basal bands. Above brown with glassy forewing spots and glassy postmedian band and basal spot on hindwing. Rarely (if ever) found with Python Skipper.
🌿 **Larval foodplant:** Bamboo muhly.

SHEEP SKIPPER   *Atrytonopsis edwardsii*

Can be common in dry canyon country at low and middle elevations in its limited southwestern range. Males perch on rocks along gullies or up on steep canyon walls in morning to find females before retreating to shade during afternoon heat. Flies late spring and late summer (2 broods). ► Fringes *checkered;* wings *more rounded* than those of other dusted-skippers. Below variable, hindwing powdered gray with glassy white spots (sometimes greatly reduced or absent). Above brown with glassy forewing spots, hindwing spots may or may not be present. 🌿 **Larval foodplant:** Sideoats grama.

SOUTHWESTERN DUSTED-SKIPPERS

actual size

White-barred Skipper

Python Skipper

Cestus Skipper

Sheep Skipper

variations

ROADSIDE-SKIPPERS

(genus *Amblyscirtes*) make up a challenging group. Adults are small, dark, and fast-flying, staying close to the ground. Similarities often make field identification difficult; worn specimens can baffle even the experts.

COMMON ROADSIDE-SKIPPER   *Amblyscirtes vialis*

The most widespread of the roadside-skippers, but usually found sparingly where it occurs. Prefers woodland edges, openings, and streamsides. Flies late spring and summer (1–2 broods). ▶ Fringes strongly checkered. Below hindwing black with bluish gray frosting, *heavier near margin, less on leading edge;* forewing shows *triangular white spot* near tip (may be faint or absent). Above mostly black; note triangular forewing spot. Compare to Linda's, Dusky, and Bronze (p. 346) Roadside-Skippers. 🐛 **Larval foodplant:** Grasses.

LINDA'S ROADSIDE-SKIPPER   *Amblyscirtes linda*

Limited distribution centered in the Ozark region. Uncommon in moist woods, often near streams. Flies in spring and summer (2 broods). ▶ Fringes strongly checkered. Very similar to Common Roadside-Skipper, but hindwing below has gray frosting *evenly distributed;* usually a faint postmedian band of diffuse whitish gray spots. Center of forewing below has brown scaling (often not visible). Above like Common Roadside-Skipper but with brown scaling. 🐛 **Larval foodplant:** Broadleaf uniola.

DUSKY ROADSIDE-SKIPPER   *Amblyscirtes alternata*

A small dark skipper of the southeast. Prefers open pine woods. Uncommon. Flies spring to fall (2 broods). ▶ Fringes lightly checkered, male forewings pointed. Below hindwing black, lightly but evenly dusted with bluish gray scales. Above blackish brown, with or without faint white spots on forewing. Common Roadside-Skipper has heavier bluish gray frosting on hindwing below, especially near margin; usually more obvious white spot on forewing. 🐛 **Larval foodplant:** Grasses.

PEPPER AND SALT SKIPPER   *Amblyscirtes hegon*

Widespread but local, usually uncommon, in woodland clearings, glades, streamsides. Flies late spring (mainly) to summer in south (1–2 broods), early summer in north (1 brood). ▶ Fringes *boldly checkered.* Variable. Below hindwing frosted greenish gray, usually with creamy postmedian band. Bell's Roadside-Skipper (next page) much darker below. Above brown, usually with white forewing spotband, more extensive than on similar species. 🐛 **Larval foodplant:** Grasses.

342   GRASS SKIPPERS

ROADSIDE-SKIPPERS

actual size

variations

Common Roadside-Skipper

Linda's Roadside-Skipper

Dusky Roadside-Skipper

Pepper and Salt Skipper

variations

343

CELIA'S ROADSIDE-SKIPPER *Amblyscirtes celia*

Almost entirely limited to Texas. Common in central and southern regions, especially along woodland trails, openings, or edges. Flies mostly spring to fall (2 broods), most of year in south Texas (2–3 broods). ▶ Below hindwing dark brown with white postmedian spotband, lightly overlaid with gray scales. Above blackish-brown with white forewing spots. Bell's Roadside-Skipper (next) is extremely similar. ✤ **Larval foodplant:** Guinea grass, St. Augustine grass, and others.

BELL'S ROADSIDE-SKIPPER *Amblyscirtes belli*

A dark roadside-skipper of the southeast. Inhabits streamsides, openings in moist woodlands, city gardens. Flies spring to fall (2 broods). ▶ Very similar to Celia's Roadside-Skipper; extremely difficult to separate where their ranges overlap. Bell's tends to be darker below and (especially) above; postmedian spots on hindwing below may be more connected. ✤ **Larval foodplant:** Broadleaf uniola, Johnson grass, and others.

LACE-WINGED ROADSIDE-SKIPPER *Amblyscirtes aesculapius*

A very distinctive eastern species, common near woodlands with cane. Flies spring to early summer and late summer to early fall (2 broods). ▶ Below hindwing gray-brown with *dazzling white cobweb pattern*. Wing fringes strongly checkered black and white. Cobweb Skipper and others (p. 316) lack checkered fringes, often show some orange above. ✤ **Larval foodplant:** Cane (*Arundinaria*).

CAROLINA ROADSIDE-SKIPPER *Amblyscirtes carolina*

Limited range in southeast, north to southern Illinois. Tends to be uncommon; usually around stands of cane in moist woods. Flies spring to fall (3 broods). ▶ Below dull yellow with *darker reddish brown spots*. Fiery Skipper female (p. 302) is larger with darker spots. Above dark brown with yellow forewing spots. Note dark spots on abdomen. ✤ **Larval foodplant:** Cane.

REVERSED ROADSIDE-SKIPPER *Amblyscirtes reversa*

Formerly thought to be a color morph of Carolina Roadside-Skipper. In its limited southeastern range it is uncommon to rare, around clumps of cane near wooded wetlands. Flies spring to late summer (2–3 broods). ▶ Below hindwing reddish brown with yellow spots (reverse of the color pattern of Carolina Roadside-Skipper). Above dark brown with yellow forewing spots. ✤ **Larval foodplant:** Cane.

Celia's Roadside-Skipper

actual size

Bell's Roadside-Skipper

Lace-winged Roadside-Skipper

Carolina Roadside-Skipper

variations

Reversed Roadside-Skipper

BRONZE ROADSIDE-SKIPPER *Amblyscirtes aenus*

Fairly common in southwest. More active in the morning, seeking shade during hot afternoons. Flies late spring to late summer (1–2 broods). ► Variable, easily confused with others. Forewings rounded. Below hindwing variable, mostly unmarked brown with gray overscaling or with faint band of diffuse whitish spots (southern Arizona populations more boldly marked). Forewing below with *cell area brown* (not always visible). Above coppery brown with yellow-tinged spots on forewing, rarely one in cell. Common Roadside-Skipper (p. 342) darker above and without brown on forewing below. ❧ **Larval foodplant**: Grasses.

TEXAS ROADSIDE-SKIPPER *Amblyscirtes texanae*

Arizona to west Texas only, in rugged canyons, washes, grassy roadsides. Males perch in gully bottoms to await females. Flies spring to fall (1–2 broods). ► Below hindwing gray with faint whitish postmedian band. Above gray-brown with creamy forewing spots, usually including spot in cell. Bronze and Oslar's Roadside-Skippers are usually less distinctly marked on forewing above. ❧ **Larval foodplant**: Bulb panic grass.

OSLAR'S ROADSIDE-SKIPPER *Amblyscirtes oslari*

A plain skipper of dry prairies in the north, canyons farther south. In southwest, from mid- to late afternoon, males perch in gully bottom sites used by other roadside-skippers earlier in the day. Flies late spring or summer depending on region (1 brood). ► Male forewing pointed, female more rounded. Fringes *gray,* checkered vaguely if at all. Below hindwing gray with muted pale postmedian band. Above mostly unmarked gray-brown, male with short black stigma. ❧ **Larval foodplant**: Side-oats grama.

SIMIUS ROADSIDE-SKIPPER *"Amblyscirtes" simius*

In short-grass prairies, males patrol areas just below hill summits. Often found with Uncas Skipper in sites that had been occupied by Rhesus Skipper (both p. 320) a month earlier. Probably not a true *Amblyscirtes*. Flies in summer (1 brood). ► Fringes gray to white, vaguely checkered if at all. Below hindwing gray to tan with pale postmedian band and basal spots of variable intensity, forewing with *orange in disk.* Above variable, orange to blackish brown (black in southern Arizona), forewing with variable pale postmedian band and usually with spot in cell. ❧ **Larval foodplant**: Blue grama grass.

ROADSIDE-SKIPPERS

Bronze Roadside-Skipper

actual size

southern Arizona

Texas Roadside-Skipper

Oslar's Roadside-Skipper

variations

variations

Simius Roadside-Skipper

LARGE ROADSIDE-SKIPPER *Amblyscirtes exoteria*

This species (which deserves the name "large" only by comparison to other roadside-skippers) is sometimes common at flowers in oak-juniper or oak-pine woodlands. Flies in summer (1 brood). ▶ Somewhat larger than its close relatives. Below hindwing brown with light gray overscaling; has a white postmedian spotband with one spot jutting outward. Above blackish brown with coppery cast and white forewing spots. 🌿 **Larval foodplant:** Bullgrass.

DOTTED ROADSIDE-SKIPPER *Amblyscirtes eos*

Widespread in southwest, may be expanding its range. Males perch in gully bottoms in the morning to await females. Flies spring to fall (mostly 2 broods, perhaps partial third brood). ▶ Small. Below hindwing brown, often with heavy gray overscaling, and with postmedian band of *bold white spots outlined in black.* Spots are more sharply defined than on Celia's Roadside-Skipper (p. 344). Above blackish brown with white forewing spots, but no spot in cell, and no spots on hindwing. 🌿 **Larval foodplant:** Obtuse panic-grass.

TOLTEC ROADSIDE-SKIPPER *Amblyscirtes tolteca*

Southeastern Arizona only, generally rare. Most active in early morning, seeking shade during sunny hot afternoons. Formerly called Prenda Roadside-Skipper. Flies in summer (1–2 broods). ▶ Below hindwing brown (sometimes gray) with white spotband and usually with white spot in middle of trailing margin. Above forewing with white hourglass-shaped cell spot, white broken spotband, hindwing with short row of white spots. Dotted and Elissa Roadside-Skippers lack the white spot along trailing margin below and the hourglass-shaped cell spot above. 🌿 **Larval foodplant:** Grasses.

ELISSA ROADSIDE-SKIPPER *Amblyscirtes elissa*

Barely extending north of the Mexican border, this skipper is uncommon in oak-mesquite-juniper woodland. Adults are most active early in the morning. Flies in midsummer (1 brood). ▶ Below brown with light overlay of pale yellow or olive scales and pattern of small white spots. Above blackish brown with small round white spot in cell, white forewing spotband and olive hair basally, lacks spots on hindwing. Dotted Roadside-Skipper lacks white spot in forewing cell; Toltec Roadside-Skipper has white spots on hindwing above. 🌿 **Larval foodplant:** Side-oats grama.

SOUTHWESTERN ROADSIDE-SKIPPERS

Large
Roadside-Skipper

actual size

Dotted
Roadside-Skipper

variations

Toltec
Roadside-Skipper

Elissa
Roadside-Skipper

NYSA ROADSIDE-SKIPPER *Amblyscirtes nysa*

Uncommon in varied habitats from dry canyons to gardens. Males perch in wash bottoms, road depressions, or along trails very early in the morning before retiring to shade for the afternoon. Flies spring to early fall (1–3 broods). ► Small. Readily identified by distinctive *mottled black and brown pattern* on hindwing below. Above blackish brown with few white spots on forewing, no spot in cell. 🌿 **Larval foodplant:** Grasses.

CASSUS ROADSIDE-SKIPPER *Amblyscirtes cassus*

Common in mid- to high-elevation oak-pine forests of southwest, with an isolated population in Davis Mountains, Texas. Flies in summer (1 brood). ► Below hindwing speckled brown and gray, forewing with extensive *orange in discal area.* Above orange and brown with pale yellow postmedian band on forewing. Bronze Roadside-Skipper (p. 346) is neither orange above nor speckled below. 🌿 **Larval foodplant:** Bulb panic-grass.

SLATY ROADSIDE-SKIPPER *Amblyscirtes nereus*

Uncommon in midelevation oak-juniper woodland. Flies in summer in most areas (1 brood), spring to late summer in west Texas (2 broods). ► Often found with other roadside-skippers, but *olive-yellow underside* is distinctive. Hindwing below has irregular white spotband. Above blackish brown with well-developed white spotband on forewing, no cell spot, often with white hindwing spots. 🌿 **Larval foodplant:** Common beardgrass.

ORANGE-HEADED ROADSIDE-SKIPPER *Amblyscirtes phylace*

A plain but attractive skipper of high-elevation grasslands, streamsides, moist woodlands. Males perch in gully bottoms to await females. Flies in summer (1 brood). ► *Head orange,* wings gray with *white or gray fringes.* Orange-edged Roadside-Skipper, found with this species in Chiricahua Mountains, Arizona, has orange fringes (except when worn) and more rounded forewings. 🌿 **Larval foodplant:** Primarily big bluestem.

ORANGE-EDGED ROADSIDE-SKIPPER *Amblyscirtes fimbriata*

Only in Chiricahua and Huachuca Mountains, Arizona, and Animas Mountains, New Mexico. Common in openings of pine-fir forests. Fresh adults are stunning! Flies in summer (1 brood). ► Head orange, wing fringes orange, sometimes turning creamy yellow (or disappearing in very worn condition). Below hindwing slate-gray with a purplish sheen. 🌿 **Larval foodplant:** Grasses.

ROADSIDE-SKIPPERS

actual size

Nysa Roadside-Skipper

Cassus Roadside-Skipper

Slaty Roadside-Skipper

Orange-headed Roadside-Skipper

Orange-edged Roadside-Skipper

351

EUFALA SKIPPER *Lerodea eufala*

A common plain skipper widespread in southern regions. Sometimes strays northward. Found in a variety of lowland situations and adapts well to disturbed habitats. Flies most of year in south (multiple broods), spring to fall northward (1–2 broods). ▶ Rather plain, but note behavior: adults usually perform *two rapid wing-quivers* just after landing. Below hindwing unmarked tan or sometimes with trace of paler postmedian band. Above brown with white forewing spots. Three-spotted Skipper (p. 308, Florida only) is similar but has longer antennae, hindwing below browner and usually with a curved row of faint postmedian spots. Julia's Skipper (p. 310, mostly south Texas) has forewing shorter with fewer white spots, and hindwing more brown or yellowish brown below. 🌿 **Larval foodplant:** Bermuda, Johnson, and other weedy grasses.

VIOLET-CLOUDED SKIPPER *Lerodea arabus*

Rare in southwest. Inhabits arid desert canyons and washes, also urban gardens. Males perch in gully bottoms in late afternoon to find females. Flies early spring to late fall (2–3 broods). ▶ Below hindwing brown with *dark postmedian patch,* sometimes faint or absent, often (but not always) bordered inwardly by small spots or lighter patch. Above similar to Eufala Skipper, but with extra white spot just above center of trailing edge of forewing. 🌿 **Larval foodplant:** Bermuda grass, barnyard grass, and other weedy species.

OLIVE-CLOUDED SKIPPER *Lerodea dysaules*

South Texas only, uncommon. Considered a subspecies of Violet-clouded Skipper by some. Reported summer to fall (2 broods). ▶ Similar to Violet-clouded Skipper, but on hindwing below, the postmedian patch is often lighter and less contrasting. Above sometimes lacks the extra white spot near center of trailing edge of forewing. 🌿 **Larval foodplant:** Probably grasses.

TWIN-SPOT SKIPPER *Oligoria maculata*

A large brown skipper of the southeast, straying northward. Inhabits pinewoods and coastal marshes. Adults are often seen feeding at thistles. Flies all year in southern Florida (multiple broods), late spring to late summer northward (2 broods). ▶ Below hindwing rich dark brown with *three distinct white spots,* two of them *together.* Above blackish brown with glassy white forewing spots. 🌿 **Larval foodplant:** Bluestem grasses.

BROWN SOUTHERN SKIPPERS

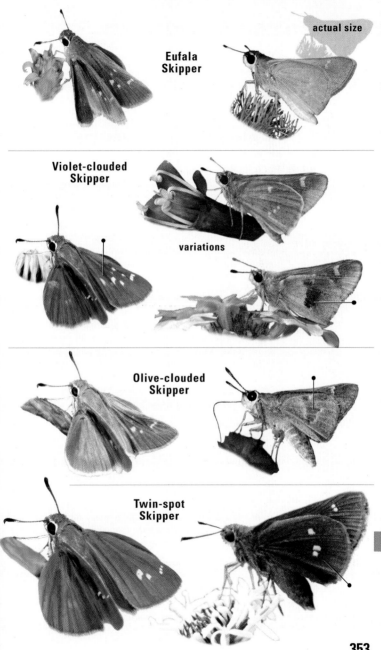

actual size

Eufala Skipper

Violet-clouded Skipper

variations

Olive-clouded Skipper

Twin-spot Skipper

(genus *Panoquina*) show a narrow "racing stripe" along the abdomen.

OCOLA SKIPPER *Panoquina ocola*

A brown skipper of the southeast. Regular fall stray to the northeast, and a rare stray to the southwest. Flies all year in Florida and south Texas (multiple broods), shorter season northward. ▶ *Forewings very long and narrow.* Below hindwing variable, darker near tip and sometimes with faint white spotband, often with purplish sheen when fresh. Above dark brown with glassy forewing spots, no spot in cell. Similar species are likely only in southern Texas. ✤ **Larval foodplant:** Grasses.

WANDERING SKIPPER *Panoquina errans*

Southern California coastal salt marshes and estuaries only. Still locally common, but many former habitats have been destroyed by development. Flies summer into fall (2 broods). ▶ Forewings long and narrow. Below hindwing yellow-brown, turning brown with wear, with small white postmedian spots (sometimes faint or absent) and *yellow veins.* Above dark brown with glassy white forewing spots. ✤ **Larval foodplant:** Saltgrass.

SALT MARSH SKIPPER *Panoquina panoquin*

A denizen of salt marshes of Atlantic and Gulf Coasts, locally common. May be found in fields near the coast, but rarely wanders inland. Flies all year in southernmost areas (multiple broods), spring to fall northward (2 broods). ▶ Forewings long and narrow. Below hindwing yellow-brown with yellow veins and distinctive *long creamy streak.* Above yellow-brown with yellowish forewing spots. ✤ **Larval foodplant:** Saltgrass.

OBSCURE SKIPPER *Panoquina panoquinoides*

Locally common in salt marshes and estuaries of Gulf Coast and Florida. Rarely wanders inland. Flies all year in southernmost areas (multiple broods), spring to fall elsewhere (2 broods). ▶ Small. Forewings not quite as long and narrow as those of Salt Marsh Skipper. Below hindwing brown with small white postmedian spots. Above dark brown with variable glassy white forewing spots. Three-spotted Skipper (p. 308) lacks dark stripe on abdomen. ✤ **Larval foodplant:** Saltgrass.

HECEBOLUS SKIPPER *Panoquina hecebola*

Regular stray to south Texas, reported in fall. ▶ Similar to Ocola Skipper but forewing above has small white flat spot in cell. Below hindwing may have slightly paler veins, rarely with postmedian band or purple sheen. See Purple-washed Skipper (next page). ✤ **Larval foodplant:** Unknown.

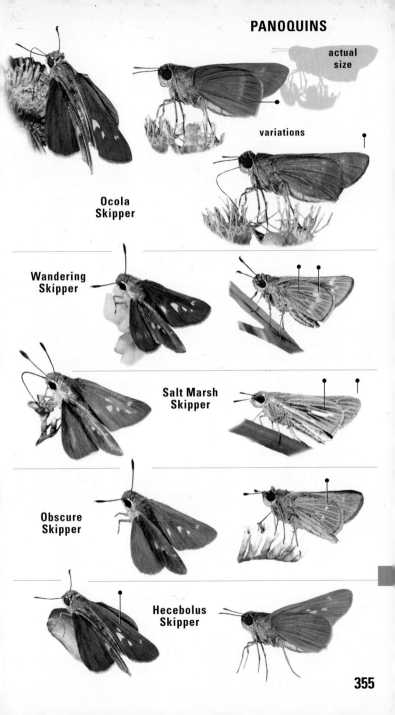

PANOQUINS

actual size

variations

Ocola Skipper

Wandering Skipper

Salt Marsh Skipper

Obscure Skipper

Hecebolus Skipper

BRAZILIAN SKIPPER   *Calpodes ethlius*

Disperses widely, but mainly resident in southern regions where canna thrives. Fast and powerful in flight, more active at dawn and dusk. Flies all year in southern Florida (multiple broods), spring to fall in southern Texas (2–3 broods), late summer to fall northward and in southwest (1 brood). ▶ *Very large.* Forewings long and narrow. Below hindwing *reddish brown* with series of glassy postmedian spots. Above brown with large white glassy spots. 🌿 **Larval foodplant:** Cannas.

MONK SKIPPER   *Asbolis capucinus*

Native to Cuba, apparently introduced into Florida years ago. It has thrived there, owing in part to the ornamental planting of palms. Flies all year in most areas (3–4 broods). ▶ Very *large and plain.* Unmarked orange-brown below, usually with narrow white fringe on hindwing; plain blackish brown above. Palatka Skipper (p. 332) is smaller, paler above, lacks white hindwing fringe. 🌿 **Larval foodplant:** Palms.

CHESTNUT-MARKED SKIPPER   *Thespieus macareus*

Rare stray to south Texas, reported summer to fall. ▶ Below hindwing mottled gray, brown, white, and red. Above brown, both wings with glassy spots. 🌿 **Larval foodplant:** Unknown.

VIOLET-BANDED SKIPPER   *Nyctelius nyctelius*

Periodic stray to south Texas, rarely to Arizona and Florida. Reported May to December in Texas. ▶ Below hindwing with purplish sheen, two darker bands and *dark spot near middle of leading edge.* Above with large squarish spot near cell on forewing. 🌿 **Larval foodplant:** Rice, sugarcane, and others.

PURPLE-WASHED SKIPPER   *Panoquina sylvicola*

Stray to south Texas, rarely Arizona, reported late summer to fall. ▶ Nearly identical to Ocola and Hecebolus Skippers (previous page) and just as variable, but with elongated white spot in forewing cell, often tiny white spots on hindwing below. 🌿 **Larval foodplant:** Grasses.

EVANS'S SKIPPER   *Panoquina fusina*

Reported a few times from south Texas in fall. ▶ Large; forewings long and narrow. Below hindwing brown with *whitish band* (most apparent on males) and purplish sheen. Above brown with large, glassy, amber forewing spots. 🌿 **Larval foodplant:** Unknown.

GREEN-BACKED RUBY-EYE   *Perichares philetes*

Rare stray to south Texas, reported in late fall. Adults active at dawn and dusk. ▶ Thorax *green,* eyes *red.* Hindwing below mottled purple, brown, and gray. Above dark brown with large glassy forewing spots. 🌿 **Larval foodplant:** Large-leaved grasses.

Brazilian Skipper

actual size

Monk Skipper

Chestnut-marked Skipper

Violet-banded Skipper

Purple-washed Skipper

Evans's Skipper

Green-backed Ruby-eye

(subfamily Megathyminae) are robust species whose larvae bore into leaves, stalks, and roots of plants in the agave family. Our largest skippers belong to this subfamily. Flight is strong and powerful. Some adults never feed, and those that do mostly visit mud, not flowers. The species on this page (genus *Megathymus*) use yuccas as larval foodplants.

YUCCA GIANT-SKIPPER   *Megathymus yuccae*

Widespread across the southern U.S. in yucca habitats. Fairly common, although sightings of adults are rare. To find females, males perch on the ground or pine trunks in east, canyon bottoms in west. Flies in spring (1 brood). ▶ Variable. Below hindwing *blackish brown* with white frosted margins and one or two large white spots near the leading edge. Above blackish brown with large yellow or cream bands and margins. Darker below than most similar species. 🌿 **Larval foodplant:** Joshua tree, banana yucca, Spanish bayonet, and other yuccas.

STRECKER'S GIANT-SKIPPER   *Megathymus streckeri*

A western species of prairie grasslands or gentle rocky slopes with yuccas. Flies later and usually at higher elevations than Yucca Giant-Skipper. Flies late spring to early summer (1 brood). ▶ Paler and grayer below than Yucca Giant-Skipper, with *more white spots* on hindwing. Unlike the *Agathymus* species on next two pages, has *pale margin* on hindwing below. Above dark brown with large yellow and white spots on forewing. 🌿 **Larval foodplant:** Yuccas.

URSINE GIANT-SKIPPER   *Megathymus ursus*

Our largest skipper. Widespread in the southwest, but sightings of adults are extremely rare. Flies mostly in summer in most areas, but reported earlier in west Texas (1 brood). ▶ *Very large* with *white antennae*. Below hindwing black with white frosting, the cell and nearby veins outlined in black. Above black with yellow forewing band (more red-orange in eastern New Mexico, broader on female). 🌿 **Larval foodplant:** Schott's yucca and other yuccas.

COFAQUI GIANT-SKIPPER   *Megathymus cofaqui*

Southeast only. Adults are rarely observed. Inhabits pine flats and coastal dunes with yuccas. Flies spring and fall in Florida (2 broods), summer in Georgia (1 brood). ▶ Similar to Yucca Giant-Skipper but *paler and grayer below*, with variable white postmedian spots; white spot near leading edge of hindwing below is usually *smaller*. Above blackish brown with broad yellow forewing band. 🌿 **Larval foodplant:** Yuccas.

GIANT-SKIPPERS

actual size

male

female

Yucca
Giant-Skipper

Strecker's
Giant-Skipper

Ursine
Giant-Skipper

Cofaqui
Giant-Skipper

(genus *Agathymus*) average a bit smaller than the yucca-feeders on the previous page. Larvae bore into agave plants, and adults fly in late summer and fall. Adults do not feed at flowers but most are attracted to mud. Identification of individual species is most reliably done by locality and larval foodplant association.

ARIZONA GIANT-SKIPPER   *Agathymus aryxna*

Mainly Arizona. Variable and common. Adults visit mud. Those in western part of range are sometimes considered a separate species, "Bauer's Giant-Skipper." Flies late summer to fall (1 brood). ▶ Below hindwing *gray* with *faint paler postmedian spots*. Above dark brown, orange basally, both wings with pale orange postmedian band, wider on female. Orange Giant-Skipper usually has broader bands and more orange above. In Huachuca Mountains, Arizona, see Huachuca Giant-Skipper. 🌱 **Larval foodplant**: Palmer's agave (and other agaves for "Bauer's").

ORANGE GIANT-SKIPPER   *Agathymus neumoegeni*

Central Arizona southeast to west Texas. A skipper mostly of rugged arid canyons and rocky slopes. Flies late summer to fall (1 brood). ▶ Variable. Below hindwing gray with faint paler postmedian spots. Above brown, orange basally with orange postmedian bands on both wings, often much wider on female. Very similar to Arizona Giant-Skipper, but their ranges barely overlap. 🌱 **Larval foodplant**: Agaves.

MOJAVE GIANT-SKIPPER   *Agathymus alliae*

Southwestern Utah to deserts of southeastern California. Essentially the only agave-feeding skipper in its range. Adults perch on rock faces with head facing upward. Flies in fall (1 brood). ▶ Below hindwing gray with faint white postmedian spots. Above dark brown, orange basally; both wings with pale orange postmedian band, wider on female. Very similar to Arizona Giant-Skipper, best identified by range. 🌱 **Larval foodplant**: Utah agave.

HUACHUCA GIANT-SKIPPER   *Agathymus evansi*

Only mid- to high elevations of Huachuca Mountains, Arizona. Adults frequent mud and often sip their own secretions. Sometimes common. Flies in fall (1 brood). ▶ Extremely similar to Arizona Giant-Skipper, but averages somewhat larger with slightly wider postmedian bands. The present species usually occurs at *higher elevations* and associates with a different agave. 🌱 **Larval foodplant**: Huachuca form of Parry agave.

AGAVE GIANT-SKIPPERS

actual size

"Bauer's"

Arizona Giant-Skipper

Orange Giant-Skipper

female

male

female

male

Mojave Giant-Skipper

Huachuca Giant-Skipper

CALIFORNIA GIANT-SKIPPER   *Agathymus stephensi*

Very limited distribution in southern California at the western edge of the Colorado Desert; common in and around Anza-Borrego State Park. Flies in fall (1 brood). ▶ Most easily identified by range, as the sole *Agathymus* in its area. Below mottled gray and cream. Above pale brown with creamy yellow postmedian spotband, a bit wider on female. 🌱 **Larval foodplant:** Desert agave.

POLING'S GIANT-SKIPPER   *Agathymus polingi*

Uncommon in southeastern Arizona and southwestern New Mexico. A smaller *Agathymus* of hillsides covered with shindagger. Unlike others in its range, adults do not visit mud. Flies in fall (1 brood). ▶ Below gray with cream postmedian and basal spots. Above brown with orange basally and yellow postmedian spotband, wider on female. Similar to Arizona Giant-Skipper (previous page), but *smaller,* may be more contrasty below; best identified by habitat. 🌱 **Larval foodplant:** Shindagger.

MARY'S GIANT-SKIPPER   *Agathymus mariae*

West Texas and adjacent New Mexico, often on limestone hills and slopes. Flies in fall (1 brood). ▶ Variable. Below hindwing gray with or without paler postmedian and basal spotbands. Above brown, orange basally with narrow yellow postmedian spotband on both wings, wider on female. In eastern part of range, compare to Coahuila Giant-Skipper. 🌱 **Larval foodplant:** Lechuguilla.

COAHUILA GIANT-SKIPPER   *Agathymus remingtoni*

Very limited range in west Texas. Flies late summer to early fall (1 brood). ▶ Below hindwing dark brown, grayer toward margin, with postmedian band of pale *outward-pointing spots.* Above brown with postmedian band on both wings, wider on female, spots on hindwing *pointed outward.* Mary's Giant-Skipper has more orange above and spots on hindwing not pointed outward; its flight period peaks later in fall. See next species. 🌱 **Larval foodplant:** Lechuguilla.

MANFREDA GIANT-SKIPPER   *Stallingsia maculosa*

South Texas only. Quite rare, current range probably not accessible to the public; much of former habitat destroyed by development. Flies spring and fall (2 broods). ▶ Below hindwing blackish brown with gray frosting along margin and faint postmedian spotband. Above blackish brown with narrow yellow postmedian spotband on forewing. Similar to Coahuila Giant-Skipper but occurs farther east. 🌱 **Larval foodplant:** Manfreda.

AGAVE AND MANFREDA GIANT-SKIPPERS

actual size

California Giant-Skipper

Poling's Giant-Skipper

Mary's Giant-Skipper

Coahuila Giant-Skipper

Manfreda Giant-Skipper

INDEX OF LARVAL FOODPLANTS

A butterfly's most important relationship is with the plants eaten by its caterpillars, or larvae. In this index we provide scientific names for the foodplants mentioned in the text, to help you find more information on these plants in botanical texts.

PHOTOGRAPHER CREDITS

This book would not have been possible without the cooperation of many outstanding photographers, who not only allowed us to use their photographs, but also gave permission to have those photographs altered for the sake of illustration. Plates are listed by page number (in bold), followed by a dash and the number of the image. Images on each plate are numbered sequentially. Read image numbers within each species, from top to bottom and then left to right. Images created from specimens are not listed. The majority of the specimen photography was done by Samuel. P. Macomber.

INDEX OF SCIENTIFIC NAMES OF BUTTERFLIES

INDEX OF ENGLISH NAMES OF BUTTERFLIES

You can tally your "life list" here by checking off the boxes in front of the names of butterflies you've seen. A box is provided for each full species in the book.

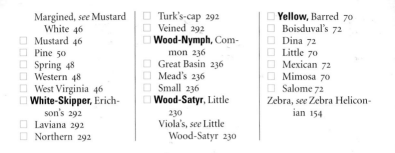
WHEN YOU SEE AN UNFAMILIAR BUTTERFLY:

1. See if you can place it in one of the groups shown in the Pictorial Table of Contents at the beginning of this Focus Guide.
2. Refer to the page numbers or color tabs and go to that section of the book. Look for the pictures that match your butterfly most closely.
3. Make sure the size is right. Always check the "actual size" figure in the upper right-hand corner of each color plate.
4. Check the range maps to see which species are likely in your area. This will help to narrow down the choices.
5. Read the text for additional pointers on habitat, behavior, flight season, and comparisons to similar species.

QUICK KEY TO THE RANGE MAPS:

Most butterflies in this guide are mapped in green. This means that the species is flying in summer (the peak butterfly season in most areas) or in more than one season. Dark green indicates areas where the species is more common. A few species fly mainly in spring or mainly in fall; these are mapped in blue for spring, orange for fall, again with a darker tone for the areas where they are more common.

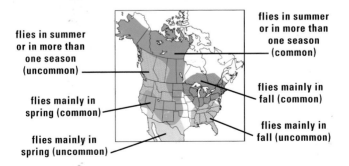

flies in summer
or in more than
one season
(uncommon)

flies mainly in
spring (common)

flies mainly in
spring (uncommon)

flies in summer
or in more than
one season
(common)

flies mainly in
fall (common)

flies mainly in
fall (uncommon)

Short index for KAUFMAN FOCUS GUIDE: BUTTERFLIES OF NORTH AMERICA
(Some rare butterflies, unlikely to be seen by most readers,
are excluded here but included in the regular index.)